The Bible Says So!

*BibleWorld*
*Series Editor:* Philip R. Davies and James G. Crossley, University of Sheffield

*BibleWorld* shares the fruits of modern (and postmodern) biblical scholarship not only among practitioners and students, but also with anyone interested in what academic study of the Bible means in the twenty-first century. It explores our ever-increasing knowledge and understanding of the social world that produced the biblical texts, but also analyses aspects of the bible's role in the history of our civilization and the many perspectives – not just religious and theological, but also cultural, political and aesthetic – which drive modern biblical scholarship.

**Published:**

*Sodomy*
*A History of a Christian Biblical Myth*
Michael Carden

*Yours Faithfully: Virtual Letters from the Bible*
Edited by Philip R. Davies

*Israel's History and the History of Israel*
Mario Liverani

*The Apostle Paul and His Letters*
Edwin D. Freed

*The Origins of the 'Second' Temple: Persian Imperial Policy and the Rebuilding of Jerusalem*
Diana Edelman

*An Introduction to the Bible* (Revised edition)
John Rogerson

*The Morality of Paul's Converts*
Edwin D. Freed

*The Mythic Mind: Essays on Cosmology and Religion in Ugaritic and Old Testament Literature*
Nick Wyatt

*History, Literature and Theology in the Book of Chronicles*
Ehud Ben Zvi

*Women Healing/Healing Women: The Genderization of Healing in Early Christianity*
Elaine M. Wainwright

*Jonah's World: Social Science and the Reading of Prophetic Story*
Lowell K. Handy

*Symposia: Dialogues Concerning the History of Biblical Interpretation*
Roland Boer

*Sectarianism in Early Judaism*
Edited by David J. Chalcraft

*The Ontology of Space in Biblical Hebrew Narrative*
Luke Gärtner-Brereton

*Mark and its Subalterns : A Hermeneutical Paradigm for a Postcolonial Context*
David Joy

*Redrawing the Boundaries*
*The Date of Early Christian Literature*
J.V.M. Sturdy, edited by Jonathan Knight

**Forthcoming:**

*Judaism, Jewish Identities and the Gospel Tradition*
Edited by James G. Crossley

*Sex Working and the Bible*
Avaren Ipsen

*Linguistic Dating of Biblical Texts: An Introduction to Approaches and Problems*
Ian Young and Robert Rezetko

*Vive Memor Mortis*
Thomas Bolin

*The Joy of Kierkegaard: Essays on Kierkegaard as a Biblical Reader*
Hugh Pyper

*From Babylon to Eternity: The Exile Remembered and Constructed in Text and Tradition*
Bob Becking, Alex Cannegieter, Wilfred van der Poll and Anne-Mareike Wetter

*Charismatic Killers :Reading the Hebrew Bible's Violent Rhetoric in Film*
Eric Christianson

*O Mother, Where Art Thou?*
*An Irigarayan Reading of the Book of Chronicles*
Julie Kelso

*On the Origins of Judaism*
Philip R. Davies

# THE BIBLE SAYS SO!

*From Simple Answers to Insightful Understanding*

Edwin D. Freed
Jane F. Roberts

LONDON  OAKVILLE

Published by
UK: Equinox Publishing Ltd., Unit 6, The Village, 101 Amies St.,
London SW11 2JW
USA: DBBC, 28 Main Street, Oakville, CT 06779

www.equinoxpub.com

First published 2009

© Edwin D. Freed and Jane F. Roberts 2009

All rights reserved. No part of this publication may be reproduced or transmitted in any form or by any means, electronic or mechanical, including photocopying, recording or any information storage or retrieval system, without prior permission in writing from the publishers.

British Library Cataloguing-in-Publication Data

A catalogue record for this book is available from the British Library.

ISBN-13    978 1 84553 163 8 (hardback)
           978 1 84553 164 5 (paperback)

Library of Congress Cataloging-in-Publication Data

Freed, Edwin D.
  The Bible says so! : from simple answers to insightful understanding / Edwin D. Freed and Jane F. Roberts.
      p. cm. — (Bibleworld)
   ISBN 13 978-1-84553-163-8 (hb) — ISBN 978-1-84553-164-5 (pbk.)
 1. Bible–Criticism, interpretation, etc. I. Roberts, Jane F. II. Title.
   BS511.3.F74 2009
   220.6–dc22
                         2007032311

Typeset by S.J.I. Services, New Delhi
Printed and bound in Great Britain by Lightning Source UK Ltd, Milton Keynes

CONTENTS

| | |
|---|---|
| Foreword | xv |
| Preface | xvii |

**Part I: Overview of Biblical Study**

| | |
|---|---|
| Chapter 1. The Bible: What is it? | 3 |
|   Introduction | 3 |
|   The Basics | 4 |
|   What the Bible Includes | 5 |
|   The Bible as History | 6 |
|   Understanding the Bible for What It Is | 7 |
|   Understanding the Bible Insightfully | 10 |
|   For Whom the Bible Was Written | 12 |
|   Chapter Summary | 13 |
| Chapter 2. Oral and Written Sources of the Bible | 15 |
|   Introduction | 15 |
|   Oral Transmission | 16 |
|   Written Transmission | 18 |
|     Manuscripts of the Bible | 19 |
|   Chapter Summary | 21 |
| Chapter 3. Translating the Bible | 23 |
|   Introduction | 23 |
|   Establishing the Text | 23 |
|   Divisions in the Texts | 25 |
|   Errors Made during the Transmission of Manuscripts | 25 |

| | |
|---|---|
| Pause for Reflection | 26 |
| Some Important English Translations | 27 |
| Translation Challenges | 27 |
| Comparisons of Different Translations | 28 |
|    Genesis 43:30 | 28 |
|    Philemon 1:12 | 29 |
|    Jeremiah 12:2 | 30 |
|    2 Samuel 20:10 | 30 |
|    Lamentations 2:11 | 32 |
|    Philippians 1:8 | 32 |
|    Leviticus 19:17 | 33 |
|    1 Corinthians 14:11 | 34 |
|    2 Corinthians 6:11-12 | 35 |
| Chapter Summary | 37 |

**Part II: The Old Testament**

| | |
|---|---|
| Chapter 4. Sources of the Pentateuch | 41 |
| Introduction | 41 |
| Source J | 42 |
| Source E | 42 |
| Source D | 44 |
|    The Deuteronomists' Views | 46 |
| Source P | 47 |
| Some Evidence of Sources | 48 |
| Sources outside the Pentateuch | 49 |
|    Influence from Ancient Sources outside the Bible | 51 |
| Hebrew Laws | 52 |
| Chapter Summary | 54 |
| | |
| Chapter 5. Creation and Garden of Eden Stories | 56 |
| Introduction | 56 |
| Creation Stories outside the Bible | 56 |
| Creation Stories in the Bible | 58 |
|    Creation in P | 58 |
|    Understanding the Discrepancies in P | 60 |

Contents     vii

| | |
|---|---|
| Comparisons between Creation in P and Ancient Accounts | 61 |
| Creation in J | 61 |
| Likenesses and Differences in the Two Genesis Accounts | 62 |
| Garden of Eden | 63 |
| Further Insights about the Stories of the Creation of Humans and the Garden of Eden Story | 65 |
| Chapter Summary | 68 |
| Chapter 6. Flood Stories and the Tower of Babel | 70 |
| Introduction | 70 |
| Flood Stories in the Bible and outside the Bible | 70 |
| Comparison of Flood Stories in the Bible | 73 |
| Tower of Babel | 77 |
| Chapter Summary | 78 |
| Chapter 7. Genesis Stories as Beginnings | 79 |
| Introduction | 79 |
| "Firsts" in Genesis | 79 |
| Further Observations on Stories in Genesis | 83 |
| Chapter Summary | 83 |
| Chapter 8. Patriarchal Narratives | 86 |
| Introduction | 86 |
| Overview of the Patriarchal Narratives | 86 |
| God's Call and Promises to Abraham about a Son (12:1-4, J; 15:1-21, J+E; 17:1-27, P) | 87 |
| Stories of the Lies | 88 |
|   Abraham and Sarah in Egypt (J) | 88 |
|   Abraham and Sarah at Gerar (E) | 88 |
|   Isaac and Rebekah at Gerar (J) | 90 |
| Understanding the Stories of the Lies | 90 |
| Stories about Ishmael (16:1-16, J+P; 21:6-21, E; 17:15-26, P) | 92 |
| Understanding the Ishmael Stories | 93 |
| Abraham Visited by Three Strange Men (18:1-33, J) | 93 |
|   Sodom Destroyed (18:16–19:28, J) | 93 |

| | |
|---|---:|
| Lot and his Daughters 19:30-38, J) | 95 |
| Abraham with Isaac as a Sacrifice (22:1-19, E) | 95 |
| Isaac and Rebekah (24:1-67, J) | 96 |
| Esau and Jacob, Sons of Isaac and Rebekah (Genesis 25:19-20, 26b, P; 25:21-26, 27-34, J) | 97 |
|    Rebekah Deceives Isaac in his Blessings (Genesis 27:1-26, J) | 97 |
|    Isaac's Deathbed Blessings (27:27-40, J) | 98 |
|    Understanding the Blessings Stories | 99 |
|    Isaac's Blessings and History | 100 |
|    Morality and Isaac's Blessings | 101 |
| Joseph | 102 |
| The Significance of Names | 107 |
|    Abraham and Sarah | 108 |
|    Ishmael | 109 |
|    Isaac | 109 |
|    Jacob and Esau | 110 |
| Chapter Summary | 111 |
| | |
| **Chapter 9. Gods Mentioned in the Old Testament** | **113** |
| Introduction | 113 |
| Elohim and Yahweh | 113 |
|    Origin and Meaning of the Term Yahweh | 114 |
|    Yahweh as "Lord of Hosts" | 116 |
| El | 116 |
| Baal | 117 |
|    Baalism and Elijah and Yahwism | 118 |
| Other Gods | 121 |
| Further Thoughts about Gods in the Old Testament | 122 |
| Household Gods | 123 |
| Henotheism and Monotheism | 124 |
| The Gender of the Deity | 125 |
| Chapter Summary | 129 |

## Part III: The New Testament

| | |
|---|---|
| **Chapter 10. Background of the Christ Movement** | 133 |
| Introduction | 133 |
| New Testament Manuscripts | 133 |
| Jesus as Messiah, Lord, Son of God, and Son of David | 135 |
| The Messiah (Christ) Movement | 136 |
| Names for Members of the Christ Movement in Paul and Acts | 137 |
|   Identifying Different Groups | 137 |
|   Christian | 138 |
|   Christianity | 139 |
| Designations for Followers of Christ | 139 |
| The Book of Acts | 143 |
| Chapter Summary | 145 |
| **Chapter 11. Church and Churches** | 146 |
| Introduction | 146 |
| Understanding Church and Churches in Paul | 146 |
|   Paul's Use of Church | 146 |
|   House Churches | 148 |
|   Understanding Church and Churches in Acts | 149 |
| Luke as "Historian" | 150 |
|   The Role of the Spirit in Luke's "History" | 150 |
|   The Role of Angels and Visions in Luke's "History" | 150 |
| Final Thoughts about the Early Church | 150 |
| Chapter Summary | 152 |
| **Chapter 12. Paul and his Thought** | 153 |
| Introduction | 153 |
| Paul's Special Religious Experience on the Road to Damascus | 154 |
|   According to Acts | 154 |
|   According to Paul | 156 |
| Understanding Paul's Supernatural Experiences | 159 |
| Paul and the Author of the Fourth Gospel | 160 |

|   |   |
|---|---|
| Justification by Faith | 162 |
| How Converts Are Made Righteous | 163 |
|    1 Corinthians 6:9-11 | 164 |
|    Romans 6:1-23 | 164 |
|    The Symbolism of Baptism | 165 |
|    Paul on Baptism and Christians Today | 165 |
| Joint Declaration on the Doctrine of Justification | 167 |
| Chapter Summary | 168 |
| **Chapter 13. The First Three Gospels** | **170** |
| Introduction | 170 |
| Oral Transmission or Oral Tradition | 170 |
| Synoptic Gospels and their Sources | 172 |
| The Priority of Mark | 172 |
| The Two-Source and Four-Source Theories | 174 |
| Literary Style of Mark | 175 |
| Special Interests of Mark | 175 |
| Literary Style of Matthew | 177 |
| Special Interests of Matthew | 177 |
| Literary Style of Luke | 179 |
| Special Interests of Luke | 180 |
| Chapter Summary | 182 |
| **Chapter 14. Jesus, Matthew, Mark, Luke, or John?** | **184** |
| Introduction | 184 |
| John the Baptist | 184 |
| The Rejection of Jesus at Nazareth | 186 |
| Jairus's Daughter and the Woman's Faith | 187 |
| What Did Jesus Really Say? | 191 |
| The Gospel of John | 193 |
|    John and the Synoptic Gospels | 193 |
|    Literary Style of John | 194 |
|    Jesus as Teacher and his Teachings | 196 |
|       Jesus as "I Am" | 196 |
| Sayings of Jesus on Specific Themes | 197 |
| Chapter Summary | 199 |

## Contents

| | |
|---|---:|
| **Chapter 15. The Stories of Jesus' Birth** | 201 |
| Introduction | 201 |
| Mary's Conception of Jesus (Matthew 1:18-25; Luke 1:26-38) | 201 |
| Mary and the Women in Matthew's Genealogy | 204 |
|    The Women in Early Christian Literature | 205 |
|    Understanding Matthew's Account of Mary's Conception | 205 |
| Ideas behind the Birth Stories | 206 |
| Date of Jesus' Birth | 207 |
| Place of Jesus' Birth | 208 |
|    The Manger Scene | 209 |
|    The Inn | 209 |
| The Family of Jesus | 210 |
| Perpetual Virginity of Mary | 211 |
| Chapter Summary | 212 |
| **Chapter 16. The Resurrected Jesus** | 214 |
| Introduction | 214 |
| Stories of Jesus' Resurrection | 214 |
| The Empty Tomb and the Women (Mark 16:1-8; Matthew 28:1-10; Luke 24:1-12; John 20:1-18) | 215 |
|    Understanding the Empty Tomb Stories | 218 |
| Resurrection Appearance in Matthew (28:16-20) | 219 |
| Resurrection Appearances in Luke | 220 |
|    On the Road to Emmaus (24:13-35) | 220 |
|    To the Eleven Disciples (24:36-49) | 220 |
|    At the Ascension (24:50-53) | 221 |
| Resurrection Appearances in John (20:19-29) | 221 |
| What Kind of Body Did the Resurrected Jesus Have? | 221 |
| Chapter Summary | 222 |
| **Chapter 17. The Man Jesus** | 224 |
| Introduction | 224 |
| "What Is This? A New Teaching – with Authority!" (Mark 1:21-28) | 225 |

| | |
|---|---|
| What Was New in Jesus' Teaching? | 225 |
| The Surprising and Unexpected | 226 |
| Concern for the Most Essential | 227 |
| Practice Goodness to the Extreme | 227 |
| "What Sort of Man Is This?" (Matthew 8:27; see Mark 4:41; Luke 8:25) | 228 |
| Questions about Jesus the Man | 230 |
| Chapter Summary | 231 |

## Part IV: Biblical Values

| | |
|---|---|
| Chapter 18. Love, Family, Marriage, and Sex | 235 |
| Introduction | 235 |
| Love as the Primary Value | 236 |
| Love for Aliens | 237 |
| Paul's Ode to Love | 237 |
| Family Life | 238 |
| Wives and Mothers | 239 |
| Husbands and Fathers | 239 |
| Children | 240 |
| Divorce | 240 |
| Paul's Views on Family Life | 241 |
| Paul on Marriage and Sex | 242 |
| Why Not to Marry | 243 |
| Paul on Divorce | 244 |
| Homosexuality | 245 |
| Homosexuality in the Old Testament | 245 |
| Genesis 19:1-11 | 245 |
| Leviticus 18:22 | 246 |
| Leviticus 20:10-16 | 246 |
| Observations and Questions | 247 |
| Homosexuality in the New Testament | 247 |
| Romans 1:26-27 | 247 |
| 1 Corinthians 6:9 | 248 |
| 1 Corinthians 5:9-11 | 249 |

| | |
|---|---|
| Food for Thought | 249 |
| Chapter Summary | 251 |
| **Chapter 19. The Bible and Selected Social Issues Today** | **253** |
| Introduction | 253 |
| The Bible in Today's World | 253 |
| Abortion, Capital Punishment, and Other Issues of Life and Death | 255 |
|    Abortion and the Bible | 255 |
|    Capital Punishment and the Bible | 257 |
|    Insightfully Understanding the Bible | 258 |
| Poverty | 259 |
|    In the Old Testament | 259 |
|       The Prophets | 259 |
|       The Pentateuch | 261 |
|       Psalms and Proverbs | 261 |
|    In the New Testament | 262 |
|       Synoptic Gospels | 262 |
|       Acts and Paul's Letters | 262 |
|       Letter of James | 263 |
|       Revelation | 263 |
| Conclusion | 264 |

# Foreword

There is a vivid memory I have from almost 50 years ago, when I was in third grade, of my parents returning home from Cambridge, Massachusetts, where my father, the primary author of this book, had successfully defended his dissertation. Coming from the garage into the basement and shaking with exhaustion and undoubtedly also tremendous relief, he held his head in his arms and poured out pent-up emotions. Since to children our parents seem all powerful, this was somewhat frightening and certainly unexpected, even with the reassurance of Mom standing right beside him, as she always has. So, with innocent confusion, I asked, "What exactly *is* a PhD?" I remember the question *only* because I very clearly remember his answer, one that has echoed in my mind at various times throughout my life. He said, "It's just something that lets you know how little you really know."

Well, from that day forward, my father has never stopped his scholarly work in pursuit of more knowledge and in a quest for more insightful understanding of the Bible. He brings to his writing – and this book – an accumulation of knowledge that is to be cherished, not just for its quantity, but also for its quality. Though too humble to openly share his accomplishments, he offers a perspective about "what the Bible says" based not only on years of dedicated study and scholarship, but also on an education that is rare today. In earning his PhD from the Graduate School of Arts and Sciences at Harvard University in 1959, he completed a very rigorous program of study that included courses from the Divinity School in addition to those within the Classics Department, from which he received a degree in Biblical and Patristic Greek. To accomplish this goal, he had to have a command of the Latin, Classical and Biblical Greek, Hebrew, and Aramaic languages and to demonstrate proficiency in reading German and French. He studied writings of the Christian Church's founding fathers and gained an in-depth understanding of the historical context in which the Bible was written.

So, as you read this book, please understand that you are reaping the benefits of years' worth of painstaking, technical study and research that have culminated in a product that clearly reflects the author's background in linguistics and his strong foundation in ancient history. It has been a privilege for me to work with my father in helping to shape this book, not simply because of the extensive knowledge that he has to share, but also because, as a gerontologist, I deeply appreciate how he can offer now – at age 87 – what he could not have possibly offered much earlier in his career. To miss out on capturing this rich resource would have been to lose a unique synthesis of ideas and insights that reflect years of scholarly work and, more importantly, wisdom possible only when superficial, simplistic answers are replaced by deeper, more thoughtful ones. I hope that you, as the reader, will appreciate this as much as I do.

*Jane F. Roberts*

# Preface

Having devoted more than 65 of my 87 years to an in-depth study of the Bible, I invite you, the reader, to join me in examining key stories from the Old and New Testaments from a scholar's viewpoint. With the help of techniques used by biblical scholars, we will reflect on these stories, comparing simple answers and explanations to more complex and insightful understanding. This is possible only when starting with an open and curious mind and a willingness to set aside preconceived attitudes and perhaps longstanding ideas about biblical "truths."

While my deep appreciation for the collection of diverse and inspiring literary works that comprise the Bible will undoubtedly be very evident, what I believe myself is a matter of personal faith. My goal is neither to share that nor to influence the reader's beliefs and faith. Instead, my intent is to discuss the results of scholarly research – both mine and that of many others over the past decades – in an effort to provide objective evidence about the content, origin, and meaning of the Bible. This insightful understanding is gained primarily by examining the languages in which the Bible was originally written, considering the historical contexts of the Bible's authors, and analyzing critically what interpretations most accurately capture not only what biblical writers were trying to convey, but also their reasons for doing so.

Thus, written from a non-denominational perspective and using a critical thinking approach, this book is intended for all persons who want to gain new insights into what the Bible really says. We will study subjects in the Bible from alternative points of view and then try to decide, on the basis of evidence or lack of it, which is the most accurate representation of what the Bible says about those subjects. There will often be times when we will be unable to say, with absolute certainty, that "The Bible Says So!" Some questions will have several possible answers, while others might have none that are plausible.

Although disconcerting, at first, to readers who have been taught about the Bible without actually questioning those teachings or without exploring deeply its many discrepancies and uncertainties, the critical study of the Bible provided in this book will lead to insightful understanding that is far more gratifying than simplistic, dogmatic approaches. It lays the foundation for an informed appreciation of the best-selling book of all times, with more than six billion copies sold!

For that reason, the book is recommended for all individuals who seek to explore the Bible through the lens of critical thinking. Although intended primarily for lay readers, it is provocative enough to offer food for thought for scholars and clergy. It certainly is written to provide insightful understanding for Christian and Jewish teachers in biblical studies, for Sunday School or Parish School of Religion teachers and others who provide instruction or leadership within their faith-based communities, and for persons who study the Bible, either in groups or individually. For the growing movement in the United States that supports teaching the Bible as literature within public schools, the book can also provide invaluable background information and insights.

You will learn the most in reading this book if you have a copy of a modern translation of the Bible with you, so you can look up the many passages that are cited. Reading them in their entirety will enhance your understanding of the material that I present. While any number of different translations of the Bible are satisfactory, my recommendation is that you select one of the following: the *New Revised Standard Version* (New York/Oxford: Oxford University Press, 1989); *The Revised English Bible* (Oxford/Cambridge: Oxford University Press and Cambridge University Press, 1989); or *The New Jerusalem Bible* (New York/London: Doubleday, 1999).

Unless indicated otherwise, the translations in this book are from the *New Revised Standard Version* (*NRSV*) and are used by permission. Sometimes I have also used my own translation in order to bring out a more precise meaning of the original Hebrew or Greek. And, at other times, I have included translations from other versions to show differences in meanings of the original languages of the Bible and to illustrate how difficult it is to be positively certain about what the Bible says.

Most scholars today believe that the Bible was written over a period of twelve centuries. In this book, when dating persons and events within that broad historical context, I have chosen to use BCE and CE instead of the well-known BC and AD. For five centuries Christians used the Roman calendar, and the Jews used one of their own. In the sixth century Christians began to date things from the time of Jesus' birth, *anno domino*, "in the year of our Lord," beginning with the year 1. Gradually they began to use AD, understood as "after Christ," and BC, for dates "before Christ." Recently, many Jewish and Christian scholars, realizing their common interests and beliefs, began using BCE, "before the common era," and CE, "the common era." The difference is in nomenclature only: 200 BC = 200 BCE and 200 AD = 200 CE.

During my many years of studying the Bible, I have been indebted to numerous scholars abroad and in America, to whom in a general way I express my gratitude. Along with the individuals mentioned in the body of this work, I am indebted to Jacob M. Myers, a seminary professor of mine, for introducing me to the study of the sources of the first five books of the Bible that appear often in this book. I am greatly indebted, as well, to my professor of Old Testament at Harvard University, Robert H. Pfeiffer, whose volume, *Introduction to the Old Testament* (New York: Harper & Brothers, 1948), I have used repeatedly. And, for his in-depth lectures on Judaism, I am indebted to Professor Harry A. Wolfson.

I am also grateful to Arthur Darby Nock, also of Harvard, from whom I received new insights into early Christianity. He was a co-mentor with Professor Cadbury, for whom no words can fully express my continuing gratitude for his influence on me as a person and for my instruction in New Testament studies. For this work I owe much of what I say about Jesus to his *Jesus: What Manner of Man* (New York: Macmillan, 1947). I also repeat, for the benefit of lay persons, some of the things I wrote about the apostle Paul and his thought at a more advanced level in my *The Morality of Paul's Converts* (London/Oakville: Equinox, 2005).

For the publication of this work I am grateful to the staff of Equinox Publishing, especially Professor Philip Davies of the University of Sheffield, Janet Joyce, and Valerie Hall. I am also grateful to Audrey Mann for careful and helpful copy editing.

In many ways this book would not have been possible without the continuing help and support of my wife Ann. For that and for specific suggestions in the manuscript, I thank her very much. Finally, I am most grateful to our daughter, Jane F. Roberts, a professor at the University of Akron Wayne College, for her patient endurance in editing the whole manuscript to make it intelligible to persons who have had no training in biblical studies. She clarified my language, smoothed many rough spots, rearranged and wove the whole together, even writing and rewriting parts, to make it a much better literary work. However, for whatever errors there may be, I am completely responsible. To Jane this work is affectionately dedicated by listing her name with mine as co-author.

*Edwin D. Freed*

Part I

OVERVIEW OF BIBLICAL STUDY

# Chapter 1

## THE BIBLE: WHAT IS IT?

### *Introduction*

"What is the Bible?" is a question that might seem almost insultingly simple. In reality, however, the answer is far more complex than any single reply and raises yet other, even more challenging, questions. Is the Bible the "Word of God"? Is it the most sacred book in the world? Is the Bible obsolete in today's world, or does it still provide relevant guidance and inspiration? Some people might say that, since they are Christians, it is the holy book that dictates how they live and what they believe. It is the source they turn to for answers about moral issues, perhaps supporting their conclusions by declaring "The Bible Says So!"

We will see that any one response to the seemingly simple question that is the focus of this introductory chapter really does not do justice to it. The Bible is a virtual library of books comprised of many literary types or genres written by many different authors who had diverse religious viewpoints, used various sources, and reflected diverse circumstances in different environments. Not only is the Bible regarded by Christians and Jews as a holy book, it has, in fact, also influenced the thought, literature, institutions, values, and mores of Western culture for many centuries. Yet, to understand the Bible insightfully is a daunting task. After spending my entire adult life dedicated to biblical study, at the age of 87 I remain amazed at its complexities and challenged by continuing unanswered questions and new insights.

Rarely is it possible to say "The Bible Says So!" as a definitive answer, because what the Bible says depends upon what specific passages are being cited and from what particular version. The Bible has been translated into more than 370 different languages and dialects and, among the English translations alone, there are more than 60 different versions. Adding to this complexity is the question of whose specific interpretation to accept. Our search for insightful understanding will include some references to the Hebrew and Greek words of the original texts of the Bible, and the meanings, though often difficult to transpose into our present use of language, will offer clues for scholarly and meaningful interpretations.

## The Basics

The word Bible is derived from the two Greek words *biblion*, meaning "book," and *biblos*, used for Egyptian papyrus or the paper made from that reed-like plant. *Biblos* also means "scroll" or "book." While these words gradually acquired the connotation of holiness or sacredness, no writing in the Bible was regarded as holy or sacred until long after it was composed. By the time the New Testament (NT) was written, its writers considered the Old Testament (OT) to be sacred, as is evident in Luke 3:4: "As it is written in the book [*biblos*] of the words of the prophet Isaiah" (see also Matthew 1:1; Acts 1:20). But writings became incorporated in the Bible because of their content, *not* their sanctity.

From about 200 BCE–200 CE some Jewish writers referred to literature they considered holy or sacred as "Scriptures" (from the Latin *scribō*, "write"). The author of First Maccabees writes: "We have as encouragement the holy books (*ta biblia ta hagia*) that are in our hands" (1 Maccabees 12:9). The Jewish historian Josephus (c. 37–100 CE) writes about receiving a gift of "sacred books" (*Life of Josephus* 418).

Christians also regarded the Hebrew Scriptures as sacred, and they were "the Bible" of the early Church. However, most Christians did not use the Jewish Scriptures in their original Hebrew language but used, instead, a Greek translation known as the Septuagint (from the Latin "seventy"). According to ancient tradition, 70 Jewish scholars translated the Hebrew Torah (the first five books of the OT) into Greek. That tradition says that each scholar worked independently, yet all came back with identical translations. Later the whole Old Testament plus the Apocrypha (books not in the Hebrew Bible) came to be included in the Septuagint, abbreviated LXX in scholarly works.

Christians eventually composed and assembled a collection of sacred writings that they called the New Covenant, because they believed Jesus had initiated a new covenant – or agreement – with his followers (Luke 22:20; 1 Corinthians 11:25; 2 Corinthians 3:6) as the prophet Jeremiah had predicted (Jeremiah 31:31-34; see also Romans 11:26-27). Christians believed that their covenant replaced the ones made by God with Abraham (Genesis 17:1-21) and Moses (Exodus 6:2-9; 34:10-28; Acts 7:8).

## The Bible: What Is It?

The word "testament" is derived from the Latin *testamentum*, for which the equivalent Greek word is *diathēkē*, meaning "covenant." Christians, obviously with a sense of pride and prejudice, called their sacred writings the *New* Testament. And, after Christianity separated from Judaism, Christians referred to the Hebrew Scriptures as the *Old* Testament. However, writers of the NT did not write to replace or supplement the Jewish Scriptures but to provide proof for their views of Jesus' birth, life, death, and resurrection; to support theological beliefs and moral exhortation; and to explain special events in early Christian history.

### What the Bible Includes

The word "Bible" does not always bring to mind the same group of writings to all people. Although many Jewish scholars use the word Bible when referring to the Hebrew Scriptures, many prefer the term *Tanak*. It is actually an acronym in which the consonants represent the three divisions of the Hebrew Scriptures: *Torah* (Law), *Nebiim* (Prophets), and *Kethubim* (Writings). The *Torah* is comprised of Genesis, Exodus, Leviticus, Numbers, and Deuteronomy. The *Nebiim* include the Former Prophets: Joshua, Judges, 1 and 2 Samuel, 1 and 2 Kings; Latter Prophets: Isaiah, Jeremiah, Ezekiel; and the Twelve (Minor Prophets): Hosea, Joel, Amos, Obadiah, Jonah, Micah, Nahum, Habakkuk, Zephaniah, Haggai, Zechariah, Malachi. The *Kethubim* include Psalms, Proverbs, Job, Song of Solomon, Ruth, Lamentations, Ecclesiastes, Esther, Daniel, Ezra, Nehemiah, and 1 and 2 Chronicles.

Arranged in a slightly different order, these books are called the OT by Christians. But even among Christians, the word Bible sometimes signifies different things. Roman Catholics, Eastern Orthodox, and some Protestants include additional writings in the OT. These extra writings are called "deuterocanonical," meaning "secondarily canon," because they were added to the other books that are referred to as "canon."

*Canon* comes from the Hebrew word *qaneh*, meaning "reed," which was properly prepared and used as a writing material. The Greek noun *kanōn* was used for a carpenter's rule, and the word acquired the meaning of "norm" or "standard." The biblical canon, then, is the sacred literature of Jews and Christians regarded as authoritative for worship, study, teaching, doctrine, and moral life. Protestants have generally regarded the deuterocanonical works as "apocryphal," or of doubtful authenticity. However, many scholars have long recognized the importance of those writings for understanding the literary and religious developments of

Judaism after the biblical period, so they are often included in modern translations of the Bible.

## *The Bible as History*

Trying to understand the Bible insightfully is difficult because thousands of years separate us from the past we try to recover. Often we must even work with documents written centuries after the reported events occurred. Such accounts were frequently idealized to enhance the present by bringing the past into it or to enhance the past by reading present ideals or viewpoints back into ancient narratives. In much biblical literature the line between history, legend, and myth is very fine, and it is often difficult to distinguish among fact, faith, and fiction.

If we think of history as the record of past events as they actually happened, then there is little in the Bible. Although today we often learn about things as soon as they happen or even before, it was not that way in the ancient world. No persons recorded or even reported orally what was going on at the time things were happening. Documents discussing past events were not written until cultures advanced enough for citizens to become aware of their ancestors' past existence. But that consciousness was expressed as recollections or memories, not as historical facts. Recollections are often only partial, inaccurate, and imaginative, and they are also often consciously or unconsciously selective, recalled, or forgotten.

The word "history" comes directly from the Latin *historia*, which came from the Greek *historia* or *historiē*, meaning "inquiry," "knowledge," or "information" obtained through research. The root form of the word is the verb *historeō*, meaning "inquire into or about" a person or thing. "History," then, in the Greek understanding is the "written account of one's inquiries," which is why Herodotus, the Greek historian (fifth century BCE), has been called "the father of history." He was the first to use the scientific method of asking questions, seeking pertinent information, and then drawing conclusions from the data collected. In trying to answer questions about the wars between the Persians and the Greeks, for example, Herodotus sought information through his travels and evidence from archaeology.

Old Testament writers certainly did not begin their accounts with questions about the persons and events of concern to them and then seek answers through formal research. In fact, there is no biblical word equivalent to the word "history," nor was there a word for "history" in Near Eastern literature. That does not mean that there is no "history" in the Bible; rather, biblical writers did not do careful research beforehand to verify their accounts. The word in the Hebrew Bible sometimes translated as "history" is *dabar*, but its primary meaning is "word," whether spoken or written. Among the many meanings of *dabar* are "saying," "speech," "news," "thing," "incident," "cause," and, rarely, "history." In the *NRSV* it is translated as "history" only in 2 Chronicles 9:29: "Now the rest of the acts of Solomon... are they not written in the history of the prophet Nathan?" *Dabar* would be rendered better as "record," as it is in 1 Chronicles 4:22, 29:29; 2 Chronicles 12:15, 33:19; and Esther 6:1. Such an understanding accords well with the fact that such records were kept by officials in the courts of Hebrew kings. Jehoshaphat was the recorder for David and Solomon (2 Samuel 8:16) and Joah, for Hezekiah (2 Kings 18:18).

Ancient historians like Herodotus were concerned not only with the events they were recording but also with the reasons for them. Writers of both the OT and NT believed that their God was behind the persons and events they wrote about, even if their convictions appear in confusing or contradictory statements. A main purpose of the writers, in fact, was to judge whether their characters' actions followed God's will, whether each one did what was right or evil "in the sight of the Lord." For example, "Solomon did what was evil in the sight of the Lord" (1 Kings 11:6); David and Hezekiah "did what was right in the sight of the Lord" (1 Kings 15:5; 2 Kings 18:3); "The Israelites did what was evil in the sight of the Lord" (Judges 6:1). Both Zechariah and Elizabeth "were righteous before God, living blamelessly according to all the commandments and regulations of the Lord" (Luke 1:6).

*Webster's Ninth New Collegiate Dictionary* defines "history" as a "chronological record of significant events (as affecting a nation or institution) often including an explanation of their causes." Given that definition, the writings from Joshua through Ezra-Nehemiah qualify, at least in part, as histories, with the exception of the short story, Ruth. Those writings give chronological accounts of Israelite "history" from the conquest of Canaan after 1250 BCE through the mid-fifth century BCE with the works of Ezra-Nehemiah.

### Understanding the Bible for What It Is

There are various ways of understanding the Bible. Some persons approach it from an extreme fundamentalist point of view that the Bible was verbally inspired by God, whose actual words were transmitted by human hands. For such persons the Bible is "the words of God." They regard it with extreme reverence as infallible and believe that it is valid for both faith and life.

However, it is impractical or impossible to observe many of the laws in the OT. For example, accepting what is written at face value would mean that it is wrong for men to shave their faces, menstruation is dirty and unclean, and children who curse their parents should be put to death. Some material is clearly antiquated, such as sections in Leviticus regulating animal sacrifices.

For many morally/ethically sensitive Jews and Christians, some passages in the Scriptures seem offensive, even abhorrent. See, for example, the stories of Lot, who offered his daughters to sexually crazed men (Genesis 19:1-17); the rape of Dinah by a non-Israelite from Shechem, with its aftermath of bloody killing, plundering, and taking wives and children as prey by the sons of Jacob, brothers of Dinah (Genesis 34:1-31); Tamar, who disguised herself as a prostitute in order to entice Judah, her father-in-law, to have sexual intercourse with her so that she could bear a child (Genesis 38:6-26); Saul, David, and the foreskins of Philistines (1 Samuel 18:20-30); and David, who had Bathsheba's husband killed so that he could marry her (2 Samuel 11:2-27).

In the OT there are passages filled with hatred toward personal or foreign enemies, such as the imprecatory psalms (e.g., parts of Psalms 5, 18, 55, 69, 104, 109, 143) and the poem of hate for Nineveh in Nahum. In the same way, the writer of the gospel of John shows a marked antipathy toward some Jews who did not believe in Jesus. "The Jews" is the author's distinctive title for the opponents of Jesus, and he writes to defend the Jews who believed in Jesus as the Messiah in contrast to those who did not. "The Jews had already agreed that anyone who confessed Jesus to be the Messiah would be put out of the synagogue" (John 9:18-23; see also 5:19-47; 8:12-59; 10:22-39; 12:36-43). And, in John, Jesus and his disciples are set apart from the Jews in a way very different than in the other gospels.

The book of Revelation contains numerous passages of hatred and vengeance toward non-Christians. See, for example, the vivid expression of the wrath of God and Christ as "the Lamb" (Revelation 6:12-17), which concludes: "Fall on us and hide us from the face of the one [God] seated on the throne and from the wrath of the Lamb; for the great day of their wrath has come, and who is able to stand?" (see also Revelation 14:8-11).

The stories presented in no way reflect the behavior of the people of their times in general, nor do we truly grasp their meaning by taking them literally. Using a more scholarly approach, we seek insights from the Bible about the many authors whose writings are included and about their circumstances and purposes for writing. For example, Tamar's action in tricking her father-in-law into having sexual relations with her can be partially explained by the fact that Hebrews believed that blood ties in the family line were extremely important for survival. Consequently, they instituted a law known as the "Levirate marriage." According to that law, when a brother who had no son died, another brother was to take the deceased brother's wife in marriage in order to produce a son and thereby perpetuate the deceased brother's name in the family line (Deuteronomy 25:5-10).

Tamar's husband, the first-born son of Judah, had died, but his living brother, Judah's last son Shelah, was too young to be given to Tamar in marriage. Judah promised that he would do this when Shelah was old enough, and Tamar went back to live in her father's home. However, after Shelah grew up, Judah delayed in fulfilling the promise he had made to Tamar. When Tamar heard that Judah was to be in the area, she disguised herself as a prostitute, covered her face so that Judah would not recognize her, and tricked him into having sex with her. She asked what he would give her in return, and he promised to send her a kid from his flock. He left his staff and his seal, including the cord used to carry it around his neck, with her as a pledge.

Three months later, Judah was told that Tamar was pregnant as the result of being a prostitute, which was an abomination to Hebrews. Judah said, "Bring her out, and let her be burned." On the way out, Tamar showed Judah the pledge, which he acknowledged. Realizing that Tamar was not a wanton prostitute, he said, "She is more in the right than I, since I did not give her to my son Shelah" (Genesis 38:26). Judah's confession of guilt that Tamar was more in the right than he shows a moral awareness that was unusual in the male-dominated society of that time. And, Tamar's actions, although probably not condoned by many modern readers, reflect Levirate law and her concern with protecting family lines. By understanding the context of the story, including customs of that time, we can gain some insight into the incident.

While some passages certainly illustrate that biblical writers reported not only nice and good stories but also the ugly and evil, many other passages in the Bible counterbalance those that seem distasteful or abhorrent. The story of Tamar and Judah is followed by that of Joseph and the temptation by his master's wife (Genesis 39:6-23). She could not resist the "handsome and good-looking" Joseph and asked him to have sex with her. By yielding Joseph would betray his master's trust, so Joseph replies: "How then could I do this great wickedness, and sin against God?" (Genesis 39:6-9). When the woman took hold of him to tempt him further, Joseph left his garment in her hand and fled. She falsely accused Joseph, and he was put into prison. Ultimately, he was vindicated "because the Lord was with him."

The stories of Tamar and Judah and Joseph and the Egyptian woman are from the same source, as we discuss in a later chapter. In the first story the author sees no wrong with the actions of the characters. Apparently he was aware of the obligation of a brother to marry the widow of a brother who died without a son. On the other hand, the same author presents Joseph as realizing that yielding to the woman's temptation was wrong. And the woman's actions were exposed as wicked and sinful.

Other stories show a solicitous concern for all persons and all nations. Increased understanding of how the literature of the Bible developed can help us appreciate why very different kinds of passages exist. The Bible is first and foremost a collection of religious writings, not the record of historical events or scientific facts. Biblical writers were thoroughly committed to their religious faith and were not concerned with history and certainly not with science. So, studying stories of persons and events in the Bible reveals only what the writers believed happened, not necessarily what actually occurred. The story of creation, for example, is not scientific fact but a confession of religious faith: "In the beginning when God created the heavens and the earth" (Genesis 1:1).

### Understanding the Bible Insightfully

Because biblical documents were not intended to convey historical truth, there is often insufficient information to separate historical fact from religious faith. The biblical documents themselves contain many differences, even contradictions. Understanding the Bible insightfully requires trying to understand *why* there are differences and contradictions. We must act precisely as judges do in the Greek sense of the terms *krinō* ("judge") and *kritikos* ("able to discern," "critical") and apply to the Bible the same kind of critical analysis applied to the works of Homer, Virgil, and Shakespeare and to other literary masterpieces. In other words, to study the Bible insightfully, we must approach it with open and inquisitive minds, acting as judges in trying to determine the most likely answers to questions we are investigating. However, often in biblical studies we can reach only tentative answers, not conclusive facts, and we must be satisfied with a consensus of opinions among scholars, if even that exists.

This type of critical study has roots in the Enlightenment in Europe (eighteenth century CE), when philosophers became especially conscious of Western history and prided themselves on their ability to reason and to think objectively. The Enlightenment provided special incentives for learning and critical and skeptical moods with respect to social and political thought. Such moods not only altered thinking about traditional worldviews but also led to questions concerning authorship, purpose of writing, and date and place of composition for literary works of all kinds.

The same moods of inquisitiveness, quest for learning and understanding, and even critical and skeptical thought were then applied to biblical history and literature in the nineteenth century. Biblical scholars began trying to determine what each biblical document revealed about the historical, political, and social contexts out of which it developed. Today scholars focus on helping us imagine ourselves living in biblical times. This means, then, that we let the OT enlighten us about the history and culture of the ancient Israelites and the NT about the history and social conditions during the rise of the early church in the Roman Empire.

Trying to understand the Bible insightfully involves the difficult process of trying to separate legend and myth from fact. It also involves asking and seeking answers to challenging questions. For example, why are there differing accounts of the creation and the flood in Genesis? How could Jesus have been born of a virgin (Matthew 1:18-25; Luke 1:26-35) and yet have a human father (Matthew 1:16; Luke 2:48, 4:22)? Why is a saying of Jesus sometimes reported in different words in two or three of the gospels?

Remember that writings of the Bible originated from individuals or communities committed to their Hebrew/Jewish or Christian faith. The writers' faith enabled them to deal with particular historical, social, and political situations of their own times. Therefore, different emphases appear in different writings because all addressed specific situations, and the particular social and cultural background of each writer affected what was written.

We can detect certain circumstances behind some writings more readily than others. The laws of the Pentateuch (for the Jews, Torah) were surely intended to provide regulations for the personal, social, and religious lives of the Hebrews/Israelites. The Hebrew prophets, those great social reformers of their times, believed God had called them to proclaim his will for people facing political, social, and economic injustice. They generally appeared in times of peace and prosperity and predicted adversity for those who heard their messages but did not obey. As the Hebrews/Israelites/Jews tried to preserve their identity in hostile environments and the Christians were striving to establish their own identity independent of Judaism, different beliefs and practices appeared in different biblical writings. And during the writing of the NT, both Jews and Christians were trying to accommodate themselves to a pagan environment in the Greco/Roman Empire without losing their individual identities.

## For Whom the Bible Was Written

Some OT writers began to look forward to a glorious age to come, free from oppression, and NT writers in general believed that the end of the world was coming soon. That's why biblical authors wrote for their own generations, *not* for future generations. When some persons in the church at Thessalonica were concerned that their faithful brothers who had died before Jesus returned would be left out, Paul wrote to reassure them. "We who are alive, who are left until the coming of the Lord, will by no means precede those who have died." The dead who were faithful "will rise first" and then those who are alive (1 Thessalonians 4:13-17). The phrases "we who are alive" and "who are left," which Paul mentions twice, clearly show his belief that he and other members of the church at Thessalonica would still be alive when Christ returned.

Paul wrote to the Philippians while he was in prison and apparently facing death because of sickness, persecution, or some other difficulty. He is hard pressed between wanting to die or remain alive. To die would mean to "be with Christ," but to remain alive would be better for the Philippian church members. He knows that he will remain alive and help them continue and grow in their faith (Philippians 1:12-26). Paul's choice was probably more difficult because he believed the end of the world was near, and he wanted to make the best of the time left. He told the Philippians, "The Lord is near," so they are not to "worry about anything" (Philippians 4:3-6).

The first three gospel writers agree that Jesus proclaimed that the Kingdom of God was near (Mark 1:14-15, 13:5-37; Matthew 3:2, 4:17, 24:4-36; Luke 10:8-11, 21:8-36). Some early Christians who were expecting the End thought that they had nothing to do but wait for that glorious day. We read that some people in the church at Thessalonica had become lazy and were not working. The author wrote to tell them to get to work and that "anyone unwilling to work should not eat" (2 Thessalonians 3:10).

Time was passing, and the Lord Jesus had not returned. When 2 Peter was written (end of first or beginning of second century CE), some evil scoffers were saying, "Where is the promise of his coming?" (2 Peter 3:4). The author gives two answers. First, "one fact" is not to be ignored (2 Peter 3:8), which – as with many Christians since his time – he found "in the Bible": "With the Lord one day is like a thousand years, and a thousand years are like one day" (2 Peter 3:8). This is an allusion to the first part of Psalm 90:4: "For a thousand years in your sight are like yesterday when it is past." By inverting the years and day of the psalmist, and by changing "yesterday" to "one day," 2 Peter makes the text applicable to his own day and to the future, not the past. The End is still to come.

Having stated his "one fact" from the Bible, the author of 2 Peter gives his theological arguments for explaining the delay of the Lord's return. The Lord is not delaying his promise but is patient so that everyone has time to repent. Moreover, "the day of the Lord will come like a thief" (2 Peter 3:10), a belief that is part of early Christian tradition elsewhere (1 Thessalonians 5:2-4; Matthew 24:42-43; Luke 12:33, 39-40; Revelation 3:3, 16:15). The author of Revelation uses the word "soon" (at least nine times) and the phrase "the time is near" in order to stress that the time of the End is close (Revelation 1:3, 22:10).

Since writers of the Bible were not writing for us today, they were also not telling us what to believe or what to do. This is true even for biblical ideas about God. We cannot actually learn about God, but only what those who wrote about God believed. When seeking religious "truths" in the Bible, we do so only by agreeing or disagreeing with what is written and then responding with faith and actions that seem appropriate for us personally.

When considering two or more accounts of similar sayings, persons, or events in the Bible, it is important to be careful in making a decision about which one to accept. To believe one and ignore the others or to reject both because of the contradictions or discrepancies in different accounts runs counter to what one faithful Bible writer declares: "All scripture...is useful for teaching, for reproof, for correction, and for training in righteousness" (2 Timothy 3:16). Later, when we consider some examples of what "the Bible says" in more than one way, our aim will be to understand why two or more accounts of the same person or phenomenon by equally faithful Bible writers often differ.

*Chapter Summary*

The word Bible derives from two Greek words and is generally translated "book." When declaring that "The Bible Says So!" people are definitely referring to that well-known "book" that has come to be considered the absolute authority or source regarding how Christians and Jews are supposed to live, behave, and believe. Yet, when seeking to understand the Bible in a more insightful way, we discover that it is really a collection of works written by many different authors at many different times using many different sources, both oral and written. It is, more accurately, a book of books. And, the Bible is not even the same collection of writings to all individuals, whether Jewish or Christian.

Although regarded today by many people as "*The* Holy Book," the writings incorporated into it were not considered holy or sacred at the time they were written. In fact, the authors were writing for a variety of reasons, and by careful study of the contexts in which they were writing, we can find clues to their purposes for writing and gain insight into the intended meaning of what they wrote. First and foremost, we must remember that the Bible's authors were not writing for us. They were writing because of a deep commitment to their religious faith. Over time, as the Bible was used in worship by faithful religious followers, its writings came to be designated as Scriptures, and it developed the authority that it has for us today.

Considered by fundamentalists to be the literal word of God, the Bible has many stories that actually have a fascinating origin in ancient writings and customs, including polytheism. And numerous laws and teachings, though pertinent to the times in which they originated, are impossible for us to follow today. Yet despite antiquated material and contradictions and discrepancies that make simple answers about the Bible and what it says invalid, we can gain invaluable insight about this remarkable collection of literary works and the religious messages its many authors were trying to communicate. Though biblical writers were not striving to report historical truths, the techniques used by scholars can help us understand not only the religious faith of the Bible's writers, but also the times in which and about which they wrote.

Chapter 2

ORAL AND WRITTEN SOURCES OF THE BIBLE

*Introduction*

Since humans learned to speak before learning to write, and speaking was the chief means of communication for centuries, especially among the uneducated, remembering what was spoken was extremely important. Consequently, ancient peoples, including the Hebrews and the Greeks, relied on memorization. We also see an emphasis on learning by memory or remembering in some ancient Mesopotamian documents, as illustrated in the following two quotations:

> The scribe who learns this text by heart escapes
> the enemy, is honoured [in his own land]...

> The sage and the learned shall together ponder [them], father shall tell [of them] to son and teach [them to] him, the ears of the shepherd and the herdsman shall be opened...this tradition that an old man had related in days long ago [he wrote down, and] left it as an instruction to coming generations.

These quotations from Eduard Nielson (*Oral Tradition* [Studies in Biblical Theology, 11; London: SCM Press, 1954], pp. 19-20) show the significance given to memory in preserving tradition. The words "the sage and the learned" indicate the origin of the quotation in an educational milieu. At the same time, shepherds and herdsmen are to listen (their ears "shall be opened"), presumably to learn and remember. The last quotation also shows, significantly, that the oral tradition was written down in order to preserve it for readers in the future. Thus, both memory and writing were sometimes simultaneous functions in passing along tradition from one generation to another. Likewise, the authors of the Bible used a variety of different sources, both oral and written, which are the focus of this chapter.

## Oral Transmission

According to 1 Chronicles 17:20, David is reported as saying: "There is no one like you, O Lord, and there is no God besides you, according to all that we have heard with our ears." This reflects the existence of oral transmission. However, it is doubtful that the Hebrews had come to believe that their God was the only god by David's time (c. 1000-961 BCE). Therefore, the monotheistic theme of passages in the latter part of Isaiah, written about the same time as 1 Chronicles (c. 600-400 BCE), was attributed to David by the biblical author. See "There is no God besides him" (Isaiah 45:14; see also Isaiah 44:8, 45:5-6, 45:21).

Messages, sometimes referred to as oracles, were transmitted in oral form until some occasion made it practical to write them down. See, for example, "The words of King Lemuel. An oracle that his mother taught him" (Proverbs 31:1) and "Now these are the last words of David: The oracle of David, son of Jesse" (2 Samuel 23:1). According to Jeremiah 36:2, the Lord speaks to Jeremiah: "Take a scroll and write on it all the words that I have spoken to you against Israel and Judah and all the nations, from the day I spoke to you." The context of this passage indicates that the scroll was to be read immediately by Baruch, Jeremiah's scribe, who had written it in order to warn the people what God would do to them unless they repented and changed their ways. However, an oracle of the prophet Isaiah was written for the future: "Go now, write it before them on a tablet, and inscribe it in a book, so that it may be for the time to come as a witness forever" (Isaiah 30:8).

For the Hebrews, memory was not regarded as a mere activity of the mind or intellect but also a part of the deepest emotions, a matter of the heart. Hebrews remembered what they had learned about the past as though they had been there when it happened. Memory of the past meant to relive it in the present as part of their religious experience. It was the responsibility of Hebrew fathers to keep the oral traditions of their people alive in the experiences of their families (see, e.g., Exodus 12:25-27; Deuteronomy 4:9-10, 11:18-21; Joshua 4:20-24).

The most important tradition that the Hebrews learned never to forget was their deliverance from Egypt. Expressed in prose and poetry, this is a repeated theme in the OT. And the act of remembering the Egyptian experience was frequently meant to evoke response or further action. Moreover, the Hebrews themselves not only remembered, but they also thought of God as remembering. And the act of remembering on the part of God or the people was to evoke action in response to what was remembered.

The sacrifice of the first-born served as a memorial of what God had done for the Hebrews:

> Moses said to the people, "Remember this day on which you came out of Egypt... You shall tell your Child... 'It is because of what the Lord did for me when I came out of Egypt.' ...You shall keep this ordinance...from year to year" (Exodus 13:3-10).

The Hebrews remembered because they thought that their God also remembered. God made a covenant with Noah never again to destroy the earth with a flood:

> When I bring clouds over the earth and the bow is seen in the clouds, I will remember my covenant that is between me and you... When the bow is in the clouds, I will see it and remember the everlasting covenant between God and every living creature (Genesis 9:14-16; see also Psalm 105:42-45).

God not only remembered his promises to Abraham, but he also fulfilled them. Sometimes remembering is contrasted with forgetting. Memory will bring good results, but forgetting will bring evil. The Israelites are to remember the Lord their God, so that he may confirm the covenant he made with their ancestors. If they forget their God and follow other gods to serve and worship them, they will surely perish by not obeying his ways (Deuteronomy 8:18-19; see also Deuteronomy 11:1-8).

While memory functioned to preserve the tradition of God's action in the history of his people, especially his act of deliverance through the Exodus experience, it also served to reinforce the subsequent and everlasting covenant of God with his people and their obligation to obey his commandments. In fact, nothing was more important in the Hebrew religion than learning and observing the commandments (laws) that the Hebrews believed were given by God. In the Pentateuch there are frequent references to hearing them as spoken, for example, Deuteronomy 6:3: "Hear therefore, O Israel, and observe them [God's commandments] diligently." In Deuteronomy 6:4-9, there is an excellent example of listening to what was spoken, memorizing what was heard, reciting it to family members and, finally, writing it down for others to read.

For insightful understanding of oral traditions that came to be written in the Bible, we must remember that memory is never infallible. Indeed, oral traditions became subject to misinterpretation, exaggeration, omission or repetition, and even abuse. This led to the necessity of preserving those traditions in written forms. Naturally, because memories preserved by the first transmitters faded with the passing of time, and the generations of persons who kept them alive died, some writings assumed a greater significance with passing decades. Gradually those writings were regarded as authoritative for use in worship and study and became the norms for religious life and practice.

### Written Transmission

The abundance of written documents from ancient Mesopotamia provides evidence of the enthusiasm for writing in that part of the world. One document, dating from about 2000 BCE, indicates that among the daily activities of a schoolboy was an exercise in learning to write. It is also clear from the OT itself that writing existed in Israel before any books of the Bible were written. Important experiences in the life of Israel were already recorded in books such as the "Book of the Wars of the Lord," from which a passage is quoted in Numbers 21:14-15. A passage is quoted from the "Book of Jashar" in Joshua 10:12-13. The "Book of the Acts of Solomon" is referred to in 1 Kings 11:41 and the "Book of the Annals of the Kings of Israel" in 1 Kings 14:19.

In the OT, writing is usually attributed to scribes, or reading and writing professionals, and to prominent persons like the prophets. However, one passage indicates that writing was also practiced by some of the common people. In a section that proclaims punishment for Assyria, Isaiah says that the remnant of the trees of Assyria's forest (symbolism for Israelite survivors taken to Assyria) "will be so few that a child can write them down" (Isaiah 10:19). Presumably, in the time of Isaiah (eighth century BCE) some children had learned how to write.

The Israelite monarchies came to an end in 587-586 BCE with the destruction of Jerusalem by the Babylonians and the deportation of many people to Babylon. Many Jews (Israelites from the tribe and land of Judah) remained in exile. But, beginning in about 538 BCE, groups of Jews periodically returned to their homeland in Palestine (see, e.g., Ezra 4:7-16; Nehemiah 1:1-3). The period from about 538 BCE to 334 BCE is part of the post-exilic era in Jewish history. Scholars generally agree that the writing of 1 and 2 Chronicles, Ezra, Nehemiah, Esther, and Ecclesiastes, among others, date from that period. Hebrew/Aramaic words for books and writing occur in those writings more often than in the rest of the OT together. This indicates that, during the post-exilic period of Jewish history, writing had gained ascendancy over memory and oral tradition. The writer of

Ecclesiastes puts it succinctly: "Of the making of books there is no end" (Ecclesiastes 12:12).

*Manuscripts of the Bible*
Not a single fragment of an original biblical writing has been preserved. However, thousands of manuscripts written over several centuries exist, for which there are two closely related methods of study. They are *Paleography* (ancient writing) and *Textual Criticism*, which are much too difficult for us to explore. Persons adept in these methods must have special skills in ancient spelling, languages and numerous scripts, and knowledge of writing instruments and the materials on which the writing occurs. Because most ancient manuscripts have no titles, names of authors, or dates of writing, paleographers decipher the manuscripts and try to establish dates of writing based on archaeological evidence, types of scripts and spelling, and modern technological methods such as carbon dating.

Although textual criticism is important for the best understanding of the Bible, most persons lack the tools to use the method adequately. Its aim is to determine the oldest texts of the Bible in their original languages and the history of the transmission of texts from the earliest to latest. Textual criticism is difficult, complex, and requires knowledge not only of biblical languages but also of the Latin, Syriac, Coptic, and Ethiopic languages of important early versions or translations of the Bible. Except for parts of Ezra and Daniel which were written in Aramaic, manuscripts of the OT were written in Hebrew. All manuscripts of the NT were written in Greek. That's why most of us have to be content to accept the judgments and conclusions of experts in textual criticism.

Until the invention of the printing press in the sixteenth century, every manuscript was written by hand, either by the one who composed it or by someone else. Indeed, m*anuscript* means "written by hand." Manuscripts were written in one of two forms, scrolls or codices ("leaf-books"). Writing was done on either papyrus, a paper-like product made in Egypt as early as 3,000 BCE, or on vellum (parchment), leather specially prepared from the skins of sheep, goats, or calves. The skins were stretched and glued together side by side to make them into scrolls, on which writing was done in columns. The manuscript of Isaiah from Qumran consists of 17 strips of leather sewn together. The scroll is 24.5 inches long and 10.5 inches wide, with 54 columns and a division that shows two parts of the work of 66 chapters.

Manuscripts were written with pen and ink. Pens, which were made from a hollow reed that was dried and cut on a slight angle, were more like our small brushes than later pens. They were flexible and therefore suitable for writing on the rough surfaces of papyrus and skins. There were two main colors of ink. One was made from the black powder deposited on ancient lamps and mixed with gum and water. The other was brown, made from the tissue of the galls on some plants.

The oldest Hebrew manuscripts are those discovered from 1947 onwards in the caves of Qumran, located in the desert of Judah near the northwestern shore of the Dead Sea. There are fragments from Qumran of every book in the OT except Esther, including very small fragments, whole books, and several complete copies of books. Although scholars disagree about the dating of the scrolls, a reasonable estimate is between the third century BCE and the first centuries CE. Before the discoveries at Qumran, the oldest OT manuscripts known to us, with the exception of a fragment of Deuteronomy, had not been written before the ninth century CE.

The oldest NT manuscript is a fragment of John 18, which probably dates from the beginning of the second century CE. There is also a codex of ten letters of Paul from about 200 CE and one of the gospels of Luke and John from the third century. Manuscripts of the whole NT, which date from the fourth and fifth centuries CE, were written in capital letters (uncials) and not divided into chapters and verses. Eventually, others were written in small letters. Christians came to prefer codices for writing in order to distinguish them from scrolls, which were used by Jews in the synagogue, as they are today. There are about 3,000 manuscripts of the NT, although four uncial codices are generally regarded as the most important for NT study.

We learn about the practice of dictating and writing from the book of Jeremiah and Paul's letters. Here are some examples: "Jeremiah called Baruch [his secretary]…and Baruch wrote on a scroll at Jeremiah's dictation all the words of the Lord that he had spoken to him" (Jeremiah 36:4). Later, officials from the court of King Jehoiakim asked Baruch how he wrote the words and if Jeremiah dictated them. Baruch replied: "He dictated all these words to me, and I wrote them with ink on the scroll" (Jeremiah 36:17-18).

Because manuscripts were handwritten, many factors entered into their production and/or reproduction. Naturally, mistakes would be made in the course of writing or copying a document. If the content was dictated, a copyist could hear something incorrectly and, if copying a manuscript, he could misread a word or words. By comparing copies of manuscripts, textual critics can detect not only differences in spelling and improvements in the language, but also more serious changes. For instance, copyists sometimes added short explanations, added or omitted words or phrases, or changed something to reflect their own opinions.

Textual critics must decide the most likely probabilities for recovering the author's words, and the text established by their critical study of the manuscripts is known as the *critical text*. Variations from that text in other manuscripts are given in footnotes called the *apparatus criticus* ("critical apparatus"). Translators of the Bible, such as those responsible for the *NRSV*, will sometimes have a note at the bottom of a page (e.g., "Other ancient authorities read" or "Another reading is") in order to let readers know that there are textual variants for a word or phrase. To see good illustrations of this, check the *NRSV* at Habakkuk 2:5; John 8:8, 8:11 and 17:21.

## Chapter Summary

The Bible today provides its readers with a rich array of writings that have been collected, edited, and translated over a period of hundreds and hundreds of years. Although not even a single remnant of any original biblical writing has survived, literally thousands of manuscripts of the Bible exist. Methods such as Paleography and Textual Criticism help to determine the dates of these manuscripts and to ascertain the historical transmission of different texts in their original languages. With the use of the very complex process of textual criticism, scholars have established what is known as the critical text, that is, the translations of the early texts that best represent the biblical authors' words and purported meaning.

Trying to capture the true essence of what biblical writers were hoping to communicate is a challenging process, however, especially since the OT was written primarily in Hebrew and the NT in Greek. Anytime a written work is translated from one language to another, there are certain words or phrases for which an exact match does not exist. Therefore, at least some meaning is lost in the translation process itself. This is complicated even more by the fact that the Bible's authors used many different oral and written sources to inform themselves about the people, places, and events they wrote about, with their own religious beliefs and other circumstances of their lives a strong motivating force for what and how they chose to write. This is reflected in varying accounts of the same event or story, often within the same book of the Bible, and in sometimes discrepant or even contradictory passages.

By the post-exilic period of Jewish history, writing became more prominent than oral transmission, and specific writings were used in worship and gradually considered to be sacred. The process of oral and written transmission that culminated in the Bible as we know it today was, by no means, without error. The fallibility of memory, which was so important in the transmission of oral traditions, was not the only problem. Written sources were handwritten until the sixteenth century, and a variety of errors occurred in that process as well. In the next chapter, we will focus on translating the Bible, including the most common errors in written transmission and challenges in translating the Hebrew and Greek texts into languages that are accurate, yet also understandable, to modern readers.

## Chapter 3

### Translating the Bible

*Introduction*

Given the vast number of manuscripts of the Bible, it was necessary to develop a process for establishing a basic, unified text. This process, of course, began by working with written Hebrew and Greek texts. Even today, regardless of the reasons or motives for studying the Bible, it is important to begin by seeking insight about the meanings of the original Hebrew or Greek texts and to use translations of them that capture, as much as possible, what the biblical authors intended to communicate.

Over time, literature that was recognized as being sacred became part of the Bible and was used in Jewish synagogues during worship services and for study by the scribes and rabbis (teachers in the synagogues). And, when individuals could no longer read the original languages of the Bible, needs arose for translations of biblical works into other languages. In this chapter, we consider the many challenges of this process.

*Establishing the Text*

The oldest manuscripts of the Bible were written only in consonants, without any spaces between words or divisions into chapters and verses. And, Hebrew texts have always been written and read from right to left. Naturally, it was hard to know how to pronounce words without vowels when reading texts aloud. Take, for example, the simple Hebrew word "son" (*BN*), for which the consonants are the equivalent of our "b" and "n." Should it be pronounced "BaN," "BeN," "BiN," or "BoN"?

During the years from about 500-1000 CE, a group of Jewish scholars invented a series of signs that became known as "vowel pointings." When placed under a consonant and/or in a consonant of a word, the word was pronounced in a certain way. So, the word for "son" was written from right to left (*NB*), with a dot in the middle of the B and two horizontal dots under it, and pronounced much as our word "bane." Scholars who invented the vowel pointings became known as *Masoretes*, from the Aramaic word *msr* (*mesar*), meaning "to transmit" or "hand down." The complete texts of the Hebrew Scriptures that those "transmitters" handed down during succeeding centuries are known as the Masoretic Text (MT). It became the accepted text and has been the basis for most translations of the Hebrew Scriptures. There are various editions and revisions of the Masoretic Text, with an especially well-known one by Rudolf Kittel (1853–1929). The latest edition of Kittel's work is *Biblia Hebraica Stuttgartensia*, edited by H. P. Ruger and others, with a critical apparatus by G. E. Weil (Stuttgart, 4th edn, 1990).

An accepted text for the Greek NT was also established. In 1516 CE, Erasmus Desiderius (c. 1469–1536) published an edition of the Greek NT that was the basis for the German NT of Martin Luther in 1522 and for the English NT by William Tyndale in 1525. Erasmus's work also influenced later editions of the Greek NT, especially those of B. F. Westcott and F. J. A. Hort (1881–1882), who published *The New Testament in the Original Greek*, and Ehrhard Nestle, who published the Greek NT entitled *Novum Testamentum Graece* in 1898. Nestle's work has been revised through many editions, the latest in 1998 by Kurt and Barbara Aland and others. A committee of scholars from America and abroad published *The Greek New Testament*, intended primarily for persons wanting to study and translate a Greek text. The Nestle text and *The Greek New Testament* are used by most New Testament students. The Masoretic Text by Kittel and others continues to be the basis for translations of the Hebrew Scriptures. That text and sometimes translations based on it are enhanced by references to the Greek OT, the Septuagint.

The basic text of the Bible for most Catholic translations is that of Jerome (c. 345–420 CE), probably the best biblical scholar in the Church of the era when the use of Latin prevailed. He translated various books of the Bible into Latin at different times, completing his work in 405 CE. In about 500 CE, Jerome's translations were collected and bound into a single volume, which later became known as the *Vulgate*. That word is derived from the Latin verb *vulgo*, meaning to "make common to all" or "make accessible to all," that is, "the public." As the name suggests, Jerome's translations were intended primarily for the common people of his time. The *Vulgate* was declared the official Bible of the Roman Catholic Church by the Council of Trent in 1546 CE. In that edition, however, not all of the translations go back to Jerome.

## Divisions in the Texts

From ancient times, scholars began to realize that in order to direct readers to specific passages in the Bible they had to make that process easier. During the Babylonian captivity of the Jews (fifth century BCE), some Rabbis marked scrolls into sections and subsections and designated them with Hebrew or Aramaic numerals. The Hebrew Torah (or Greek Pentateuch) was the first to be divided into larger and smaller units based on subject matter. In Babylonia the Torah was read at services of worship on a one-year cycle, so the text was divided into 53 or 54 units. However, in the rabbinic schools of Palestine, the Torah was read in a three-year cycle, so it was divided into 154 units. Sectional divisions appear also in the Qumran Scrolls, although they differ from later divisions.

Beginning about 1205, editions of the Latin Bible were divided into chapters and verses. In 1551, an English printer named Robert Stephens published a Greek and Latin NT in which verses were numbered in a similar way to our modern translations. And, in 1555, he published an edition of the *Vulgate*, the first complete Bible with verse numbers and including the Apocrypha.

## Errors Made during the Transmission of Manuscripts

While the oldest manuscripts of the Bible were written in capital letters (uncials) in solid lines from beginning to end, scribes, perhaps because they were interested in writing faster, developed a type of writing known as "minuscules," meaning "small." As manuscripts were being studied, copied, transmitted, and translated into different languages throughout several centuries, lines were separated into words, sentences, and ultimately chapters and verses. Remember that all manuscripts were written by hand before the invention of the printing press in 1450 CE and the first use of movable type in 1456. If a copyist made a mistake, he either continued or sometimes rubbed smooth a text and wrote over it again. Such a text is called a *palimpsest* (meaning "rubbed off" or "smooth again").

Obviously, such processes were not free from errors, but the situation is not as bad as it might seem. Paleographers have given the following technical names to the most frequent kinds of scribal errors made in the transmission of manuscripts:

> *Dittography* ("written twice") was the accidental repetition of a letter, word, or line meant to be written only once.

*Haplography* ("single writing") was the accidental omission of a word, syllable, line, or sentence because it was similar to material near it. It is the opposite of dittography.

*Homoioarchton* ("like beginning") and *homoioteleuton* ("like ending") were the two main reasons for haplography. These were omissions of a syllable, word, or line(s) because the copyist's eye fell on a similar beginning or ending. After copying the one, he went to the similar material, skipping all in between.

*Homography* ("like writing") was mistaking Hebrew consonants that looked almost alike. For example, the Hebrew letters roughly the equivalent of the English B and K, D and R, and W and Z, which look very different, were easily confused in Hebrew because they were very similar.

*Metathesis* ("placing after") was transposing letters in a word or changing the order of words as, for example, in the English "crud" and "curd" or "mats" and "mast."

## *Pause for Reflection*

Despite errors in the making and transmission of biblical manuscripts through the centuries, the complete manuscript of Isaiah from Qumran, probably dating from the beginning of the second century BCE, differs by only about five to eight percent from the Masoretic Text of the beginning of the tenth century CE. That is a good test of the accuracy of biblical manuscripts in general. Ancient Hebrew and Greek texts used for biblical study are as reliable as can be expected. However, since most people today cannot read the biblical languages, they must rely on modern translations, of which there seems to be no end.

The groundwork for scholarly study of the Bible has been done for us through modern translations. Some translations, though, especially the so-called "standard translations," convey the meaning of original texts better than others. Interestingly, there are sometimes more differences among translations than in the ancient texts. Translations sometimes do not convey the precise meaning of the ancient texts, because translators have numerous challenges, especially in choosing the right words in their language for those of the Hebrew and Greek texts. And it is not only a matter of words. There are seven voices in Hebrew and three in Greek grammar, compared with only two in English, that is, active and passive. Sometimes meanings of words differ according to the voice of the verb, so translators must choose meanings according to the context. In fact, members of the committee responsible for the *Revised Standard Version (RSV)* and the *New Revised Standard Version (NRSV)* chose among proposed meanings of words by majority vote. The passages compared below illustrate differing results of the translation process.

## Some Important English Translations

For three centuries the most widely used Bible in the English language was the *King James Version (KJV)*, also known, especially in America, as the *Authorized Version (AV)*. Published in 1611, it was based on older English versions going back to that of William Tyndale of 1525, which the translators considered to be no longer adequate. From 1881–1885 the *Authorized Version* was revised, and a version of it was edited by the American Version Committee and published in 1901 as the *American Standard Version (ASV)*. It was then revised by a committee of scholars and is known as the *Revised Standard Version (RSV)*. The New Testament was published in 1946, the Old Testament and New Testament together in 1952, and the Old and New Testaments together with the Apocrypha in 1956.

Until 1965 there were two English versions of the Bible authorized by the Roman Catholic Church, one known as the *Douay Bible* and one later translated by Ronald A. Knox, a Monsignor in the Church. The Douay version got its name from the city Douai in Italy, and later its name was changed to the *Douay-Rheims Version*. The New Testament was published in 1582 and the whole Bible in 1609–1610. Several more versions were published in the centuries after that.

In addition to the *KJV*, the *ASV*, and the *RSV*, there have been other noteworthy English translations, including the *New International Version (NIV)*, 1978; the *New King James Version (NKJV)*, 1982; the *Revised English Bible (REB)*, 1989; the *New Revised Standard Version (NRSV)*, 1989; and the *New Jerusalem Bible (NJB)*, 1998, which is a Catholic version.

## Translation Challenges

Throughout the centuries, new manuscripts have been discovered, and new and improved methods and tools for the study of ancient manuscripts and the Bible have evolved. This has led to the creation of new translations, as have changing times, customs, and traditions. For instance, much of the spelling and other aspects of the language used in the *KJV* and the *ASV* are outdated. Examples are the pronouns "thee," "thine," "ye," "thou," and similar expressions and verbal endings in -est, -st, and -th in such words as "sayest," "saith," "shouldest," "knoweth," and "hast." Similarly, "which" is generally no longer used with persons, having been replaced by "who" or "that." Meanings of words are constantly changing, and new words are being added to our vocabularies. Over two thousand words and phrases of the *KJV* are now archaic, as affirmed in the various translations below. Many Hebrew and Greek words have more than one meaning, so translators must decide not only which meaning best fits the context but also ensure it will be clear to modern readers who may lack an understanding of that context.

Translators are confronted with other challenges, as well. They must choose between a more accurate translation or a more familiar one, so that readers clearly understand the meaning of the text. Likewise, they must decide how literally to translate a passage. Simple narratives such as the stories of creation, narratives of Abraham, and the gospels, for example, do not cause as much difficulty as Paul's letters and the book of Hebrews. Translations that are too literal might be confusing, if not misunderstood. There is also the question of how much to paraphrase and to what extent to convey lifestyles and customs of the worlds of the Bible. For some things there simply are no equivalents in modern languages, for example, types of clothing, values of coins, and kinds of foods.

### *Comparisons of Different Translations*

In the following pages are examples of passages from the eight different versions mentioned above that help to illustrate challenges of the translation process. Their order is *KJV, ASV, RSV, NIV, NKJV, REB, NRSV,* and *NJB*. Of the numerous translations after the *RSV*, I have chosen the last five because they are neither too loosely nor too literally translated to be accurate, nor are they misleading as paraphrases sometime are.

The first passage shows how a change in the meaning of a word can affect translations. For example, the bowels and the heart, in Hebrew and Greek thought, referred both to emotions and to human anatomy. Joseph's feelings for his brothers are expressed as follows:

*Genesis 43:30*
- *(KJV)* "His bowels did yearn upon his brother: and he sought where to weep; and he entered into his chamber, and wept there."
- *(ASV)* "His heart yearned over his brother: and he sought where to weep; and he entered into his chamber, and wept there."

(RSV) "His heart yearned for his brother, and he sought a place to weep. And he entered his chamber and wept there."
(NIV) "Deeply moved at the sight of his brother, Joseph hurried out and looked for a place to weep. He went into his private room and wept there."
(NKJV) "Now his heart yearned for his brother, so Joseph made haste and sought somewhere to weep. And he went into his chamber and wept there."
(REB) "Joseph, suddenly overcome by his feelings for his brother, was almost in tears, and he went into the inner room and wept."
(NRSV) "Overcome with affection for his brother, and he was about to weep. So he went into a private room and wept there."
(NJB) "So strong was the affection he felt for his brother that he wanted to cry. He went into his room and there he wept."

There are other interesting examples of the use of "bowels," sometimes translated as "heart," in ways unlike those of today. When Paul writes to Philemon asking him to take back his runaway slave Onesimus, he says:

*Philemon 1:12*
(KJV) "Whom I have sent again: thou therefore receive him, that is, mine own bowels."
(ASV) "Whom I have sent back to thee in his own person, that is, my very heart."
(RSV) "I am sending him back to you, sending my very heart."
(NIV) "I am sending him – who is my very heart – back to you."
(NKJV) "I am sending him back. You therefore receive him, that is, my own heart."
(REB) "In sending him back to you I am sending my heart."
(NRSV) "I am sending him, that is, my own heart, back to you."
(NJB) "I am sending him back to you – that is to say, sending you my own heart."

The Greek word (*splanchna*), translated as "bowels" or "heart," is literally "viscera" and is used metaphorically of the emotions or feelings. The versions using bowels and heart are literal, although antiquated. Actually, Paul does not get around to asking Philemon to take back Onesimus until verse 17, but inserting the idea of taking him back here makes Paul's intentions clear from the start. At the same time, it detracts from his sincere desire to keep Onesimus himself. Perhaps it would be more in keeping with the text here and what follows to say simply: "I am sending him back to you as if he were me." This coincides with what Paul says in Philemon 1:17: "Welcome him as you would welcome me."

Sometimes the kidneys were thought to be the seat of the emotions, as the following passage illustrates.

*Jeremiah 12:2*
- (*KJV*) "Thou art near in their mouth, and far from their reins" (kidneys).
- (*ASV*) "Thou art near in their mouth, and far from their heart" (with a footnote: "Heb. *Reins*").
- (*RSV*) "Thou art near in their mouth and far from their heart."
- (*NIV*) "You are always on their lips but far from their hearts."
- (*NKJV*) "You are near in their mouth But far from their mind."
- (*REB*) "You are ever on their lips, yet far from their hearts."
- (*NRSV*) "You are near in their mouths yet far from their hearts."
- (*NJB*) "You are on their lips, yet far from their heart."

This is an excellent example of translators trying to be true to the Hebrew text but at the same time modernizing the prophet's thought with the use of "heart(s)" instead of kidneys. The point of Jeremiah is that some persons who have turned from the Lord continue to confess or praise him, but they are not sincere. It was difficult, though, even for the *NRSV* to give up entirely the language of the *KJV*.

"Bowels" is used in the physical sense in the vivid description below of Joab's assassination of Amasa. In the *KJV*, *rib* in italics indicates that the word is not in the text and was supplied by the translators.

*2 Samuel 20:10*
- (*KJV*) "He smote him therewith [the sword] in the fifth *rib*, and shed out his bowels to the ground."
- (*ASV*) "He smote him therewith in the body, and shed out his bowels to the ground."
- (*RSV*) "Joab struck him with it in the body, and shed his bowels to the ground."
- (*NIV*) "Joab plunged it into his belly, and his intestines spilled out on the ground."
- (*NKJV*) "He struck him with it in the stomach, and his entrails poured out on the ground."
- (*REB*) "Joab struck him with it in the belly and his entrails poured out to the ground."

below, for example, that the word "suffer" was used with several meanings that no longer make sense.

*Leviticus 19:17*
- (*KJV*) "Thou shalt in any wise rebuke thy neighbour, and not suffer sin upon him."
- (*ASV*) "Thou shalt surely rebuke thy neighbor, and not bear sin because of him."
- (*RSV*) "You shall reason with your neighbor, lest you bear sin because of him."
- (*NIV*) "Rebuke your neighbor frankly so you will not share in his guilt."
- (*NKJV*) "You shall surely rebuke your neighbor, and not bear sin because of him."
- (*REB*) "Reprove your fellow-countryman frankly, and so you will have no share in his guilt."
- (*NRSV*) "You shall reprove your neighbor, or you will incur guilt yourself."
- (*NJB*) "You will reprove your fellow-countryman firmly and thus avoid burdening yourself with a sin."

This text seems to mean that persons should reprove others who sin so that they are not responsible for the sins of the others. Otherwise, they would be sinning themselves if they did not reprove other sinners. Who today would understand the meaning of the *KJV*: "not suffer sin upon him"? Later translators were all trying to convey the meaning of the passage.

The word "suffer" sometimes meant "let" or "permit." See, for example, Exodus 22:18, where "suffer" is used in the *KJV* and the *ASV*, but in the others it is translated either as "permit" or "allow." Perhaps a better known passage is Jesus' words in Mark 10:14 (Matthew 19:14; Luke 18:16), where the *KJV* and the *ASV* read: "Suffer the little children to come unto me," while the others have "let." Similarly, in the New Testament the Greek word for "love" (*agapē*) is translated as "charity" in the *KJV* but with "love" in all the others. For example, see the well-known poetic piece of Paul in 1 Corinthians 13:1: "Though I speak with the tongues of men and of angels, and have not charity" (*KJV*). Today, the word "love" conveys the meaning of *agapē* better than charity.

When the *RSV* first translated the Hebrew word *almah* in Isaiah 7:14 as "young woman" instead of "virgin" as in the *KJV*, the reaction varied from consent to condemnation. Those who objected said that it threatened the

Christian doctrine of the virgin birth of Christ. However, Matthew's quotation from LXX Isaiah 7:14 in Matthew 1:23, where the Greek *parthenos*, meaning "virgin," occurs, can be used to support that doctrine. See also Luke 1:27. In the *ASV* there is a note at "virgin" in Isaiah 7:14: "Or, maiden." Some translators of the *RSV* were reluctant to change, so at "young woman" they inserted a note: "Or *virgin*." "Virgin" is retained in the *NIV* and *NKJV*, and "young woman" is given in the *REB*, *NRSV*, and the *NJB*, although the latter has a note: "For young woman Gk reads virgin, interpreted by Mt of Mary."

Numerous passages demonstrate how some words or phrases have changed in meaning or can be translated differently. Consider Mark 1:30, where the Greek adverb *euthus*, which basically means "immediately," is rendered as follows in our eight translations: "anon," "straightway," "immediately," omitted in translation (in *NIV*), "at once," "as soon as," "at once," and "at once." In Mark 2:4 (*KJV*), some persons were trying to take a paralyzed man to Jesus to be healed, but "they could not come nigh unto him for the press." The antiquated words "come nigh unto" are one word in Greek, and "press" is for the Greek word *ochlos*, meaning "crowd" or "multitude." The *ASV* retains "come nigh" but has "crowd." Our other translations modernize "come nigh" in various ways and generally have "crowd."

Additional examples of diverse translations of antiquated words include Acts 13:16, in which the same word is variously translated as "give audience," "harken," "listen," and "listen to me." In 1 Corinthians 14:11, quoted below, Paul is writing about converts at worship and speaking in tongues, that is, strange and ecstatic language that might not be understood by others. It shows the change in meanings of Greek words and the difficulty translators have in trying to convey the meaning in lucid English. To fully appreciate the differences among translations, it is necessary to read the passages in their contexts.

*1 Corinthians 14:11*

(*KJV*) "If I know not the meaning of the voice, I shall be unto him that speaketh a barbarian, and he that speaketh shall be a barbarian unto me."

(*ASV*) "If then I know not the meaning of the voice, I shall be to him that speaketh a barbarian, and he that speaketh will be a barbarian unto me."

(*RSV*) "If I do not know the meaning of the language, I shall be a foreigner to the speaker and the speaker a foreigner to me."

(NIV) "If then I do not grasp the meaning of what someone is saying, I am a foreigner to the speaker, and he is a foreigner to me."

(NKJV) "Therefore if I do not know the meaning of the language, I shall be a foreigner to him who speaks, and he who speaks will be a foreigner to me."

(REB) "If I do not know the speaker's language, his words will be gibberish to me, and mine to him."

(NRSV) "If then I do not know the meaning of a sound, I will be a foreigner to the speaker and the speaker a foreigner to me."

(NJB) "But if I do not understand the meaning of the sound, I am a barbarian to the person who is speaking, and the speaker is a barbarian to me." (At "barbarian" there is a note: "i.e., someone who does not understand Gr.")

The use of the antiquated verbs and prepositions of *KJV* is discontinued after the *ASV*. The word translated as "meaning" is *dynamis*; it originally meant physical "power," "might," or "strength" and then came to mean the "force" or "meaning" of a word. The word translated "voice" is *phonē*, which originally meant "sound" or "tone" made with the lungs and throat of humans or animals and then "the sound of a voice." So, the phrase "meaning of the voice" is accurate, but it no longer is used and, therefore, is vague for modern readers.

The word "barbarian" is an accurate translation of the Greek *barbaros*, but it is misleading. For us a barbarian is someone from another land, culture, or people often thought to be uncivilized and inferior to us. For the Greeks, however, a barbarian was a person who did not know or speak the Greek language. The *REB* varies most from the Greek text, but it makes perfect sense in light of the context. As with "barbarian," "foreigner" is misleading because for us a foreigner is a person from another country, no matter what language is spoken. "Meaning," used in all translations except the *REB*, is correct, and use of "sound" with it (*NRSV, NJB*) goes back to the earliest meaning of the word *phonē*. "Grasp the meaning of what someone is saying" in the *NIV* is less literal but conveys the meaning precisely.

*2 Corinthians 6:11-12*
In the following passage, Paul is writing about his difficulty in trying to win back the Corinthian converts' support for his work after it had been challenged by some adversaries. Here is what he says in the words of our eight translations, illustrating how hard it is to understand Paul's Greek and to put it into good English:

(KJV) "O ye Corinthians, our mouth is open unto you, our heart is enlarged. Ye are not straitened in us, but ye are straitened in your own bowels."

(ASV) "Our mouth is open unto you, O Corinthians, our heart is enlarged. Ye are not straitened in us, but ye are straitened in your own affections."

(RSV) "Our mouth is open to you, Corinthians; our heart is wide. You are not restricted by us, but you are restricted in your own affections."

(NIV) "We have spoken freely to you, Corinthians, and opened wide our hearts to you. We are not withholding our affection from you, but you are withholding yours from us."

(NKJV) "O Corinthians! We have spoken openly to you, our heart is wide open. You are not restricted by us but you are restricted by your own affections."

(REB) "We have spoken very frankly to you, friends in Corinth; we have opened our heart to you. There is no constraint on our part; any constraint there may be is in you."

(NRSV) "We have spoken frankly to you Corinthians; our heart is wide open to you. There is no restriction in our affections, but only in yours."

(NJB) "People of Corinth, we have spoken frankly and opened our heart to you. Any distress you feel is not on our side, the distress is in your own selves."

The most literal translations are the *KJV* and *ASV*. The word translated as "straitened" is *stenochōreō*, which literally means "straiten," "cramp," or "compress" and hence "restrain" or "restrict." Paul had used that word in 2 Corinthians 4:8, the only other place it occurs in the NT. There he writes about his troubles and begins by using the word *thlibō*, followed by *stenochōreō*. *Thlibō* literally means "make narrow by pressure" or "compress" and then metaphorically "oppress," "afflict," "distress," which is almost the same meaning as *stenochōreō*. Here is how our translations render the two words: "troubled – distressed"; "pressed – straitened"; "afflicted – crushed"; "hard pressed – crushed"; "hard pressed – crushed"; "hard pressed – cornered"; "afflicted – crushed"; "subjected to every kind of hardship – distressed." "Crushed" seems a bit too severe here because it implies being utterly defeated. Facing opposition, Paul was emotionally in a tough situation, and there was not much affection on the part of either Paul or the Corinthians. All translations agree that Paul thinks the Corinthians are responsible for this situation.

## Chapter Summary

Over the years, the Bible has been translated many different times from its original Hebrew, Aramaic, and Greek languages. Innumerable challenges are involved with that process, perhaps most importantly the difficulties in attempting to convey in modern languages what the authors wrote in their ancient languages. It is difficult, if not impossible, to capture completely the meanings they were intending to communicate. And that is just one aspect of the challenges involved in the translation process. Indeed, thousands of manuscripts of the Bible existed, and it became necessary to establish the basic text, that is, a text that is generally accepted for use in scholarly study. What is known as the Masoretic Text became the established text for the OT, and *The Greek New Testament* became one of the most accepted NT texts.

While a variety of different errors were made in the written transmission of biblical manuscripts, a process that most scholars believe occurred over a period of twelve centuries, it was a surprisingly accurate process. In fact, today some translations of the Bible have more differences among them than differences among the ancient texts. And, some translations of the Bible definitely convey what scholars believe to be the message ancient writers were trying to communicate more accurately than others. In a comparison of eight different standard translations of the Bible, it is possible very quickly to see differences among translations and the difficulty in understanding language that varies considerably from modern usage or that is simply archaic.

While written neither to be historical nor scientific fact, the Bible was the means for its authors to share their *religious beliefs* and *how they understood their faith within the context of their times.* It is tempting to read meaning into biblical passages based on our current thinking or beliefs or to take those passages out of context to support a particular point of view. That is why it is so important to study the original Hebrew or Greek words to gain insight into what biblical authors were most likely trying to communicate. Before learning more about how the use of words and their translations help us understand biblical texts insightfully, we focus on the sources of these texts in the next chapter.

Part II

THE OLD TESTAMENT

# Chapter 4

## SOURCES OF THE PENTATEUCH

### Introduction

During the nineteenth and early twentieth centuries, when the Bible was subjected to increased scrutiny by the power of reason, biblical scholars were becoming more willing to make critical judgments about the Bible as a collection of religious literary works. They began to recognize differences in literary style, words for the deity, and viewpoints. They also observed repetitions and contradictions, evident even within a few verses in the book of Genesis and certainly in other writings in the OT, as well.

Already in the first half of the eighteenth century a French doctor, Jean Astruc, detected the occurrence and reoccurrence in Genesis of two Hebrew words for God, *Yahweh* and *Elohim*, which are not used interchangeably. Sometimes the one occurs more frequently and sometimes the other does. Although Astruc still believed that Moses wrote the Pentateuch (the first five books of the Bible), he concluded that the words represented two different sources used by Moses. Astruc designated the sources A and B. This marked the beginning of the study of sources or *source criticism.*

Most OT scholars today continue to subscribe to a basic theory of OT source criticism that identifies four main sources of the Pentateuch: J, E, D, and P. Each one of these has special local, national, and religious interests and particular literary styles, as well. The theory has been modified and expanded, for example, by the elimination of one source and the addition of others, and applied to books beyond the Pentateuch. While the names of the sources' authors are unknown, the oldest source, according to the German scholar who suggested the hypothesis, is J. Although estimates vary, perhaps the best date for J as written material is the tenth/ninth centuries BCE.

## Source J

The designation of J derives from the German word *Jahve*, representing the Hebrew word for the deity (*YHWH*), which in English is Yahweh. Yahweh is usually rendered as "the Lord" in English translation, although the *NJB* uses "Yahweh." "Jehovah" is the predominant usage in the *ASV*, although the *KJV* rarely uses it. Yahweh is the favorite word for the deity in the J source, although the combination "Lord God" (*Yahweh Elohim*) is also often used.

J shows a special concern for persons and places in the southern kingdom of Judah, and this is another reason for the designation J. Its principal theme is the exploits of Abraham and his descendants from humble beginnings to a great nation under the leadership of Yahweh. For that reason, it has sometimes been called a religious and patriotic epic, the theme of which is stated in Genesis 12:1-3:

> Now the Lord (*YHWH*) said to Abram (Abraham), "Go from your country and your kindred and your father's house to the land that I will show you. I will make of you a great nation, and I will bless you, and make your name great, so that you will be a blessing. I will bless those who bless you, and the one who curses you I will curse; and in you all the families of the earth shall be blessed."

The Yahwist (name for the author of J) has woven oral legends, folktales, and memories into a rather unified account. He takes for granted an agrarian way of life and a religious cultus. For J the deity is openly anthropomorphic, that is, in human form. For example, Adam and Eve "heard the sound of the Lord God (*Yahweh Elohim*) walking in the garden" (Genesis 3:8), and God himself often spoke to Moses from Mount Sinai (e.g., Exodus 19:2-3).

Theologically, in spite of the disobedience of the humans he has created, Yahweh spares them from death. However, the woman must bear children in pain, and the man must earn his food by the sweat of his face (Genesis 3:1-24). The author of J had observed the realities of pain in childbirth and hard labor in life and then explains the reasons for them. Although humans had become so wicked that their thoughts were continually only evil (Genesis 6:5), J's flood story shows that Yahweh is in control of humans and events as he destroys the wicked and saves the righteous Noah.

## Source E

The second source of the Pentateuch is designated E from *Elohim*, another Hebrew word for deity. According to E, the name Yahweh was revealed for the first time to Moses (Exodus 3:13-15), but after that the Elohist (name for the author of E) uses Yahweh as well as Elohim. And P, the fourth source, sometimes also uses Elohim for God. The E source is rejected by some scholars, and others think it was combined with J (J+E) near the end of the eighth century BCE. Verses assigned to a particular source by some scholars may not always be the same as those of other scholars, but the point of different sources is valid, nevertheless.

E is generally dated from the ninth or eighth century BCE, and it shows a special interest in people and places of the northern kingdom Israel, where Ephraim, son of Joseph, was the most important tribe. This is one of the reasons why E is used as the designation for this source. In a supplementary way, E parallels the J account and, like it, begins with the story of Abraham. It begins, though, with Abraham in Canaan, not in Haran (J+P), where God renewed his promise to Abraham in the form of a vision. The following verses from Genesis 15:1-5 illustrate the view of some scholars that sources may sometimes be combined.

> (J) The word of the Lord came to Abram in a vision, "Do not be afraid, Abram, I am your shield; your reward shall be very great." But Abram said, "O Lord God, what will you give me, for I continue childless, (E) and the heir of my house is Elizer of Damascus?" And Abram said, "You have given me no offspring, (J) and so a slave born in my house is to be my heir." But the word of the Lord came to him, "This man shall not be your heir; no one but your very own issue shall be your heir." (E) He brought him outside and said, "Look toward heaven and count the stars, if you are able to count them." Then he said to him, "So shall your descendants be."

The Elohist is usually more sensitive ethically than the Yahwist. According to J, Abram was afraid that, when Pharaoh saw the beauty of his wife Sarai (Sarah), he would want her and kill him. The Yahwist has Abraham say that Sarah is his sister instead of his wife (Genesis 12:10-20). In a similar story the Elohist modifies the lie by having Abram say that his wife Sarah is his half-sister, that is, "the daughter of my father but not the daughter of my mother" (Genesis 20:12).

The Elohist is occasionally more emotionally expressive than the Yahwist. In the account of the test of Abraham's faith by his willingness to sacrifice his only son Isaac (Genesis 22:1-14), the Elohist is at his literary best in arousing his readers' emotions. See also the forceful questioning of their father Jacob by Rachel and Leah concerning their inheritance (Genesis 31:4-16, E), Joseph weeping after seeing his brothers (Genesis 42:24, E), and Jacob's astonishment and disbelief when learning that his son was alive and the joy the reader shares with him at his words, "Enough! My son Joseph is still alive. I must go and see him before I die" (Genesis 45:26-28, J+E).

### Source D

The third source is designated D from the Deuteronomic Code of Jewish laws (Deuteronomy 12–26). That code was probably the result of, or gave rise to, the religious reformation under King Josiah, about 621 BCE (2 Kings 22:1–23:27). In contrast to Kings Manasseh and Amon, who "did evil in the sight of the Lord," King Josiah "did what was right in the sight of the Lord." He ordered the high priest Hilkiah to repair the Temple, and he reported that he found "the book of the law" there (2 Kings 22:8, 11). The prophetess Huldah warned Josiah that disaster would fall upon the city of Jerusalem because the people of Judah had forsaken the Lord, the God of Israel, and "made offerings to other gods." Josiah ordered that "the book of the covenant" be read and its commandments and statutes be put into effect (2 Kings 23:2, 21). This book was probably some or all of Exodus 21–23 (see also Exodus 24:7) and was likely the first piece of Hebrew literature to be regarded as sacred and, therefore, to be obeyed. It was based on the codes of Hammurabi and those of Sumer and Akkad from the second millennium BCE.

A royal housecleaning in Jerusalem followed Josiah's orders. The vessels made for the gods Baal and Asherah were brought out of the Temple of Yahweh and burned. Josiah deposed the idolatrous priests, removed those who sacrificed to Baal, and destroyed the houses of the male prostitutes who were in the house of Yahweh, where the women wove hangings for the Asherah. Shrines where other gods were worshiped were destroyed, the Temple became the only legitimate place of worship, and the Passover was reinstituted. Many other actions were taken to subdue evidence of Baalism.

There are some clear parallels between the laws of Deuteronomy, especially chapters 12–26, and the reforms of Josiah reported in 2 Kings. The destruction of idolatrous places of worship is emphatic: "You must demolish completely all the places where the nations...served their gods... Break down their altars, smash their pillars" (Deuteronomy 12:2-3; 2 Kings 23:6-15, 19). Worship is restricted to Jerusalem (Deuteronomy 12:4-7, 13-14; 2 Kings 23:4-15). Deuteronomy 17:3 forbids worship of heavenly bodies, and 2 Kings 23:4-6 reports the destruction of the vessels used in such worship. Passover, reinstituted by Josiah (2 Kings 23:21-23), is legislated in Deuteronomy 16:1-8. According to Deuteronomy 18:10-12 and 2 Kings 23:10, 24, child sacrifice, divination, soothsaying, augury, sorcery, and casting of spells are prohibited. As with the reformation of Josiah, Levites are the only legitimate priests according to Deuteronomy 12–26. Furthermore, sacred prostitution is forbidden by Josiah (2 Kings 23:7) and outlawed in Deuteronomy 23:17-18.

Among other things, such parallels have led scholars to assume a close relationship between the reforms of Josiah and Deuteronomy. That is why the reformation recounted in 2 Kings is referred to not only as the Reformation of Josiah, but also as the Deuteronomic Reformation. Although the present book of Deuteronomy was formalized after the time of Josiah, most OT scholars believe that "the book of the law" found by Hilkiah was most of Deuteronomy (chapters 5–26, 28), written well before Josiah's time. Therefore, we would expect to find that "book of the law" within the Pentateuch. Indeed, 2 Kings 14:6 quotes Deuteronomy 24:16 as "what is written in the book of the law of Moses."

Not all portions of Deuteronomy were written by the person(s) responsible for chapters 5–26 and 28, usually referred to as the Deuteronomic Code. Although some scholars include chapters 1–4 and perhaps also 27–30 in the Code, others do not. Most scholars think Deuteronomy 31–34 are from one or more redactors (editors). So, some scholars use the term "Deuteronomists" for the authors/compilers of Deuteronomy and some other parts of the OT from Genesis through 2 Kings. They do so because those books reflect the literary style and theological views of Deuteronomy, although scholars do not agree about the extent of influence.

While some scholars call Deuteronomy through 2 Kings "the Deuteronomic History," it is generally agreed that it is not a single work by a single author. "Deuteronomic Histories" (plural) would be a more accurate term, because there are many inconsistencies and contradictions within those works, to say nothing about diverse theological viewpoints that raise doubts about actual history. For example, according to the book of Joshua, Canaan was conquered under Joshua's leadership with almost no opposition. But, according to Judges, there was opposition from all sides that had to be overcome gradually through warriors called "judges."

Many similar examples indicate that the literary development of the Deuteronomic Histories is complicated and reflects numerous sources utilized by several authors. Sources mentioned are the Book of Jashar (Joshua 10:12-13), either a poem or a collection of poetry; the Book of the Acts of Solomon (1 Kings 11:41); the Book of the Annals of the Kings of Israel (1 Kings 14:19); and the Book of the Annals of the Kings of Judah (1 Kings 15:7; 2 Kings 8:23). And, it is quite apparent that Judges 4 is a prose account of the poetic version of the same story in Judges 5, one of the oldest literary units in the Bible. Besides these written sources, there were also folktales, sagas, especially hero sagas, legends, anecdotes, and curses and blessings from pre-Deuteronomic oral traditions that eventually developed into written forms and were adapted to the Deuteronomic historical framework.

*The Deuteronomists' Views*
The Deuteronomists believed that the fall of Israel was due to the Israelites' loss of faith and that, in permitting it to happen, God hoped their suffering would lead them to repent and obey his laws. They were greatly influenced by the beliefs of the prophets of the eighth century BCE that Yahweh wanted moral life, not sacrifice, but it took the Israelites a long time to comprehend and practice the teaching of their prophets. According to the prophets, the rites of sacrifices and offerings were insignificant for God, who despised the immoralities associated with pagan sacrifices. God demanded moral life – what was *right* – not rites. What God expects is expressed in Hosea 6:6: "I desire steadfast love and not sacrifice, the knowledge of God rather than burnt offerings." Micah 6:7-8 contrasts viewpoints with respect to rites and what is right:

> Will the Lord be pleased with thousands of rams, with ten thousands of rivers of oil? Shall I give my firstborn for my transgression, the fruit of my body for the sin of my soul? He has told you, O mortal, what is good; and what does the Lord require of you but to do justice, and to love kindness, and to walk humbly with your God?

The words "my firstborn" and "the fruit of my body" refer to the sacrifice of children, a regular part of the pagan religion of the Canaanites. For the Deuteronomists, as with the prophets, the essence of religion is love for God and obedience to his laws. In Deuteronomy these feelings are emphatically expressed in 6:5; 10:12-13:

> You shall love the Lord your God with all your heart, and with all your soul, and with all your might. Keep these words that I am commanding you today in your heart... So now, O Israel, what does the Lord your God require of you? Only to fear the Lord your God, to walk in all his ways, to love him, to serve the Lord your God with all your heart and with all your soul, and to keep the commandments of the Lord your God...that I am commanding you today, for your own well-being.

## Source P

The latest source of the Pentateuch (about 500 BCE) is designated P, because it reflects the concern of the Jewish priests and the regulations and rituals for the temple cultus. As usual, scholars do not agree about precise texts that belong to P. However, all agree that P, or influence from it, occurs in parts of Genesis, Exodus, much of Leviticus and Numbers, and perhaps some of Deuteronomy 32 and 34.

P is a kind of philosopher of history. He believes that, from the time when God created the world, the only God in existence, the God of Israel, wanted to set apart that nation from others. God also wanted to make a covenant with the Israelites, provide them a homeland, and give them laws of their own. The P source must have originated from a person or a community of experts in history and cultic legal practice concerned with genealogies, lists of nations, and cultic regulations. There are also literary formulas in P, repeated in precisely the same words, for example: "Then God said, Let there be" (Genesis 1:3); "These are the generations of" (Genesis 2:4a); and "This is the list of" (Genesis 5:1; 6:9; 11:10).

P thought of God as transcendent, above and beyond the comprehension and experience of human beings. Apparently P was aware of ancient Near Eastern cosmologies and mythologies (see Genesis 1:2) that said the world emerged from original chaos, with the god of order, Marduk, and the goddess of chaos, Tiamat, struggling with each other. For the author of P, the world did not come as the result of such a struggle, nor did God have to conquer dragons as in the Babylonian creation myth. The Hebrew deity was above all that when he created the world by his word – "creation by fiat."

It may be, though, that P got some of his ideas from the very old Hebrew Psalm 18 (duplicated in 2 Samuel 22): "The Most High uttered his voice" (Psalm 18:13; 2 Samuel 22:14). See also Psalm 46:6: "He utters his voice, the earth melts" and Psalm 33:6-9: "By the word of the Lord the heavens were made... For he spoke, and it came to be; he commanded, and it stood firm." These psalms are very old and show influence from the Canaanite religion, which we discuss more when studying the stories of creation. The idea that God created the world by fiat was taken over by the Christian Church. See, for example, Hebrews 11:3: "By faith we understand that the worlds were prepared by the word of God" (see also 2 Corinthians 4:6; Romans 4:17).

## Some Evidence of Sources

Most OT scholars believe that each of the Pentateuch's sources has been redacted by one or more persons, that J and E were combined as JE by a redactor, and that the sources JEDP, along with others, were combined into final form about 400 BCE when the Pentateuch was finalized in essentially the same composition it is today. The best way to insightfully understand the sometimes discrepant, disparate, and disjointed accounts of biblical stories is to think of them as due to different sources.

Biblical writers were not as conscious of consistency, literary style, and logical thought as authors are today. They probably did not seek out and study critically materials but used those they already had. They wanted to convey their belief that God was ultimately responsible for the outcome of every stage in their history and religion, whether good or bad. Moreover, when an author read a source that came into his hands, he did not rewrite it in order to make it consistent with another account he may already have read. Biblical writers probably regarded all sources at their disposal as valid and, therefore, were reluctant to change them.

The following examples from Genesis of two or more versions of the same incident undoubtedly suggest different sources. In times of danger, Abraham twice said that his wife was his sister: with Pharaoh in Egypt (12:10-20, J) and with Abimelech at Gerar (20:1-18, E). Three times Abram was promised an heir from his own family: by Yahweh in a vision (15:1-2a, 3b-4, J; 5, 13-16, E); when El Shaddai (God Almighty) speaks to him (17:15-21, P); and by three strange visitors (18:9-15, J). Isaac is named four times: God tells Abraham to call his son Isaac (17:17-19, P); the name is implied with the verb "laugh" (18:9-15, J); Abraham names his son Isaac (21:2b-5, P); the name is implied in wordplays on laughing (21:6-7, E).

Hagar leaves home twice: Sarai treated her so harshly that she ran away (Genesis 16:4-6, J), and, at Sarai's demand, Abraham packed Hagar a lunch and sent her off (21:8-16, E). Jacob twice named Luz Bethel: after his dream about a ladder reaching from earth to heaven (28:19, J) and when he returns to Luz and names it Bethel because God spoke to him there (28:19, J; 35:15, P). Twice Jacob's name is changed to Israel: after he wrestled with the man (God), God named him Israel (32:22-28, J); God appeared as El Shaddai (God Almighty) to Jacob and named him Israel (35:9-11, P). Three times Joseph is sold: to a caravan of Ishmaelites going to Egypt (37:25-28, J); to Midianites (37:29-36, E); to Potiphar in Egypt by the Ishmaelites (39:1, J).

There are also contradictory accounts of the same event. According to P, man and woman were created at the same time after the rest of the creation

(Genesis 1:11–2.4a). According to J, man was created, then a garden with trees bearing fruit, animals, and birds. Finally, God created a woman from the man's rib (2:4b-24). In the accounts of the flood, P (6:19-22) reports that two of every living thing, male and female of birds and animals, along with food for humans and the animals, were taken into the ark. According to J (7:1-5), Noah was told to take seven pairs of all clean animals, male and female; a pair of unclean animals; and seven pairs of birds, male and female. According to J (7:12), rain fell for 40 days and 40 nights; according to P (7:24), waters were on the earth for 150 days.

## Sources outside the Pentateuch

Not all scholars agree about specific sources used by the authors of 1 and 2 Samuel, but all do agree that the books are composite works from various sources. Some scholars think that the sources J and E can be found in those books, while others do not. Some think other sources can also be detected, while others deny that there is enough evidence to affirm any theory of sources. There were probably several traditions about persons and events that arose locally and were preserved in court records of the kings of Israel and Judah. Without trying to identify them, the use of sources in the following examples seems plausible.

According to 1 Samuel 8:10-22, God opposed the idea of a king for Israel because the people rejected him and told Samuel how devastating a king would be for them. Then Yahweh is said to have approved Saul as king after Samuel had anointed him in private (1 Samuel 10:1-2). And later Saul seems to be rejected by Yahweh in 1 Samuel 13:13-15 and again in 15:1-35. In another account, Saul is chosen by lot at a public assembly at Mizpah, where he is proclaimed king – "Long live the king!" – after having been introduced by Samuel (1 Samuel 10:17-24). And in a third account, at another assembly, this time at Gilgal, the people "made Saul king before the Lord" (1 Samuel 11:12-15), again at the direction of Samuel. These contradictions could certainly indicate different sources.

As happened with Saul, David is anointed in secret at his home in Bethlehem (1 Samuel 16:1-13). Three times it is mentioned that a daughter of Saul is to be given to David in marriage: unnamed in 1 Samuel 17:25, Merab in 18:17-20, and Michal in 18:20-29. David is introduced to Saul in three different ways. First, it is said that David became Saul's musician in order to soothe his mental state, that Saul loved him greatly, and that David became his armor-bearer (1 Samuel 16:14-23). Second, David meets Saul in his army camp (1 Samuel 17:31-39). Third, when David brought the head of Goliath to Saul, Saul did not recognize David, even though he had been his beloved musician, and asked: "Whose son are you, young man?" (1 Samuel 17:57-58). It is reported twice that David defects to the king of the Philistine city of Gath (1 Samuel 21:10-21; 27:1–28:2) and twice that David spares Saul's life (1 Samuel 24:1-7; 26:1-25).

From information in the books of Samuel, some scholars conclude that historically David did much to lessen the Philistine threat to the new kingdom and that he was significant for other reasons. Undoubtedly, David became the hero par excellence of the Israelites/Jews. Both Jews and early Christians believed the Messianic ruler was to be descended from him (e.g., Isaiah 7:10-25; 9:1-7; Matthew 1:1–2:12; Luke 1:26-38, 67-80; 2:1-14). In spite of David's enduring popularity, that he killed the giant Goliath in the ways narrated is hardly historical fact. Or, if it is fact, which is the historical account? Legends developed around a king the Israelites came to regard as a great hero. Let's see how several biblical writers report legends by studying the most widely known and popular account in 1 Samuel 17:1-25:

> There came out from the camp of the Philistines a champion named Goliath, of Gath, whose height was six cubits and a span [c. 9.473 feet]. He had a helmet of bronze on his head, and he was armed with a coat of mail; the weight of the coat was five thousand shekels of bronze [c. 125.92 pounds]... The shaft of his spear was like a weaver's beam, and his spear's head weighed six hundred shekels [c. 15.11 pounds] of iron (1 Samuel 17:4-7).

The details, especially the height of the giant and the weights of his armor, were not likely to be recorded by a historian in the time of battle. The details are an embellishment to the nucleus of a story by a person who admired David as a special hero. They were probably added not so much to describe the strength and size of Goliath as to impress the readers of the prowess and gallantry of David.

Two other passages indicate that there were at least three traditions of a giant killer. In recounting a battle of the Israelites with the Philistines, the writer of 2 Samuel 21:19 names another man as the slayer of Goliath: "There was another battle with the Philistines at Gob; and Elhanan son of Jaareoregim, the Bethlehemite, killed Goliath the Gittite, the shaft of whose spear was like a weaver's beam."

The books of Chronicles are a rewriting of much of the material recorded in the books of Samuel and Kings. The writer of 1 Chronicles 20:5 apparently was aware of the conflicting traditions about the slaying of the giant, so he writes: "Again there was war with the Philistines; and Elhanan son of Jair killed Lahmi the brother of Goliath the Gittite, the shaft of whose spear was like a weaver's beam."

By the time the Chronicler wrote his account, the earlier tradition about David killing Goliath had been established. So the chronicler modified the account in 2 Samuel, where it is said that Elhanan killed Goliath, by saying that Elhanan killed the brother of Goliath. In this way the David tradition remained the prevailing one. Obviously, the tradition of David and Goliath that has survived among Jews and Christians is the glorified account in 1 Samuel. Read the magnificent poetic tribute to David in the Jewish deuterocanonical or apocryphal work known as Sirach (Sirach 47:1-11).

These and many other similar instances of inconsistencies, repetitions, and discrepancies indicate that the books of Samuel are composite works comprised of different sources. Most scholars agree that JEDP and other sources of the OT were based on a variety of oral traditions from the political and social life of the Israelites that have been preserved and redacted into numerous literary forms, including sagas, laws, hymns, confessions of faith, prophetic oracles, sermons, historical writing, legends, and myths. There are differences in vocabulary, style of writing, and other literary features, as well as different points of view with respect to history and religious experiences, that are due to editorial influence.

Most readers think that when they read the books of the prophets they are reading what the historical persons themselves said. While much in the prophetic books may come from the historical characters, there is evidence of compilation and editorial work. The popular book of Isaiah, for example, contains 66 chapters, but many scholars think that only chapters 1–39 actually came from the prophet Isaiah during the middle to end of the eighth century BCE. Many scholars think that, even in those chapters, actual words of Isaiah appear mostly in chapters 1–11 and 28–32. Much editing has resulted in a complex book. On the basis of historical events referred to, literary style, vocabulary, names for and characterizations of the deity, and religious ideas, some scholars believe that chapters 40–66 comprise a second book and refer to it as the Second Isaiah. Others say that chapters 56–66 are a third separate book and refer to it as the Third Isaiah.

*Influence from Ancient Sources outside the Bible*
It is interesting to examine more specifically the influence of ideas in ancient literature on some OT material. For example, the words "the deep" reflect influence from both Mesopotamian and Ugaritic literature (fourteenth century BCE). According to the creation myth in *Emuna Elis,* Marduk killed Tiamat, goddess and dragon of the deep. In Ugaritic literature the primeval

sea ("the deep") was the abode of El where several gods went (James B. Pritchard [ed.], *Ancient Near Eastern Texts Relating to the Old Testament* [Princeton University Press, 1969], pp. 133, 136, 153, hereinafter referred to as *ANET*). In the OT the phrase is most often used for the primeval ocean of creation as in Genesis 1:2. In the flood story "the great deep" is contrasted with "the windows of the heavens" as the sources of the waters that burst forth (Genesis 7:11; see also Genesis 49:25; Deuteronomy 33:13; Psalm 104:6). According to Proverbs 8:22-27, Yahweh created wisdom as the first of his work, "when there were no depths" and "when he established the heavens" and "drew a circle on the face of the deep." The ancient mythological struggle between primeval chaos and the gods, although suppressed, appears at several places in the OT as the struggle of Yahweh against chaos, sometimes disguised as sea monsters (Genesis 1:21; Job 7:12; Psalm 148:7; Isaiah 27:1), Leviathan (Job 3:8; 40:25–41:26; Isaiah 27:1), the Dragon (Job 7:12; Isaiah 27:1; 51:9), and Rahab (Job 9:13; 26:12; Psalm 89:10; Isaiah 51:9).

Perhaps the most interesting OT passage that shows influence from ancient cosmological myths in which the god kills the monster of chaos is Isaiah 51:9-10: "Awake, awake, put on strength, O arm of the Lord! Awake, as in days of old, the generations of long ago! Was it not you who cut Rahab in pieces, who pierced the dragon? Was it not you who dried up the sea, the waters of the great deep...?" The probable prototype of this passage is the Canaanite myth (*ANET*, 130-31) in which Baal defeats Yamm (Sea) and Nahar (River):

> O Prince Baal... O Rider of the Clouds. Now thine enemy. O Baal, Now thine enemy wilt thou smite... Chase Yamm from his throne, [Na]hor from his seat of dominion. Yamm collapses... He falls to the ground; His joints bend, His frame breaks. Baal would rend, would smash Yamm, Would annihilate Judge Nahor.

Isaiah 51:10 presents the crossing of the Red Sea in Exodus 14:15-31 as a replay of Yahweh's defeat of the sea monsters.

## *Hebrew Laws*

There are a number of biblical accounts of the giving of laws to the Hebrews/Israelites, although most scholars today acknowledge that these laws were influenced by sources outside the Pentateuch. According to Exodus 20:1, the Lord spoke words of the law to Moses. And, according to Exodus 24:4, "Moses wrote down all the words of the Lord" that he has spoken to him (see also Malachi 4:4). In Exodus 24:12, the Lord told Moses to come up to the mountain and he would give him the laws and commandments that he had written on tablets of stone for the Israelites.

Exodus 31:18 is more emphatic in saying that God was responsible for the laws: "When God finished speaking with Moses on Mount Sinai, he gave him the two tablets of the covenant, tablets of stone, written with the finger of God." After Moses got angry and broke the tablets of stone, God told Moses to cut tablets of stone like the ones that were broken and that he would write the words that were on the former stones (Exodus 34:1-6).

Deuteronomy also contains accounts of the giving of the laws. According to Deuteronomy 4:12-13, the Lord wrote the Ten Commandments on two stone tablets. In another account, Moses recites the laws to the Israelites and then tells them that the Lord wrote them on the two tablets and gave them to him (Deuteronomy 5:22; see also Deuteronomy 9:8–10:5). In each of these accounts, a deity gave the Israelites their laws, which were inscribed on stone tablets. The prototype for that belief was the Babylonian account of the deity giving the Babylonians their laws inscribed on stone. And in both the Babylonian account and the Bible a human was the mediator in transmitting the laws from the deity to the people.

Throughout the centuries various theories of the origin of Hebrew laws developed. The Hebrews believed that God himself wrote the laws and then gave them to Moses. This view is reflected in almost every book of the OT and was taken over by the early Christians. Many orthodox Jews and some Christians today still believe that God himself was responsible for Hebrew laws. Then, some persons believed that Moses himself wrote the laws or that he was largely responsible for them. This is the view of biblical writers in general, including those of the NT. See, for example, "the book of the law of Moses" (Joshua 8:31; 23:6; 2 Kings 14:6; Nehemiah 8:1); "the law of Moses" (1 Kings 2:3; 2 Kings 23:25; Joshua 8:32; 2 Chronicles 23:18; Ezra 3:2; 7:6; Daniel 9:11; Luke 2:22; 24:44; John 7:23; Acts 13:39; 15:5; 28:23; 1 Corinthians 9:9). The view that Moses was responsible for Hebrew laws is reflected by the persons responsible for the *KJV* in which each book of the Pentateuch is attributed to Moses, for example, "The First Book of Moses, Called Genesis."

The question of how much Hebrew law, if any, goes back to Moses is still debated. Answers range from none to some to the view that Moses was the great lawgiver, which need not be questioned. However, after the development of the theory of sources of the Pentateuch, scholars generally came to believe that Hebrew laws were written over a long period by a number of different persons and based on ancient prototypes, such as the

Code of Hammurabi. Hammurabi was King of Babylon from 1728–1686 BCE, and the laws incorporated into his code were based partly on earlier laws from Sumer in southern Babylonia. Therefore, ancient codes of law are an important source to consider when studying the Pentateuch.

The Code of Hammurabi was written on a stela, a stone slab with writing on it that was set up in commemoration of some person or event. An image of the sun-god Shamash handing the laws to the worshiper Hammurabi standing before him is on the top of the stela, with the laws of Hammurabi inscribed below that scene. The examples below seem to confirm the influence of the Code of Hammurabi on Hebrew laws.

As in the Hammurabi Code, Mosaic laws contain a prologue (Exodus 20:1; see also Exodus 20:22; Code I-V), the body of laws (Exodus 20:23–23:19; Code VI-XXIII), and an epilogue (Exodus 23:20-33; Code XXIV-XXVIII). In the Code, laws dealing with property are given priority over those dealing with persons, whereas in the OT the reverse is true. Below is a list of some subjects dealt with in the Pentateuch and the Code of Hammurabi given by number as in *ANET,* 163-80. They may also be found on the Internet under "Code of Hammurabi."

> *False witness*: Exodus 20:16; 23:1-3; Leviticus 19:11-12; Deuteronomy 5:20; 19:15, 18-20; Code 3-4.
> *Stealing (theft)*: Exodus 20:15; 21:16; 22:1-8; Leviticus 19:11-12; Deuteronomy 5:19; Code 7-10, 22, 25, 259-260.
> *Treatment of a thief*: Exodus 22:1-8; Code 21-23.
> *Buying and selling slaves*: Exodus 21:2-11; Deuteronomy 15:12-18; Code 117-19.
> *Adultery*: Exodus 20:14; Deuteronomy 5:18; 22.22-27; Code 129-32.
> *Sexual relations*: Leviticus 15:19-24; 18:6-23; 20:10-21; Numbers 5:11-31; Deuteronomy 27:20-23; Code 127-32, 154-58.
> *Personal injuries*: Exodus 21:12-27; Code 195-223.
> *Law of retaliation (lex talionis)*: Exodus 21:23-27; Leviticus 24:17-21; Deuteronomy 19:21; Code 195-205.
> *Harm to a pregnant woman*: Exodus 21:22-25; Code 209-14.
> *Goring of an ox*: Exodus 21:28-36; Code 250-51.
> *Disputed ownership*: Exodus 22:9-13; Code 120-26.

## Chapter Summary

With careful and critical scrutiny of the Pentateuch, a scholar in the first half of the eighteenth century proposed a method of biblical study known as *source criticism*. It is based on the idea that it is possible to detect different sources responsible for the Pentateuch and remains a generally accepted theory today. In fact, four primary sources have been identified and designated J, E, D, and P. By analyzing biblical passages, scholars attribute them to one or more sources and use the method of source criticism to help provide insight into the meaning of differing or even contradictory accounts of the same stories or events.

Other sources outside the Pentateuch are also evident in OT writings. For example, ancient Near Eastern laws, especially the Code of Hammurabi, influenced Hebrew/Israelite laws that are an important part of the Pentateuch. In the next chapter we study the creation and Garden of Eden stories in Genesis in light of some ancient literature that probably served as a background for them and that can be regarded as influential sources outside the Pentateuch.

Chapter 5

CREATION AND GARDEN OF EDEN STORIES

*Introduction*

As with the subject of sources, the study of the backgrounds of the OT is difficult, complicated, and requires special linguistic skills. Bible writers did not produce their works in a vacuum, sealed off from the environments in which they lived, so many of the thousands of ancient documents from Egypt, Mesopotamia, and Syria/Palestine offer insights for biblical study. Although those literary texts were probably not direct sources, they show that some of the most well-known stories in the OT, including the creation and Garden of Eden stories, were influenced by similar stories from the civilizations where they originated.

Given the controversy that exists even today regarding the role of creationism in modern education and thought, it is especially important to contrast simple answers about the beginning of the world with more complex and insightful ones. First and foremost, the Bible offers absolutely *no* scientific evidence or facts. Scientific research as we know it did not come into being for hundreds of years after the Bible was written. Yet, putting aside that undeniable truth, to suggest that we should believe that God created the world in six days and rested on the seventh just because "The Bible Says So!" is to ignore significant insights we can gain from a more careful examination of the Bible itself. As a starting point, we need to acknowledge that the Bible actually has two different accounts of the creation.

*Creation Stories outside the Bible*

Both creation stories in Genesis (1:1–2:4a; 2:4b-24) reflect how ancient peoples thought the world and human beings came into existence and show knowledge of and influence from ancient cosmological and mythological views. Bible writers took for granted the accepted view of their time of a three-tiered structure of the universe, with the flat earth in the middle, heaven or the heavens above (Genesis 1:1, 20; 2:1, 4; 14:19-22), and seas underneath the earth. The Israelites shall not make an idol "in the form of anything that is in heaven above, or that is on the earth beneath, or that is in the water under the earth" (Exodus 20:4; see also Deuteronomy 4:16-19; 5:8).

There is a long Babylonian epic poem on the creation, probably written down about the twelfth century BCE, called *Enuma Elish*. As with Genesis, the epic gets its name from the first words, which mean "when on high": "When on high the heaven had not been named, Firm ground below had not been called by name" (*ANET*, 60-61). The author of the epic writes about the origin of the earth, heavenly bodies, and human beings. In Genesis the deity is responsible for the creation, as are the gods of the *Enuma Elish*. Although God and gods are involved in creation, the means of creation are different. The biblical deity created by fiat and by action: "God said, Let there be…and it was so *[fiat]*." "So God made the dome and separated the waters *[action]*" (Genesis 1:7). "The Lord God formed man *[action]*" (Genesis 2:7). According to the Babylonian epic, Marduk, god of the city of Babylon and god of order, killed the monster Tiamat, goddess of chaos. Then he cut her dragon-like body into two parts from which he created the world: the upper part, the sky with luminaries, and the lower part, the earth.

The *Enuma Elish* and the Genesis narratives are alike in that the supreme deity brings order out of chaos (the Epic) or something less than the created order (Genesis). The creation stories in Genesis, however, are far different from the Babylonian epic in that there is nothing in them of the bloody violence in the Babylonian account.

There is a carryover from the Babylonian polytheism when the biblical writer has God say: "Let *us* make humankind [Hebrew, *adam*] in *our* image, according to *our* likeness" (Genesis 1:26). Here the Hebrew word for God is *Elohim*, a plural noun in form but grammatically taken as a singular in most places (see discussion of gods mentioned in the Bible in Chapter 9). Here are two other examples of the same kind: "Then the Lord God said, See, the man has become like one of *us*" (Genesis 3:22) and "The Lord said… Come, let *us* go down" (Genesis 11:7). These expressions reflect the ancient Near Eastern view that the gods determined the fate of humans. Other hints from the *Enuma Elish* occur in the narrative of God's primordial defeat of Rahab, a sea monster representing chaos. "You crushed Rahab like a carcass" (Psalm 89:10; see also Job 9:13). See also the crushing of Leviathan (Psalm 74:13-14; Isaiah 27:1).

## Creation Stories in the Bible

While the Bible's two accounts of the creation of the world and humans, especially the first one, are based on prototypes from ancient Egyptian and Babylonian accounts, they are attributed to two different sources. The first account (Genesis 1:1–2:4a) is from P and the second (Genesis 2:4b-24) from J. Because this second account is older than the first, we cannot say that the author of the later one copied or even used the earlier one. Besides, there are many differences in the stories regarding how creation occurred and in details of the process, which we discuss below.

### Creation in P

Scholars often point out the number of creative acts in the P account and generally find from seven to ten. We get a more accurate understanding of the creation story in P by dividing the creation into two parts: creation by *fiat* ("God said, Let there be...and it was") and creation by a subsequent *action*, indicated by a verb of action, such as "created," "separated," and "made" (Genesis 1:1, 4, 7, 16). Here is a list from Genesis 1:1–2:4a that shows the phenomena created by fiat, those resulting from an action on God's part, and the response to each. It also reveals inconsistencies in the author's literary style.

- 1:1-2: *fiat*: none; *action*: "God created...wind from God."
- 1:3-5: *fiat*: light; response: "light was good"; *action*: "God separated" and "called."
- 1:6-8: *fiat*: "Let there be a dome...and let it separate"; *action*: "God made...and separated"; response: "And it was so"; *action*: "God called."
- 1:9-10: *fiat*: "Let the waters...and let the dry land"; response: "And it was so"; *action*: "God called" (twice); response: "And God saw that it was good."
- 1:11-13: *fiat*: "Let the earth put forth"; response: "And it was so...and God saw that it was good."
- 1:14-19: *fiat*: "Let there be lights...and let them be" (twice); response: "And it was so"; *action*: "God made...and set them"; "And God saw that it was good."
- 1:20-23: *fiat*; "Let the waters...and let birds"; *action*: "God created"; response: "And God saw that it was good"; *action*: "God blessed them"; *fiat*: "Be fruitful and multiply...and let birds multiply."

## Creation and Garden of Eden Stories 59

1:24-25: *fiat*: "Let the earth"; response: "And it was so"; *action*: "God made"; response: "And God saw that it was good."

1:26-27: Here there is not the typical fiat of earlier ones, "Let there be." Instead, there are two *exhortations*: "Let us make" and "Let them have dominion." An exhortation is intended to encourage someone to do something. The plural "let us make" coincides with the plural *elohim* ("gods"), which is unusual since it is used mostly with singular verbs. The plural usage, therefore, may be a carryover from early polytheism in the Hebrew religion. It has also been suggested that the plural here may imply a female companion deity. Notice the plural, too, in "our image" and "our likeness." Does that suggest that male and female humans were created in the image of the male god and the female goddess? In what follows, though, the author implies monotheism: "God created man in his image, in the image of God he created him."

1:28: *action*: "God blessed"; *exhortations*: "Be fruitful and multiply, and fill the earth and subdue it; and have dominion."

1:29-31: summary of what God gave humans and a double response: "And it was so" and everything he had made "was very good."

Observe that God created all kinds of vegetation by fiat (1:11-12), and that by fiat he also created living creatures in the waters and birds in the skies (1:20). By action he "created" sea monsters and other living things (1:21); by fiat, living creatures of all kinds; and by action, wild animals of all kinds (1:24-25). And then God reminds the humans that he had given all kinds of plants for them for food and the same for animals (1:29-30). Apparently, the author viewed both humans and animals as completely vegetarian.

Genesis 2:1-3 may be understood in several ways. The word translated as "multitude" in the *NRSV* is *sebaoth* and means "heavenly hosts" or "heavenly beings," either angels or luminaries (see Genesis 1:14-18). "Luminaries" (*NJB*, "all their array") makes good sense, along with heaven and earth, which were readily observable in the writer's time. In the *REB* the concept is broadened: "the heavens and the earth and everything in them." But understanding the word *sebaoth* is not the only difficulty in the passage.

The author gives the impression that, at the end of the sixth day, the creation was "finished." Then he says that, on the seventh day, God finished the work he had done and rested. This is not only a contradiction (see also verse 3), but it has God working on the Sabbath, thus breaking his own commandment: "The seventh day...you shall not do any work" (Exodus 20:10; Deuteronomy 5:12-13). The author of P was probably aware of the sanctity of the Sabbath as stated in Deuteronomy but takes its origin back to the creation.

*Understanding the Discrepancies in P*
Scholars have tried to resolve the discrepancies mentioned in various ways. Some say that the numeral seventh is an error and should be read as "sixth," so God finished his work on the sixth day and rested on the seventh. However, there is no substantial evidence for that view. At Genesis 1:1 the *NRSV* gives a footnote for "In the beginning when God created," which some translators understand: "When God began to create" or "In the beginning God created." With this in mind they take the verb translated as "finished" or "completed" in 2:1-2 as "fulfilled." God has now fulfilled the task that he set out to do when he began to create the world. This view seems to be an accommodation to the traditional belief that God created the world in six days and rested on the seventh.

Biblical writers were not concerned with logical development or consistency of thought. Their only priority was to convey religious truth as they believed it. For P that truth was twofold: God created the world and everything in it, and he gave his blessing on the seventh day as a "holy day." Many Jews and Christians are so convinced of the truth of God's creation of the world and the Sabbath as a sacred day that, like the author of P, they do not notice the difficulties in the passage.

Two interesting issues arise with the six days: the beginning of time and the invention of a calendar. Naturally, persons had to be aware of time before developing a calendar. Philo, a Jewish philosopher and allegorist from Alexandria, Egypt (c. 20 BCE -50 CE), has written many works in Greek, including *On the Creation*. When allegorizing on Genesis 1:1 he writes that "the beginning" cannot be taken in a chronological sense, as some of his time did. Why? Because there was no time before there was a world; time began either with the world or after it. Time is determined by the movement of the world; therefore, time began either simultaneous with or later than the creation of the world (*On the Creation*, 7).

Sometimes it is argued that a day in the time of creation was not the equivalent of one in our time, but longer. This is thought to make the creation in six days more believable. But that is a rationalization that is totally false, because peoples of Mesopotamia, as early as the third millennium BCE, had lunar/solar calendars of roughly the same number of days in a year as current calendars. Likewise, the common belief that God created the world *ex nihilo*, "from nothing," cannot be supported by the biblical creation stories. This view first appears in 2 Maccabees 7:28, where the mother of one of her sons about to suffer martyrdom says to him as he looks at heaven and earth and everything in them that he should "recognize that God did not make them out of things that existed." However, according to Genesis 1:2, there was a void, darkness, and the deep (a primeval ocean?) before God began to create the world.

### Comparisons between Creation in P and Ancient Accounts

It is clear that several ideas in the creation story in Genesis 1:1–2:4a have trickled down, if not directly derived from, ancient Egyptian and Babylonian accounts (see *ANET*, 4-12). Here are some specific parallels between the Egyptian and Genesis stories: creation by fiat ("mouth" or "tongue" in ancient texts) and the creation of men, cattle, creeping things and everything that lives, food, and fertility of humans and the soil by acts of the deity. There is no mention in the ancient texts of the creation of woman as such. In both P and the ancient myths, God or the gods showed pleasure at the work done.

Despite striking similarities, the Egyptian stories do differ from the biblical accounts in that they have polytheism throughout; a god creating other gods; violence involved in the creation; a god who has in mind the things he wants to make and then creates them by utterance; and gods involved in the fertility of humans. Many more details differ, as well.

### Creation in J

The second story of creation and the Garden of Eden story belong together as a unit (Genesis 2:4b–3:24) and are attributed to J. The writer's favorite expression for the deity is *Yahweh Elohim*, "the Lord God." It could reflect the Near Eastern custom of using the name of a god with a qualifying word to accentuate the god named. Perhaps the original form was simply *Yahweh*, in keeping with the usage of J, and a later editor added the *Elohim* from Genesis 1:1.

At the outset, other differences show immediately that the two stories of creation are from different sources. "God created" (Genesis 1:1, P) and "the Lord God made" (2:4b, J); and "God created mankind" (1:27, P) and "the Lord God formed man" (2:7, J). In P there is "the heavens and the earth." In P the writer's main interest is the majesty of God and his creation, and man comes in almost incidentally. In J there is "the earth and the heavens" (2:4), and the earth is the main interest of the writer and man the center of the stage. And, whereas in P the creation occurred over six days plus (1:31–2:3), in J it happened on one day (2:4b).

Genesis 2:4b-7 is an introduction to the Eden story and gives the reason for the creation of man. There was no vegetation when God created the earth, because he had not yet brought rain. But there would be a stream to water all the earth, and that river came from Eden to water the vegetation God had planted in the garden.

The Yahwist says twice that there is no partner for the man (2:18, 20), but between the statements comes the creation of all sorts of animals and birds for the man to name. In J, though, there is nothing about humans having dominion over all created life, which P stresses, although it may be implied by the bringing of animals for the man to name. However, would we think that if we were not reading the account of J after that of P? We must be careful not to try to reconcile two such obviously diverse accounts of the creation.

In P there is nothing about a partner for the man or his naming of the animals, and there is no mention of a specific woman and her role with the man. In J the woman having pain in childbirth and the man earning his bread by the sweat of his face and tilling the ground from which he was made are punishments for disobedience. And the man is to rule over the woman, a reflection of the male-oriented society in which the author lived. Indeed, the universal experiences of life helped shape the author's account.

## Likenesses and Differences in the Two Genesis Accounts

Most readers probably notice the likenesses rather than the differences in the two biblical accounts of creation, so we'll consider some of the most important differences. Each author has a favorite word for the deity, *Elohim* for P and *Yahweh Elohim* for J, usually translated as "the Lord God." The origin of the dual name is uncertain, but it is one of the most frequently used designations for the Hebrew deity. In P's account of creation there is an emphasis on action or work. In Genesis 2:2-3 the phrase "the work that he had done" is repeated three times. But P also has creation by fiat, whereas J's account has nothing of creation by fiat.

In Genesis 1:2 the words "while a wind from God" are an accurate translation and have a prototype in an Egyptian text: "The All-Lord says...I made the four winds that every man might breathe thereof" (*ANET*, 7). The same text may be a prototype for J, too, in the statement in Genesis 2:7 that the Lord God "breathed" into the man's nostrils "the breath of life." On the other hand, "the spirit of God" in the footnote to Genesis 1:2 in the *NRSV* is also a correct translation; it appears in the texts of the *RSV* and the *REB*, while the *NJB* reads, "a divine wind." "Spirit of God" coincides with the more spiritual or transcendent idea of the deity in P and may give some insight into that author's concept of "the image of God" in Genesis 1:27.

P's conception of God in the creation contrasts with the older and more primitive concept of God in J's account. The Yahwist writes: "The Lord God formed man from the dust of the ground." The image to be understood here is "as the potter shapes the clay." God also "breathed into" the man's nostrils and "planted a garden" (Genesis 2:7-8; see also Genesis 2:19-22). See the vividly anthropomorphic, anatomical statements of ribs, rib, bones, and flesh in the creation of the woman in Genesis 2:23. The statement that the Lord God "took one of his ribs and closed up its place with flesh" coincides with standard surgical procedure.

In trying to understand the creation of humans, two cautions are important. In spite of some similarities, the differences between the Bible's two stories are too evident and numerous to say that one author was including, omitting, supplementing, or even aware of the other's account. And above all, we must try not to bring into the texts things that never entered the minds of the authors. As with other Semites, the Hebrews used concrete images to express thoughts and feelings. This is precisely what the authors of the creation and Garden of Eden stories were doing. Here the story of the creation of a woman from the rib of a man is particularly apt. While scientists may eventually be able to create another human from a person's rib or other cell tissue, the point to remember is that the biblical account is not scientific fact. Instead, it is a concrete expression of the author's belief about the origin of human life, especially with respect to that of the first woman.

When we were discussing the story about the rib in one of my classes, a boy seated beside his girlfriend asked: "Does this mean that men have one less [sic] ribs than women?" I suggested that he do a little research and report next class period. And, indeed he did. Though not saying what research he did or how he did it, he reported that a man does *not* have fewer ribs than a woman!

## Garden of Eden

As with the creation stories the narrative about Eden as a place of bliss has its prototype in older literature. Aspects of it occur in the *Enuma Elish* and especially in the Gilgamesh Epic, which is extant in several versions from about 2000 BCE. Gilgamesh, the hero of the epic, was king of the city of Uruk in Mesopotamia during the middle of the third millennium BCE.

The central theme of the Gilgamesh Epic is the quest for immortality (see "the tree of life" in Genesis 2:9; 3:22), a theme well known in the ancient world. Gilgamesh set out on the quest, and although he had it in his grasp, it got away from him. Why? Because the gods had destined him for mortality. Gilgamesh was told: "Gilgamesh, whither rovest thou? The life thou pursuest thou shalt not find. When the gods created mankind, Death for mankind they set aside, Life in their own hands retaining" (*ANET*, 90). Near the end of the story of the flood in the Epic, Utnapishtim, who had joined the assembly of the gods and was given eternal life, tells Gilgamesh that there is a plant with thorns like a rose. If he gets it, he will find new life. Gilgamesh found the plant and named it "Man Becomes Young in Old Age." But a serpent smelled the fragrance of the plant and took it away. Thus, Gilgamesh did not succeed in his quest for eternal life (*ANET*, 96).

The plant conveying eternal life in the Epic becomes "the tree of life" in the Genesis story of Eden. However, its author was not primarily interested in immortality for the humans he believed God had created, although that aspect of the story comes out in the serpent's words to Eve: "You will not die" (Genesis 3:4). Instead, the biblical writer has another tree – "the tree of the knowledge of good and evil" (Genesis 2:9, 17). The desire to "be like god" (3:5) and the quest for wisdom reflect very ancient beliefs. Notice that in this second story of creation the objection to being like God is counter to the first story of creation in Genesis 1:1–2:4), where the author says that both male and female were created "in the image of God" (1:27).

The woman becomes more prominent than the man as the Garden of Eden story progresses: "The man named his wife Eve [chawa, similar to *chayah*, the word for "living"], because she was the mother of all living" (Genesis 3:20). Notice that the author has not yet said there were other humans living (see Genesis 4:1). The name "Adam" does not appear in the text until Genesis 4:25, because grammatically the definite article "the" is not used with a proper name. So "the man" has not been called Adam anywhere in the passage we have been considering (Genesis 2:8–3:24).

In Genesis 3:1-24 J is at his literary best. The story moves along at a rapid pace in dramatic fashion, mostly in prose with poetry in 3:14-19. The whole passage depicts the anthropomorphic and experiential aspects of human beings as the author understood them. There are sexual intimations, beginning already with 2:24-25 and appearing again in 3:7, 21. Subtle temptations to disobey appeal to the senses: good for food, a delight to the eyes, and make one wise. Only after they disobeyed God did the couple become aware of their nakedness and cover their genitals. They have now become fully aware of their sexuality. The suspense comes to an unexpected conclusion in that the couple achieved the knowledge of good and evil like God, who had not wanted that to happen, and although punished, they did not die as God had promised.

The idea of a special place in nature where humans and animals live together and a man becomes aware of his sexuality and becomes wise occur in the Gilgamesh Epic. Enkidu ran with the gazelles until a woman was not bashful in laying aside her clothes to bare her body for sexual enjoyment. After seven days of such enjoyment to the fullest, the gazelles ran away from him, and life was not as before. But now he has wisdom and broader understanding. The woman, a prostitute, tells him he is wise and has become like a god. Later the woman clothed the man and herself (*ANET*, 75, 77).

As the Garden of Eden story ends in Genesis 3:22-24, the author returns to both trees. He repeats what he had said earlier about eating from the tree of the knowledge of good and evil and now adds what seems to have been implied earlier – that eating from the tree of life would bring life forever. This echoes the words of the serpent: "You will not die" (3:4). Thus, the second story of creation ends with the primordial quest for immortality, which in the Bible as in the Gilgamesh Epic was thwarted by a snake.

Surely the similarities between the Epic and the J account of Eden are not just happenstance. The familiarity of the author of J with the ideas expressed in the Epic can hardly be denied. As we have learned, the Yahwist (J) has blended together the story of the creation of the world and that of Eden. Now let's explore several aspects of these stories in a little more depth.

## *Further Insights about the Stories of the Creation of Humans and the Garden of Eden Story*

In Genesis 2:7 the Hebrew word translated as "dust" is *apar*, which may also mean "clay" or "soil." A good translation is: "Yahweh God (God Yahweh) formed the man (*haadam*) of clay from the ground (*haadamah*) and breathed into his nostrils the breath of life; and the man became a living being." The translation of *apar* with "clay" fits in well with the idea of "forming" the man as a potter shapes the clay. There is a close parallel to this story in an ancient Babylonian myth about the creation of man by a mother goddess. It is said of her who creates humans: "Let him [man] be formed out of clay, be animated with blood!" A god is slain, and then the mother goddess is told: "With his flesh and his blood Let Ninhursag [name for the goddess] mix clay. God and man" (*ANET*, 99-100).

Another text, one that dates from the last half of the fifteenth century BCE, gives instructions for an Egyptian king and provides insight into both Genesis stories of creation. The Egyptian account includes, among other things, the creation of heaven and earth, cattle, animals, fowl and fish, and light of day created by a god. Then, concerning the creation of humans by a god, the author writes: "He made the breath of life (for) their nostrils. They who have issued from his body are his images" (*ANET*, 417).

In the Genesis stories, clearly influenced by the Babylonian and Egyptian counterparts, there is the clay and the life-giving breath, although in the Babylonian account the blood gives life. In both the biblical and ancient accounts humans are created or formed by the deity. Again, we should notice that the major difference is the refinement of the biblical accounts because of their authors' monotheistic faith.

Now let's take a look again at the Yahwist's story of the creation of a partner for the man and the naming of the animals brought to him by the Lord God (Genesis 2:18-20, J). As we have learned, some interpreters think that these verses indicate that the man has dominion over every living thing (see Genesis 1:26-28, P). However, we also learned that if we did not have P's account first, we probably would not think so. However that may be, if you look at Genesis 2:18-20 carefully, you will see that God created the man and then decided that it was not good for him to be alone and that he would make a helper/partner for him. Then he made every kind of animal, as though thinking, perhaps, that one would be a partner for the man. Immediately after the statement that the man had named every animal, the author says: "but for the man there was not found a helper as his partner."

The words translated as "a helper as his partner" in the *NRSV* are better translated as "a helper suitable (fit) for him." These words, along with those about no partner for the man among the animals, may be the Yahwist's repudiation of beastiality – humans having sex with animals – so prominent in much of the ancient world. In the Gilgamesh Epic, Enkidu spent six days and seven nights mating with an ass (*ANET*, 77). Hebrew law is emphatic in condemning such practices for both men and women: "Whoever lies with an animal shall be put to death" (Exodus 22:19). For the law applying to both men and women, see Leviticus 18:23; 20:15-16.

According to the Yahwist, a man should have a different kind of partner, someone originating with himself. The human couple become one again in their sexual relationship. Thus, the Yahwist has marriage originate with the creation of human beings. It was not long, though, until the man accused the woman he had named Eve as the reason for his own disobedience to God.

We have discussed the creation of a woman from the rib of a man and bones and flesh. Now let's consider the "woman" and the "man" in Genesis 2:23. The word for "woman" is *ishsha*, and the word for "man" is not *adam* but *ish*, obviously a wordplay. The *adam*, a human being, has now become an *ish*, a mortal male, in contrast to the immortal deity from whom the mortal came. This sets the stage for the emphasis on the man's mortality. Although he became wise like God, he was denied immortality, so he was put out of the garden to be sure he did not eat from the tree of life and live forever. Notice that "the Lord god" (Yahweh Elohim) said, "has become like one of us" (Genesis 3:22), another inadvertent clue to the primitive polytheism of the biblical source.

The word for "Eve," the name given to her by the man, is *chawwah*, and the word for "living" is *chayah*. Both come from the same root and are probably meant to show that, as a human, the woman is to be the mother of humans, not one of the goddesses so prominently mentioned in ancient mythologies. The drama ends in an unexpected fashion. The man does not suffer the punishment of death as decreed by God if he ate from the tree of the knowledge of good and evil (Genesis 2:17). Instead, he became wise like a god, as in ancient mythology. And, as in the ancient Akkadian Epic, the *Adapa*, the human was denied immortality. In that Epic its author says that Ea, god of wisdom, arts, and crafts, had created the hero as "the model for men." The author also says, "to him he had given wisdom; eternal life he had not given him" (*ANET*, 101).

Another thing to consider is that, if the first and only man and woman created by God were to "be fruitful and multiply" and populate the earth (Genesis 1:27-28, P), their children would have had to commit incest for Eve to be "the mother of all living" (Genesis 3:20; 4:1-26, J). The writer of the apocryphal work known as *Jubilees* (second century BCE) says, "Cain took Awan his sister" as his wife, and she gave birth to Enoch (*Jubilees* 4.9; see Genesis 4:17). So, did the apocryphal writer create a sister so as to eliminate the need for Cain to have sexual relations with Eve?

The Bible never mentions that Cain had a sister, but it does say later that he had sexual relations with his wife when he was in exile after killing his brother Abel and that she bore a son Enoch (Genesis 4:17, J). Apparently, when the Genesis stories of the creation of humans were written, the author must have believed that there were humans already in existence besides Adam and Eve. Moreover, Adam and Eve had a third son, Seth, and, according to Genesis 4:26, "To Seth also a son was born, and he named him

Enosh. At that time people began to invoke the name of the Lord." Not only was there someone who bore Seth's son, but this passage refers to other people, as well.

Additional questions are raised if we take the stories of creation and Eden literally. If Adam and Eve had that fantastic encounter with God in the Garden of Eden, isn't it strange that they would not have told their sons about it? And, doesn't God's rather mild punishment of Cain for killing Abel – exile to a strange land – seem inconsistent with the punishment for murder in Hebrew law: "Anyone who kills a human being shall be put to death" (Leviticus 24:17, 21)?

These stories clearly demonstrate the importance of insightful understanding rather than simple, literal answers about "what the Bible says." The biblical author was only writing what he believed about the origins of human existence, not history, nor were the authors of J and P writing anthropology or sociology, much less modern ethics. They probably never thought about the moral ramifications of the things they were writing or the obvious contradictions, because their sole purpose was to explain the origins of humans on the earth from their own religious perspectives.

## Chapter Summary

When tempted to say "The Bible Says So!" to support a literal interpretation of the creation and Garden of Eden stories, remember that what the Bible says reflects clear influence from ancient, polytheistic ideas like those in the *Enuma Elish* and the Gilgamesh Epic. Besides that, the biblical stories of creation have been given less credibility since the time of Galileo (1564–1645), the astronomer, physicist, and pioneer in the scientific method. Among other things, he invented a superior telescope and discovered the moons of Jupiter. As a young professor he had been required to teach the accepted theory that the sun and planets revolved around the earth. Later, as professor of astronomy at the University of Pisa, he confirmed the theory of Copernicus (1473–1543) that the earth and planets revolved around the sun.

Consider the major scientific advances since then that have proven that our little planet earth is just one of many others. Earth revolves around the sun, just one of billions of stars in the Milky Way, a little galaxy observable with the naked eye and one of billions of galaxies in the universe not yet completely known. Given how difficult it is even today to comprehend the vastness of the universe, can you imagine anyone in the ancient world who could have conceived of a universe as we know it today?

The biblical creation stories, influenced by earlier traditions and void of scientific facts, are understandable given the worldview at the time they were recorded. Similarly, with its contradictions and unanswered questions, the Garden of Eden story communicates the author's religious beliefs, not history. There is no need to subscribe to every literal detail of that story to understand its central message: we are to "Obey God's will." That same message is a common thread in the flood and Tower of Babel stories that we consider in the next chapter. Indeed, man's disobedience to the will of God is a theme prominent throughout the whole OT.

# Chapter 6

## FLOOD STORIES AND THE TOWER OF BABEL

### Introduction

Just as the Bible has two creation stories, it also has two flood stories which begin in Genesis 6:5. These stories probably show more noticeable influence from ancient Mesopotamian sources than even the creation or Garden of Eden stories. Influence from Tablet XI of the Gilgamesh Epic is especially notable (*ANET*, 93-97). As elsewhere in the Epic, the polytheism of the ancient world is present throughout.

The Genesis account of the flood stories is itself a composite of two of the main sources of the Pentateuch: mostly J interspersed with some from P. As usual, scholars' opinions differ about certain verses and parts of verses that belong to each source, yet there is agreement that there are multiple sources. Unlike the stories of the creation, the flood stories are a unified narrative, and we will deal mostly with the major differences between the two sources.

### Flood Stories in the Bible and outside the Bible

Observe below the comparisons of flood stories from the accounts of J and P with the Gilgamesh Epic.

*Epic*: The gods secretly decide to cause a flood and destroy the city of Shurippak.

*J*: The Hebrew God decides to destroy the whole earth and everything on it (6:5-7).

*P*: God is also responsible for the flood (6:11-13).

*Epic*: Nothing is said about the corruption of the earth.

*J*: Great wickedness of humankind is responsible for it (6:5).

*P*: Corruption of the earth is mentioned three times and the earth filled with violence two times (6:11-13).

## Flood Stories and the Tower of Babel

*Epic*: Utnapishtim is hero of the flood (afterward "hero").
*J*: Noah, hero of the flood, finds favor with God (6:8).
*P*: Noah alone is righteous before God (7:2).
*Epic*: God Ea warns the hero.
*J*: God warns Noah that he will blot out the earth (6:7).
*P*: God warns Noah that he is about to destroy the earth (6:13, 17).
*Epic*: Hero is told to build a ship.
*J*: ....................
*P*: Noah is told to build an ark (6:14-18).
*Epic*: The ship's dimensions are equal in width and length.
*J*: ....................
*P*: The ship's dimensions are 300 X 50 X 30 cubits (6:15; a cubit is about 18 inches or 45 centimetres).
*Epic*: Hero is told to seal the ship with bitumen (pitch).
*J*: ....................
*P*: Noah is told to seal the ark inside and out with pitch (6:14).
*Epic*: Hero is told to save his life by going into the ship.
*J*: Noah is told to go into the ark with his family (7:1).
*P*: Same as J.
*Epic*: The ship had six decks, seven parts, nine divisions in floor plan.
*J*: ....................
*P*: The ark had three decks (6:16).
*Epic*: Hero is told to take on board specimens of all living things.
*J*: Noah is told to take seven pairs of all clean animals and one pair of all animals not clean, male and female, and seven pairs of birds, male and female (7:2-3).
*P*: Noah is told to take two of every living thing, male and female, including birds, and food of every kind for humans and animals (6:19-21).
*Epic*: In an awesome storm, with hatches battened down, gods are scared by the deluge and cowered like dogs.
*J*: After seven days flood waters came (7:10).
*P*: Fountains of the great deep burst forth and windows of heaven opened on a specific year, month, and day (Genesis 7:11) and waters increased (7:17-21).
*Epic*: The flood lasted six days and six nights.
*J*: The flood lasted 40 days (7:17).
*P*: The flood lasted 150 days (7:24; 8:3) and stopped on a specific month and day (8:5, 13).

*Epic*: On the seventh day the storm and flood ceased, the landscape was as flat as a flat roof, humans had turned to clay, and the hero wept.

*J*: All animals and humans were blotted out (7:22-23).

*P*: All flesh, animals, and human beings were gone (7:21).

*Epic*: The ship grounded on Mount Nisir.

*J*: ....................

*P*: The ark grounded on Mount Ararat (8:4).

*Epic*: On the seventh day the hero sends out a dove and a swallow, but both returned. A raven sent out did not return.

*J*: Noah sent out a raven, which flew about until the waters were dried up. A dove sent out returned. After seven days Noah sent out a dove again, and it did not return (8:6-12).

*P*: ....................

*Epic*: Hero made a sacrifice to the gods on Mount Nisir.

*J*: Noah built an altar and sacrificed burnt offerings to God (8:20).

*P*: ....................

*Epic*: The gods smelled the sweet savor.

*J*: God smelled the pleasing odor ("sweet savor"; 8:21).

*P*: ....................

*Epic*: The gods crowded around the Hero like flies.

*J*: ....................

*P*: ....................

*Epic*: Goddess Ishtar will never forget the flood and its destruction of her people.

*J*: God resolves never again to curse the ground and destroy every living creature (8:21-22).

*P*: God makes a covenant with Noah never again to destroy the earth and all life (9:1-11).

*Epic*: The jewels of Ishtar given to Hero by the god Anu are a sign that she will not forget.

*J*: ....................

*P*: The rainbow is a sign of the covenant that God will remember never again to destroy the earth with a flood (9:12-17).

*Epic*: Utnapishtim and his wife will henceforth be like the gods.

*J*: ....................

*P*: Noah was saved from the flood because he was a righteous man, blameless, and walked with God (6:9).

Most scholars agree that the biblical accounts of the flood go back to Mesopotamian prototypes. The following are striking similarities: a proclamation by the gods (God in Bible) to a hero that a devastating flood is coming about which only the hero knows; the building of a boat, with dimensions stated, and sealing it with pitch; cargo of every kind of living creatures taken aboard; all other life destroyed; grounding of the boat on a mountain; releasing of birds, two of which return; sacrifice to deities; gods (God) smelled the sweet savor; and a promise, with a sign, that never again would the earth be destroyed by a flood.

In spite of these similarities, there are also striking differences between the Babylonian epic and the Bible. In the epic the flood is local, confined to one city, whereas in the Bible it is universal. The polytheism of the epic is in strong contrast to the biblical monotheism. The gods of the epic disagree, blame one another, cower like frightened dogs, and like bloodthirsty flies they swarm around the sacrificer. Whereas in the epic no cause is given for the flood, in the biblical account it was the corruption of the earth. The righteousness of Noah motivated God to spare him and his family.

## Comparison of Flood Stories in the Bible

According to J (Genesis 6:5-8), Yahweh saw great wickedness of humans on earth, regretted his creation, and decided to blot out humans and all other life. Noah, however, found favor with Yahweh. The author of P says that Noah was a righteous man, blameless, walked with God, and that he had three sons, Shem, Ham, and Japheth (Genesis 6:9). Walking with God was a concrete and anthropomorphic way of saying a person was righteous (see also Genesis 5:22, P).

According to P (Genesis 6:11-22), God (Elohim) tells Noah that he has decided to put an end to all flesh because of violence (better, "lawlessness"). There are elaborate directions for building an ark with three decks. God decides to bring on a flood to destroy all life and makes a covenant with Noah that he, his wife, and his sons and their wives shall enter the ark. Noah is to take two of every kind of living thing (male and female) into the ark, along with food for the humans and animals. Noah complies with God's command.

According to J (Genesis 7:1-5), Yahweh tells Noah, who alone is righteous, to take his family into the ark, along with *seven pairs* of all *clean* animals, male and female; *one pair* of *unclean* animals, male and female; and *seven pairs* of *birds*, male and female, so that all kinds of life will be preserved. In seven days Yahweh will send rain for 40 days and 40 nights and put an end to the existence of all things he had made. And Noah did as Yahweh commanded.

The following is an outline of events according to the sources J and P:

- P: Noah was 600 years old when the flood began (7:6).
- J: Noah and his family, the animals, and birds enter the ark because of flood waters that came after seven days (7:7-10).
- P: In the six hundredth year of Noah's life, in the second month, the seventeenth day, "all the fountains of the great deep burst forth, and the windows of the heavens were opened" (7:11; poetry).
- J: It rained for 40 days and 40 nights (7:12).
- P: On the day mentioned Noah and his sons, Shem, Ham, and Japheth, and their wives entered the ark, along with two each, male and female, of every living thing, both wild and domestic animals and birds (7:13-16a).
- J: And Yahweh shut him in (7:16b).
- P: The flood came down on the earth (7:17a).
- J: Forty days the waters increased so that the ark rose high above the land (7:17b).
- P: Waters rose greatly, the ark floated, waters surged 37 feet over the high mountains, and all life on earth, including humans, was destroyed (7:18-21).
- J: All life on earth, including birds, had died; only Noah and his family were left (7:22-23).
- P: Waters crested for 150 days. God (Elohim) remembered Noah and all the animals in the ark. God caused a wind to make the waters subside, and the fountains of the deep and windows of heaven were closed (7:24–8:2a).
- J: Rain was held back, and the water gradually receded (8:2b-3a).
- P: At the end of 150 days waters had lessened so that on the seventeenth day of the seventh month the ark came to rest on the mountains of Ararat. Waters continued to lessen, and on the first day of the tenth month tops of mountains appeared (8:3b-5).
- J: After 40 days Noah released a raven that flew around until the waters on the earth dried up. Then he sent out a dove to see if the water had gone from the ground. It found no place to sit and returned to the ark because water still covered the earth. After seven days Noah sent out the dove again, and at evening it returned with an olive leaf in its bill indicating that the water

## Flood Stories and the Tower of Babel

had subsided. After another seven days, Noah sent out the dove again, and it did not return (8:6-12).

*P:* On the first day of the first month in the six hundred first year of Noah's life (see Genesis 7:11) the water was dried up on the earth (8:13a).

*J:* Noah removed the covering of the ark and saw that the ground was drying (8:13b).

*P:* On the twenty-seventh day of the second month the earth was dry. God told Noah to take his family from the ark and all the living creatures so that they might multiply on the earth. Noah and his family left the ark, and so did all the animals in family groups (8:14-19).

*J:* Noah made an altar to Yahweh and sacrificed one of every clean animal and bird. When Yahweh "smelled the pleasing odor" of the sacrifice, he promised never again to curse the ground because of humans, "for the inclination of the human heart is evil from youth." Nor will Yahweh again destroy all living things (8:20-22; in verse 22 the promise is stated in a poetic couplet).

*P:* God blessed Noah and his sons and exhorted them to be fruitful and multiply with the same formula P had used in God's blessing the man and woman whom he had created (Genesis 1:28a; 9:1-17).

P's ideas of giving man dominion over animals and plants for food in Genesis 1:28b is echoed in 9:2-3, and the creation of man and woman in the image of God (Genesis 1:27) is reflected in 9:6. The prohibition against eating meat with blood in it (Genesis 9:4-5) is a part of Hebrew law (Leviticus 19:26; see also 1 Samuel 14:32-34). God's covenant with Noah mentioned in Genesis 6:18 (J) is elaborated in 9:8-11 (P) with the confirming sign of the rainbow (9:12-17, P).

According to J, Yahweh is God; for P, God is Elohim. In both sources Noah is a good man, in the favor of Yahweh (J) and a righteous and blameless man (P). According to both J and P, the deity decides to destroy humans and all life on earth because of human wickedness. However, in J the decision is made before Noah is mentioned; in P the story begins with Noah, and the wickedness of mankind is mentioned afterward.

Ponder the questions below as you seek more insightful understanding of the biblical flood stories. If the flood lasted for 40 days and 40 nights (J), to say nothing about 150 (P), what would the stench from all the animals and birds have been like? Would some animals have been mating and others giving birth? There could hardly be so many animals of different kinds on the boat without some fighting and a lot of noise. Imagine an elephant trumpeting. Some animals may have died, so how would their bodies be disposed of from a tightly sealed boat before they began to decay? Feeding the animals would have been a real chore, and would not some of the larger animals prey on the smaller ones?

If we believe P's account in Genesis 6:19-20, Noah would have taken one pair of every living thing. However, if he sacrificed one of every clean animal and bird immediately after he got off the boat, how could the creatures surviving produce young if one of each was gone? How would they have replenished their species on earth? (See Genesis 6:19-20, P.)

Likewise, just as with Adam and Eve if they alone were to have populated the earth, similar incestuous sexual relations would have had to take place with Noah's family after the flood if they were to repopulate the earth (Genesis 9:1, P). This means that all of us as one human family are the products of numerous incestuous relationships. It has been calculated that from the time of Shakespeare we have had 16,384 ancestors and from the time of the Roman Empire trillions of ancestors.

So, how are we to understand all of this? First of all, the stories are vivid, concrete expressions of religious faith, not facts. The questions we have raised never entered the minds of J and P or their editors. They began with ancient stories and, because of their distinctive monotheism, they refined them. The biblical writers omitted the anger of the gods and their evil exploits. The Hebrew deity was sorry he had created mankind, and his decision to destroy what he had created is justified by the wickedness of humans.

The protagonist of the story is not a hero, but a righteous man who is saved because of his righteousness. Even Noah's age of 600 years is symbolic of his righteousness, not an accurate account of his chronological age. The authors were not concerned with practical matters. They wanted to convey the religious message of the wickedness of humans and the righteousness of Noah, with the respective consequences. Because of Noah's righteousness, God made a covenant never again to destroy mankind and all life on earth. Because of Noah's righteousness, "the whole earth was peopled" through his three sons (Genesis 9:19). The primary message communicated in the story – the importance of righteousness – is clear, with no need to take literally the many contradictions and impractical details.

## Tower of Babel

As with the biblical creation, flood, and Garden of Eden stories, there is a link to the ancient world with the story of the Tower of Babel. While the flood stories in Genesis were greatly influenced by the ancient Gilgamesh Epic, the Babel story is just as convincingly influenced by the ancient *Enuma Elish*. In it (*ANET*, Tablet VI, lines 60-62, 69), there is an account of the building of the Babylonian Tower (Temple Tower in Babylon), which provided the motivation for the biblical tower of Babel (biblical name for Babylon). It was built in the common ziggurat style, pyramidal, of baked bricks in successive stages, with spiral stairs going around on the outside and a religious shrine on top. The date of the tower that inspired the biblical story is uncertain.

E. A. Speiser (*Genesis* [AB 1; Garden City, NY: Doubleday, 1964], pp. 75-76) calls attention to two interesting and important parallels between the Babylonian narrative and the one in Genesis. The first is "they molded its bricks" and the biblical "Come, let us make bricks" (Genesis 11:3). The second is the meaning of the language in the line, "They raised the head of Esagila toward Apsu. Apsu is, among other things, a poetic term for the boundless expanse of the sky." And, "Esagila means literally the structure with upraised head." The words in Genesis 11:4, "with its top in the heavens" (*NRSV*) are literally "with its head in the heavens."

In Genesis 11:5-6 the author writes: "The Lord came down" and "the Lord said," both in the singular. However, in Genesis 11:7 the author writes: "Let us [plural] go down." This is clearly an unconscious echo of polytheism in the earliest stage of the Hebrew religion and provides additional evidence that the author of the Genesis story of the Tower of Babel was familiar with the Babylonian prototype. However, he used it for religious purposes.

The biblical Babel story (Genesis 11:1-9, J) follows directly after the story of the descendants of Noah. The opening statement, "the whole earth had one language and the same words," contradicts the words of P that the families of Noah each had their own language in their own lands (Genesis 10:5). The idea behind P's words is that Noah's descendants would have lands of their own given by God (Genesis 10:5, 19, 30-32). However, the "they" in Genesis 11:2 is ambiguous and does not refer to the families of Noah mentioned above. Perhaps taking it as "human beings" would be better. They migrated and settled in the land of Shinar, the biblical name for Babylonia. The migrants became haughty and decided to build a city of their own and a tower that reached toward heaven. All of this was in disobedience to the will of Yahweh.

The biblical author is not concerned with the architecture of the tower or with the literary nature of his account, although he uses wordplay in the sentence, "Therefore it was called Babel, because there the Lord confused the language." The word translated as "confuse" (in the sense of "mix") is *balal* a wordplay on *babel*, the Hebrew word for Babylon. In the simplest terms, the author uses the story of Babel to explain the existence of the many nations of his time and the origin of the different languages that he was aware were being used. The account of J about those things is in sharp contrast to the Table of Nations by P. There the descendants of Noah, according to families, had their own nations and distinctive languages (Genesis 10:5, 20, 31-32).

*Chapter Summary*

The Genesis stories about the flood and the Tower of Babel were clearly influenced by ancient stories that originated in a polytheistic world. They become colorful expressions of the biblical authors' religious faith, reflecting their monotheistic views, and share an underlying message of the importance of obeying God's will. After gaining the knowledge of right and wrong in the Garden of Eden, there followed the moral degeneration of mankind, a theme that was highlighted in the preface to the flood story. Yahweh regretted that he had made humans and decided to destroy them along with all life on earth, sparing Noah because he was a righteous and blameless man. Despite discrepant details in the flood stories, the importance of man's righteousness is very clear.

J's theme that humans must not become like God comes to its climax in the Tower of Babel story. In the words of Yahweh, the writer says that humans becoming one people and having one language is only the beginning of what they might try to do. Therefore, Yahweh mixed their languages so that they could not communicate with one another and dispersed them over all the earth. This story also shows how the author was trying to explain what he observed: the existence of multiple nations and languages.

The book of Genesis and its well-known stories are often an attempt to explain observable phenomena within the context of the writers' time. The biblical authors' understanding of the world, radically different from ours today, along with a deep commitment to their religious views, shaped what they wrote. For insightful understanding, what the Bible says must be studied with that in mind. In the next chapter, we use the same approach to study Genesis stories as beginnings.

## Chapter 7

### GENESIS STORIES AS BEGINNINGS

*Introduction*

The first book of the Bible was given its name from the Greek word *Genesis*, which means "beginning" or "origin," and it is the equivalent of the Hebrew word *bereshith*, the first word of the Hebrew text transferred to the title of the book. Genesis, therefore, is the account of how its authors believed phenomena observed or known to them began, particularly the earth, life on it, and Hebrew history. In everyday life, the author of P experienced light and darkness; day and night; morning and evening; the sky as a dome, with birds and the sun, moon, and stars; earth as dry land, with vegetation of many kinds, some for food; wild and domestic animals; creeping things on the earth; and waters, with all kinds of creatures large and small. Besides the creation of the heavens and earth, J's account in Genesis provides an explanation of how animals got their names, although none is actually named. Indeed, J's "beginnings" are at the same time explanations.

Both authors believed that the earth and all on it were created by God (Genesis 1:1–2:24). This means that they came from a theocratic (Greek, *theos*, "god," and *kratos*, "power") society. From the beginning, the God of P was in control of everything, including nature, as the formless void, darkness, and the deep indicate. Henceforth, God was in control of the earth and everything on it, including humans. God's control over nature is symbolized by the words "a wind from God."

### *"Firsts" in Genesis*

The author of P was clearly aware of the established view of the sanctity of the Sabbath and included it in his creation story by having God rest on the seventh day. While the origin of the Sabbath and its observance are uncertain, in Babylonian literature there is a word (*sabattu*) very similar to the Hebrew *shabat*. It was a day of "quieting of the heart," perhaps implying a day of rest. Interestingly, the seventh day of the month and multiples of it in certain months were regarded as evil days, because they were under the power of gods or spirits angry with humans. On those days doctors, priests, and especially royalty did not serve in official capacities.

The Hebrew word for Sabbath is derived from the verb *shabat*, meaning to "desist," "cease," "come to an end," and secondarily to "rest." Among the Israelites, the Sabbath became a day of rest; all physical work was prohibited for all members of the family, including slaves and sojourners (Exodus 20:8-11; Deuteronomy 5:12-15). It is uncertain when they began to observe the Sabbath, but during nomadic life when their only sustenance was animal husbandry, it would have been impossible to abstain from all work on one day of the week. So, the Israelites probably began to observe their holy day after they learned from the Canaanites how to plant and harvest crops and became settled in an agrarian life. An agricultural calendar from the Canaanite city of Gezer, dated about 1000 BCE, lists months for planting and harvesting crops, tending vineyards, and picking summer fruits.

From the beginning of time, according to Genesis, humans were endowed with the ability to choose between good and evil. Genesis 3:1-24 is often referred to as "the fall of man" or as "the origin of sin." Observe, though, that the author of J never says that the man and woman died because of their "sin," in spite of the fact that he said they would (Genesis 2:17). If they had died, the earth could not have become populated. Thus, the couple was sent from the garden so that they would not eat of the tree of life and live forever (Genesis 2:9, 16-17; 3:22). Humans became mortal. Made from the dust, humans return to dust (3:19), again an explanation for a universal experience. Here, as in the ancient mythologies, only gods have eternal life. The suspense comes to an unexpected conclusion in that the couple had achieved the knowledge of good and evil like God, who had not wanted that to happen. Although punished, they did not die as God had promised. Instead, woman was to bear children in the pain of childbirth, again an explanation for a universal feminine experience, and man was to earn his bread through the sweat of his labors.

The discussion of Adam and sin by the Apostle Paul in Romans 5:12, "Just as sin came into the world through one man, and death came through sin, and so death spread to all because all have sinned," is often used by Christians to support what is known as the doctrine of original sin. However, Paul says "because all have sinned," *not* that all are sinful *because* of Adam. The quip in *The New England Primer of 1805*, on the other hand, does state the doctrine of original sin succinctly: "In Adam's fall/We sinned all."

Adam fell, but only for the fruit Eve gave him. Nonetheless, Adam is said to be responsible for the "fall of man" or sin.

The wrong choice of the first woman and her husband was followed by the first murder when Cain killed his brother Abel. Factually, the Yahwist (J) does not mention the word "sin" anywhere in the Eden story. Rather, he first mentions it in the story of Cain and Abel (the sons of Adam and Eve). Typical of J's anthropomorphic conception of the deity, Yahweh speaks to Cain, who is angry with his brother: "Sin is lurking at the door; its desire is for you, but you must master it" (Genesis 4:7). As with Adam and Eve, Cain had a choice between good and evil, and like them he disobeyed and was punished (Genesis 4:1-8). Yet "the Bible says" that Cain's murder of Abel became the beginning of sin. In light of the Eden story, it seems surprising that the first sin of humans to be mentioned is the result of a man's relationship with another man, not that between a man and a woman.

The story of Cain and Abel shows that the author of J had a preference for the pastoral way of life over the agricultural, because Abel's offering from the flock was the one pleasing to Yahweh, not that of the farmer Cain (Genesis 4:2–5:12). This shows the origin of farming and the raising of livestock. The Cain and Abel story is followed by the first mention of vengeance (4:15; see also 4:23-24). The genealogies in Genesis 4:17-22 refer to the first polygamy – "Lamech took two wives"; the first music; and the making of bronze (copper) and iron implements. Genesis 4 ends with the statement that then people began to invoke the name Yahweh (4:26).

The story of "the sons of God" marrying human women (Genesis 6:1-4) is the only one of its kind in the Bible. "Sons of God" (Hebrew *bene elohim*) is a Hebrew metonym for "gods" and should probably be understood as "divine beings," distinguished from Yahweh by J. The main contrast is on immortal beings as opposed to mortals. The story is typical of ancient mythologies, beginning with those in Hittite documents based on earlier sources that date from the second millennium BCE. Those documents are the most likely source of the biblical account, which may be only a fragment of a larger story. It seems out of context, unless because of the immoral implications, the author of J used it as a preface to the evils of humans that motivated Yahweh to bring on the flood.

After the flood there is the account of the first vineyard planted by Noah. He then lost his righteousness by consuming too much of its product, becoming drunk, and exposing his nakedness (Genesis 9:20-23). Such nakedness had implications of sexual relations among family members, which was strictly forbidden by Hebrew law (Leviticus 18:6-19; 20:11, 17-21). However, J does not blame Noah, perhaps because as the first person to grow grapes he was not aware of the intoxicating effects of wine. On the other hand, he must have known how to turn grape juice into wine. Perhaps, like Eve, he yielded too much to the good taste.

The story of the descendants of Noah's three sons, Shem, Ham, and Japheth, is mostly from P (Genesis 10:1-32). Because of the title in Genesis 10:1, the lists that follow are generally referred as the Table of Nations. Since the author reflects knowledge of geographical locations and peoples in them for about two centuries before his time in mid-fifth century BCE, he must have done some research. Certain names of persons indicate places that can be identified as ancient locations, reflecting that the author had knowledge of the southern shore of the Black Sea, Asia Minor, Mesopotamia, southern Arabia, and Egypt. For example, Ashur and Elam, sons of Shem, represent places in Mesopotamia, and Aram represents Syria; Ham's sons Cush and Mizraim (Hebrew) represent Ethiopia and Egypt, respectively; and the Medes and Scythians in Asia Minor are represented in the names Gomer and Ashkenaz, sons of Japheth.

The author's statement in Genesis 10:5, "in their lands, with their own language, by their families, in their nations," indicates that the "Table" is not only ethnic-geographic, but ethnic-linguistic as well. It so happens that the peoples from Japheth used Indo-European languages, the peoples from Ham spoke African languages, and the peoples from Shem used Semitic languages.

Before leaving our discussion of "firsts" in Genesis, let's consider one more point. Some persons use Genesis to argue for the equality of man and woman in the OT by saying that God intended equality between the sexes when he created male and female simultaneously. While that is true in P's account, woman was created from the rib of the man in J's account. And, in J's account, Adam is the leading character. Because he listened to Eve and ate fruit from the forbidden tree, humans forever remain mortal. Woman will desire for her husband who will rule over her (Genesis 3:16).

To use Genesis either to support equality of the sexes or to support the need for woman to be subservient to man might provide simple, though contradictory, answers but certainly not insightful understanding. We cannot use Genesis to argue equality of the sexes any more than we can use it to support the dominance of man. Genesis reflects the context of its author, and it is in that context that we must understand its stories. When the author says that woman's husband will rule over her, he was simply reflecting the male-dominated society of his time. While we must understand the story in that context, this is not to suggest that it should direct us today.

## Further Observations on Stories in Genesis

The stories we have been considering are mostly from J, the oldest source of the Pentateuch (Genesis 2:4b–11:9), with the exceptions of one creation story and some of the flood stories from P. The author of J reveals some consciousness of the advancement of civilization. Humans were naked and lived by eating fruits from trees in the primeval era (2:4b-9, 15-17), and then the making of clothing from leaves (3:7) and skins (3:21) represents a stage above nakedness. The practice of arts and crafts began with the fabrication of tents (4:20), musical instruments (4:21), and tools from metals (4:22). The age of heroes and renowned warriors who lived as giants (*Nephilim*) upon the earth (6:1-4) followed. The planting of vineyards and wine-making (9:20-21) were probably a part of the author's own times. And, finally, there is the difference among nations and languages, living in communities, and the building of cities (11:1-9).

Although the authors of the creation and Eden stories reveal an agrarian society, each was written under different circumstances. According to P there was abundant vegetation with various kinds of plants and fruit for food (Genesis 1:11-12). According to J there were trees for fruit (2:9), but the soil was infertile, cursed, with thorns and thistles, and food was attained through hard labor (3:17-19).

The story of Cain and his descendants, which does not follow naturally among the other stories of J, shows that the author was not trying to write a consistent account. Cain is portrayed in different ways. According to Genesis 4:12, he was condemned to "be a fugitive and a wanderer on the earth." His background was that of a nomad whose soil would not yield crops. According to Genesis 4:17-21, Cain became the ancestor of successful persons who built a city, lived in tents, had livestock, and practiced arts and crafts. Lamech bragged about his valorous deeds and drastic revenge (4:23-24). The reference to metal tools indicates that the environment of Cain's descendants was the Bronze Age, whereas nothing in the Eden story shows a setting beyond the Stone Age.

## Chapter Summary

The accounts of creation, the Garden of Eden, the flood, and the Tower of Babel probably all first circulated orally as separate stories. They are diverse and of uncertain origin, although clearly based on primitive mythologies. Eventually these stories were inserted into the Bible by editors who did not make a connected or unified account. Therefore, the Bible includes two different creation stories and two accounts of the flood. Attributed to J and P, these stories, though similar, have obvious discrepancies.

Beginning with the stories of creation, both P and J are dealing with the relationship between humans and the deity, whether Yahweh or Elohim. Both authors want to assure their readers that the deity and humans are not on the same level of existence, either physically or morally. According to P, humans are above the animals and have dominion over them. There is no thought in P about humans being like God, yet the imagery of the creation of humans in the image of God occurs in P. See, for example, Genesis 5:1-2, where the author says, "When God created humankind, he made them in the likeness of God. Male and female he created them" (see also Genesis 9:6). There is no reference to the behavior of humans, nor is there a hint of antipathy between the deity and the humans he created. In P the stress is on the creation of the earth and humans and the reproduction of vegetation and animal and human life.

The author of J, on the other hand, links his brief story of the making of the man with the story of Eden. Immediately the man is made aware of the choice between good and evil when Yahweh informs him about the tree of the knowledge of good and evil. Disobedience by eating the fruit of that tree will bring punishment. The temptation to "be like God" brought with it the potential for moral awareness, "knowing good and evil" (Genesis 3:5), and, by eating the forbidden fruit, the eyes of the woman and man were opened. They became like God in that they are now aware of the difference between right and wrong. Their disobedience is the beginning of the moral decline of humans and, along with it, the beginning of antipathy between humans and the deity that created them. Humans must go no further in being like God, so he denied them the possibility of living forever by eating from the tree of life (Genesis 3:22-24).

Without any advice about how to prevent it, the theme of moral degeneration after the knowledge of right and wrong learned in Eden reached its greatest in the preface to the flood story. Yahweh regretted that he had made humans and decided to destroy mankind, except Noah who found favor with Yahweh, and all life on earth (Genesis 6:5-7). The author of P makes clear the reason for Noah's favoritism: he was a righteous and blameless man (6:9).

Throughout these stories the author of J wants to make certain that God is above the reach of humans and is in control of their lives. This is unique to J. His theme that humans must not become like God comes to its climax in the Babel story. Yahweh mixed their languages so that they could not communicate with one another and dispersed them over all the earth.

Perhaps the editors also refined these biblical stories by eliminating polytheistic elements but without inserting advice about morality, which is almost completely lacking in the J accounts.

Despite details that lack accuracy, a common thread among these stories and a theme prominent throughout the whole OT is man's disobedience to the will of God. For insightful understanding the question is not whether the stories are historical and, therefore, true, but what they meant for their authors and for the intended readers long before the Bible was compiled in its present form. They were expressions of their authors' religious beliefs and are neither history nor science. In the next chapter we examine the Patriarchal Narratives, which are yet another example of stories that reveal more about the authors' religious faith than pure historical fact.

## Chapter 8

PATRIARCHAL NARRATIVES

*Introduction*

Genesis, a book of "beginnings," includes stories about the early Hebrew nomads who came to be known in Judaism and the NT as the Patriarchs. The "origins" in Genesis were never intended to be taken as "scientific explanations," words the writers would never have understood. Rather, writing strictly from religious points of view, biblical writers were trying to tell others how they believed phenomena they observed in life and nature must have originated in an attempt to convince others to believe as they did. This is important to remember, as well, when reading the accounts in Genesis of how Hebrew "history" began.

Some OT scholars maintain that the patriarchal narratives in Genesis, the desert wanderings of the Israelites in the book of Exodus, including the character Moses, and the conquest of Canaan in the book of Joshua are of little, if any, historical value. According to those scholars, the narratives mentioned are legends, sagas, myths, and even fairy tales, written to explain the prehistory of the nation of Israel. Other scholars regard the same narratives as some of the actual prehistory of Israel. Perhaps most scholars think the narratives contain some historical truth, although they realize the difficulty in trying to determine exactly what is historically true. The discussion that follows is intended to illustrate the theory of sources, which naturally raises some questions about historicity, and to provide the basis for insightful understanding of these OT stories.

*Overview of the Patriarchal Narratives*

Names from the time of the Patriarchs (c. 2000-1700 BCE) occur in documents from the Mesopotamian cities of Mari (eighteenth century BCE) and Nuzi (fifteenth century BCE). In an ancient Mesopotamian text there is the name *Abram* in the form "abamram," which appears also in the

Mari texts. Nahor, the name of Abraham's grandfather and brother (Genesis 11:22-26), is also the name of a city near the town of Haran (Genesis 24:10). Other names occurring in the same texts are Benjamin, Levi, and Ishmael, as well as names similar to those of Gad and Dan, two Israelite tribes.

The patriarchal narratives divide naturally into the stories of Abraham (Genesis 12:1–25:18), Jacob (Genesis 25:19–37:2a), and Joseph (Genesis 37:2b–48:22), with no cycle of stories for Isaac as for Abraham and Jacob. Isaac plays a relatively passive role, and the stories about him serve as a link between those of Abraham and Jacob. The most significant thing about Isaac is that he was born to fulfill the role God gave him in patriarchal history and religion. Material about the patriarchs is presented below when it first appears in Genesis, and other accounts are considered with it. All references are to Genesis. As with other stories in that book, repetitions, intertwining of material, and differences in accounts undoubtedly reflect different sources.

### *God's Call and Promises to Abraham about a Son (12:1-4, J; 15:1-21, J+E; 17:1-27, P)*

According to P earlier in Genesis (11:31-32), Terah, Abram's father, took Abram and his family from Ur in Babylonia to Haran in Canaan. Yahweh, according to J, told Abram to leave his home and go to a land he will show him. He will be a great nation, and God will bless those who bless him and curse those who curse him (12:1-4). Then, according to P, Abram took his family and went to Haran in Canaan (12:4-5). According to J+E, the Lord came to Abram in a vision and told him that, although childless, he will have a son as heir from his own family, not through his servant Eliezer. Abram's descendants will be as numerous as the stars of heaven and have lands of their own (15:1-6).

In P the promise to Abram is longer and more dramatic and detailed. When Abram was 99 years old, Yahweh appeared to him as God Almighty (El Shaddai), but in the rest of the narrative the deity appears as Elohim. God covenants with Abram to make him "the ancestor of a multitude of nations" through his descendants and to give him the land of Canaan. For that reason, his name is changed from Abram to Abraham. Abraham must promise to Yahweh that he, with all his slaves and his descendants throughout the generations, would be circumcised. Sarai's name is changed to Sarah because she will be blessed and give Abraham a son Isaac, who will be the beneficiary of God's covenant with Abraham. Abraham asks a favor for Ishmael, Abraham's son with Sarah's slave Hagar, and God promises that a great nation will also come from him.

The documents from the ancient Mesopotamian city of Nuzi, mentioned earlier, provide insight into customs practiced among the Patriarchs and also into this story about Abraham. According to Nuzi law, couples without children could adopt a son who would be loyal to them while they lived and be their heir at death. However, if a natural son should be born, the adopted son would no longer be the heir. In Genesis 15:1-6, Abram was afraid that if he died childless his servant Eliezer would become his heir. Abraham was worried because he did not even have an adopted son to mourn his death and bury him. This clearly reflects the custom discussed in the Nuzi texts. God assured Abram that he would have a son.

## Stories of the Lies

There are three different accounts in Genesis of a man taking his wife into a strange place and lying that she is his sister. The man does so because his wife is so beautiful that he is afraid some other man will kill him to take her. With respect to the first two stories, J puts Abraham in Egypt (12:10-20), and E puts Abraham at Gerar (20:1-18). J, in the third story, has Isaac and Rebekah at Gerar (26:6-11). E seems to be a rethinking of J with the social and religious overtones lacking in J's Egypt. The three accounts must be considered in light of God's call of Abraham and promises that he will be a great nation.

### *Abraham and Sarah in Egypt (J)*
In J, as the result of Abram's lie about Sarai being his sister, officials praised Sarai to Pharaoh, who took her as his wife. For Sarai's sake Pharaoh treated Abram well by giving him livestock and female slaves. However, Yahweh sent plagues on Pharaoh and his family. Pharaoh summoned Abram and asked, "What is this you have done to me? Why did you not tell me that she was your wife? Why did you say, 'She is my sister'?" Pharaoh abruptly told Abram to take his wife and be gone. There is no reconciliation between Pharaoh and Abraham, and God does not become involved in trying to make that happen. Pharaoh orders Abraham to be sent away, and there is no further thought about justifying the conduct of either man (12:18-20).

### *Abraham and Sarah at Gerar (E)*
In E the official in the story is Abimelech, King of Gerar, and again Abraham said that his wife was his sister. After the lie, the king sent for and took

Sarah. In the first of two dialogues, God appears to Abimelech in a vision and tells him that he will die because he took a married woman. But E is careful to say that Abimelech had not approached Sarah, which means he did not have sexual intercourse with her. Abimelech, addressing the deity as "Lord," asks if he would kill an innocent person. He also asks the Lord if Abraham himself had not said, "She is my sister," and Sarah herself, "He is my brother." E stresses Abimelech's innocence even further when he has Abimelech say, "I did this in the integrity of my heart and the innocence of my hands" (20:5).

Then, still in the dream, God admits that Abimelech acted with integrity, but God himself takes credit for that: "It was I who kept you from sinning against me. Therefore I did not let you touch her." God tells Abimelech to return Abraham's wife and says that Abraham is a prophet, who will pray for him and he will live. If Sarah is not returned, Abimelech and his family will die. E again seems to stress the innocence of Abimelech by saying, "he had not approached her" (20:4), although that statement comes after God had just said that Abimelech was to die because he had taken a married woman (20:3-4). Abimelech appears more righteous than Abraham in asking God if he would destroy someone who is innocent. In fact, in E Abimelech exemplifies the kind of moral sensitivity one would expect of the righteous Abraham.

In a dialogue between Abimelech and Abraham, Abimelech asks, "What have you done to us? How have I sinned against you, that you have brought such great guilt on me and my kingdom? You have done things to me that ought not to be done... What were you thinking of, that you did this thing?" (20:9-10). Abraham's answers appear rather weak. First, he says that he did so because there "is no fear of God at all in this place" (20:11), yet its king is the one who has exemplified the Hebrew virtue of not committing adultery.

Second, Abraham answers, "She is indeed my sister, the daughter of my father but not the daughter of my mother; and she became my wife." Moreover, Abraham says that, when God told him to begin his wanderings, he (Abraham) asked Sarah to show kindness toward him by saying, "He is my brother" (20:11-13). Is this another lie? Regardless, Abimelech completely accepts Abraham's answers and does not question him further. He gives livestock and female slaves to Abraham, returns his wife, and tells him to settle where he wants; he gives Sarah silver and exonerates her before all. Abraham prays to God, who heals Abimelech and his family.

From a literary standpoint E's story of Abraham and Sarah at Gerar is a drama about God, Abraham, and Abimelech. Conflicts and emotions are expressed mainly in dialogue interspersed with action. There is suspense, followed by surprise, when readers expect the justice of God with respect to the innocent Abimelech, but God punishes him, instead. Also, contrary to expectations, readers learn that the innocent Abimelech gives gifts to Abraham. Rather than ordering Abraham to leave the place as Pharaoh did in J (12:20), Abimelech offers Abraham land for habitation, returns Sarah to him, and vindicates her, and Abraham intercedes with God on behalf of Abimelech, whose punishment is then revoked. Abraham is again saved from death so that God's promises to him might be fulfilled.

### Isaac and Rebekah at Gerar (J)

In J's story about Isaac and Rebekah at Gerar, Isaac, to save his life, lies that his beautiful wife, Rebekah, is in fact his sister. As in E, Abimelech is king (26:6-11), and the Isaac story seems to reflect the ones about Abraham. After a long time, Abimelech learned that Rebekah was Isaac's wife when he saw Isaac "fondling" her. Abimelech asks why Isaac said that she was his sister, to which Isaac replies that he thought he might die because of her. This is the same as in the other stories.

Abimelech's question, "What is this you have done to us?" reflects his similar exclamations and questions in E (20:9-10) and Pharaoh's in J (12:18-19). Whereas the innocence of Abimelech is stated clearly in E, it is only implied by J in the Isaac story. After his question about why Isaac lied about his wife, Abimelech says that one of the men might have had sex with Rebekah and brought guilt upon them. In the Isaac story Abimelech's warning further assures his innocence: "Whoever touches this man or his wife shall be put to death" (26:13). In the other two stories the couple move on after the incident, but Isaac stays. The Lord blessed him, and he became so rich and powerful that Abimelech then asked him to leave (26:12-16).

### Understanding the Stories of the Lies

The practice of a king wanting the wife of another man is well known, even in the Bible, with the story of David having Bathsheba's husband killed so that he could have her (2 Samuel 11:1-12, 25). There is no help in the Bible, however, for understanding the lies of Abraham and Isaac. A clue for insightful understanding is in the words "his wife Sarah," "she is my sister," "indeed my sister," "became my wife," "he is my brother," "his wife," and "your brother" (20:2-16). Thinking in terms of our time, the theme of wife/sister/brother relationship is hard to understand, especially in light of some biblical teaching on family relationships and morality elsewhere, but information about a social background probably familiar to E is helpful.

A people in the ancient world known as Hurrians moved into Mesopotamia from the north in the third millennium BCE. They established a number of kingdoms, the most important of which was Mitanni. The chief Hurrian city of Harran was near the center of Mitanni in the Euphrates Valley. In the OT that city is known as Haran, the home of Abraham after his father took his family from Babylonia (11:31-32, P). Eventually, the Hurrians moved westward into Asia Minor, Syria, and Canaan. Hurrians used a language of their own, with a cuneiform style of writing called "Hurrian," and hundreds of documents written on stone tablets have been discovered, which inform us about Hurrian culture. In the OT the Hurrians are known as Horites, Hivites, and Jebusites, the people who occupied Jebus (Jerusalem) before David conquered it in the tenth century BCE (e.g., Genesis 14:6; Joshua 9:7; 11:19; 15:63). These passages attest the presence of Hurrians in Canaan and their interactions with the Israelites.

The social customs of the patriarchs were influenced by the Hurrians in several ways. For instance, one custom which was peculiar to the Hurrians was that the bonds of marriage and wife/sister/brother relationships were especially strong. A wife had the legal status of a sister, even if there was no blood relationship. A man would sometimes marry a girl and adopt her as a sister at the same time, and each transaction was recorded in a separate legal document. So, when Abraham says that his wife Sarah is the daughter of his father but not of his mother (Genesis 20:12), this means that she was the daughter of Terah, Abraham's father, because of marriage to Abraham but not an actual biological offspring of his mother. According to Hurrian customs, Sarah would also qualify as Abraham's "sister."

Rebekah was from Nahor, a city near Haran, the homeland of Abraham, in Hurrian territory (Genesis 24:1-10, J), where her brother Laban gave her to a servant of Abraham for marriage to Isaac (Genesis 24:45-51, J). The formality of such a marriage agreement is stated in Genesis 24:57-58. Rebekah's brother Laban and his mother agreed to ask Rebekah if she would go with the servant: "Will you go with this man?" She said, "I will." The words "to her brother and to her mother" (Genesis 24:53, 55) indicate that Rebekah's father was dead and that her brother was performing the responsibilities of her father in giving Rebekah for marriage. In Hurrian law the same kind of pledge was given by a woman who consents to marriage: "myself and my brother (agree to this marriage)." The words about Rebekah and her brother acting in place of her father coincide with part of a marriage contract known in Hurrian marriages as a "sistership document" (Speiser, *Genesis*, pp. 184-85).

J (Genesis 12:10-20) and E (20:1-18) were probably familiar with Hurrian marriage customs, which each used in distinct ways. In J there is only the wife/sister relationship, whereas in E there is the threefold relationship of wife/sister/brother. Although we do not know how the authors became familiar with the customs, it seems unlikely that either used written documents. Rather, they were probably writing down oral traditions, choosing and omitting as they wished with additions of their own. This best explains the likenesses in the accounts and especially the differences.

### *Stories about Ishmael (16:1-16, J+P; 21:6-21, E; 17:15-26, P)*

Abraham was concerned for his son Ishmael, born of Sarah's slave-girl Hagar, should Sarah bear a son. In J childless Sarai asked Abram to have sex with her slave-girl Hagar. Abraham consented, but when Hagar conceived, she began to despise her mistress. Sarai reported it to Abram and asked God to judge between Abram and her about the wrong done. Abram told Sarai to deal with Hagar as she pleased, and after being dealt with harshly, Hagar ran away. After finding Hagar in the desert, an angel of Yahweh told her to return and submit to her mistress. Readers are never told, though, if she did return. However, the angel promised that her son would be given numberless descendants. He would also be "a wild ass of a man" at odds with everyone, including his own kin, and everyone at odds against him.

In E Sarah saw the son of Hagar (Ishmael) playing with Isaac (in LXX, not in Hebrew). She asked Abraham to put Hagar out so that Ishmael would not be an heir with Isaac. Abraham was very distressed, but God told him to do as Sarah wanted because his descendants would be preserved through Isaac, and the son of the slave woman would also have a nation. Abraham packed a lunch for Hagar and her son and sent them on their way. Having found her in the wilderness with her son about to die, God told Hagar he would make a great nation of Ishmael. While God was with Ishmael in the wilderness, Hagar, who was an Egyptian, got her son a wife from Egypt.

In P, the latest account, Abraham implores God, "O that Ishmael might live in your sight." God reassures Abraham that Sarah will bear a son, with whom he will make a covenant to give him numberless people in a great nation. Abraham then circumcised his son Ishmael and all the male members of his household.

### Understanding the Ishmael Stories

The Nuzi texts again provide insight into our understanding of the Ishmael stories. In a marriage contract in Nuzi law, a wife who is childless is obligated to provide another woman, usually a slave, for the purpose of bearing a son. That certainly explains Sarah giving her slave woman to Abraham to have a son as an heir. However, if a son is later fathered by the husband, the slave woman and her child could not be turned away. That helps to explain Abraham's distress at doing this to Hagar and her son (21:8-13, E).

From a religious point of view, authors of the Ishmael stories portray the tension between faithfulness and doubt. Both Abraham and Sarah doubt that at their age Sarah could bear a son herself, and Abraham has to be assured that God will provide for his son Ishmael. At the same time, God shows his faithfulness by fulfilling his promises to Abraham about his descendants and appears as the one in charge of all circumstances.

### Abraham Visited by Three Strange Men (18:1-33, J)

As Genesis continues, Abraham is visited by three strange men. One of these "men" was Yahweh, who promises Abraham a son from Sarah. Unaware that one of the visitors is Yahweh, Abraham addresses him as "My lord." Abraham's exemplary hospitality to guests is part of the drama that prepares the readers for the unexpected surprise announcement of the son to be born of Sarah. J stresses the faithlessness of Sarah upon hearing Yahweh's promise and then her fear before God at realizing his greatness: "Is anything too wonderful for the Lord?" After she denies that she laughed at being told about a son, the drama ends dramatically with Yahweh's words: "Oh yes, you did laugh."

### Sodom Destroyed (18:16–19:28, J)

In yet another well-known story in Genesis, the cities of Sodom and Gomorrah were destroyed because of their wickedness, but Lot, Abraham's nephew, was spared through Abraham's pleading with Yahweh (18:16–19:20). Because Yahweh chose Abraham, he expects him to charge his descendants to follow his ways by being righteous in order that his promise to Abraham will be fulfilled (18:19). In the monologue of Yahweh (18:17-21) and in the dialogue between Yahweh and Abraham (18:23-32), J becomes interested in something more than history. The questions of Yahweh and Abraham show a moral and philosophical awareness greater than heretofore in J, for example, "Will you indeed sweep away the righteous with the wicked?"(18:23). As judge of all the earth, God distinguishes between the righteous and the unrighteous in a way reminiscent of the flood stories. Abraham's plea is that Yahweh save the righteous individuals from the wicked masses. The question of the righteous and the unrighteous and their ultimate fate was first raised in Babylonian literature and is the theme of the classic Job in the Bible.

As with Noah and his family, Lot and his daughters were saved from death because of their righteousness, but Lot's wife was not. Her curiosity got the better of her, and after disobeying God's will not to look back, she was turned into a memorial of salt. This penalty seems a bit harsh compared with the lesser punishment of Adam and Eve. If J wrote both stories, would he give such diverse consequences? Was he simply recording stories, or was an editor at work in one of the stories? Or, do the stories come from two different sources? We do not know the answers to such questions, and more are raised in J's account of Lot and his daughters.

J may intend a parallel between the visit of three men with Abraham (18:1-15) and the two angels with Lot (19:1-22). Abraham is favored because he welcomes the three visitors, one of whom is Yahweh, who speaks directly to him. Lot welcomes the two men (angels), bows down, addresses them as "my lords," and invites them into the house. Young and old sexually crazed men of Sodom come to Lot's house and want to "know" the men. The words "that we may know them" (*NRSV*) are a euphemism for sexual relations and imply homosexuality forbidden by Hebrew law (Leviticus 18:22; 20:13). Sodom, in fact, is the origin of the word "sodomy" for homosexuality. The behavior at the house of Lot gives concrete evidence for the exclamation of Yahweh: "How great is the outcry against Sodom and Gomorrah and how very grave their sin!" (Genesis 18:20). The author of J had already written that Yahweh had destroyed Sodom and Gomorrah because the people were wicked, "great sinners against the Lord" (13:10, 13), but no specific sins are mentioned.

The story about Lot and his visitors is often cited as evidence that the Bible forbids homosexuality. But, is the demand of the men of the city for homosexual relations with his male guests any more or less moral than Lot's offer to give them his daughters for sexual purposes? Without trying to agree or disagree with "what the Bible says" about homosexuality, let's try to understand the Lot story in light of its times. Lot was shielding his guests from homosexual acts that later biblical writers condemned. However, by trying to be a good host, his hospitality overpowered his obligation as a father to protect his daughters. No immoral sexual acts were actually committed, though, because of dramatic divine action. Lot and his daughters were saved from acting immorally and from the men of the city, who were blinded so that they could not find the door to Lot's house. So, no homosexual acts were committed either.

Typically, J's story ends with Yahweh in control of events. Abraham was spared in the destruction of the wicked cities, and Lot was spared to remind Abraham of God's promises to him. The fact that no evil was committed by anyone may reveal a moral awareness on the part of J greater than that of the people of Sodom, whose wickedness was the sole reason for its doom. The wickedness of Sodom became traditional in the thought of the prophets, who not only were aware of its wickedness but used it as an example when proclaiming Yahweh's condemnation of the wickedness of his own people (e.g., Isaiah 3:8-9; Jeremiah 23:14; Ezekiel 16:46-49). But in none of these passages is homosexuality actually mentioned as a sin of the cities.

### *Lot and his Daughters (19:30-38, J)*

The story of Lot's daughters having sexual relations with their drunken father raises further questions about morality. Incest, that is, sexual relations between members of a family, came to be forbidden in Hebrew law (Leviticus 18:4-23). We must try to understand the story about Lot and his daughters and similar passages in light of Israel's pre-history, though, and not according to later standards of morality. Recall the stories of Tamar (Genesis 38:1-30, J) and Rahab (Joshua 2:1-25). By trying to understand the story about Lot and his daughters in light of biblical times, we can get a truer insight into the situation that gave rise to it. The story (Genesis 19:30-35) is really a long preface to the words in 19:36-38, which give the author's view of the origin of the Moabites and Ammonites, Israelite's neighbors east of the Jordan River.

Lot's older daughter bore a son, Moab, who became the ancestor of the Moabites. The younger daughter's son, Ben-Ammi, became the ancestor of the Ammonites. By assigning the origins of the two enemies of the Israelites to the ancestry of Lot, through his daughters, Abraham as the beneficiary of God's promises remained the main actor on the stage of Israel's prehistory. This helps, too, to explain the perpetual animosity between the Israelites and those nations.

### *Abraham with Isaac as a Sacrifice (22:1-19, E)*

Probably one of the best known stories in Genesis is when God tests Abraham's faith by telling him to sacrifice his beloved son Isaac as a burnt offering. It is also one of the best literary compositions in the Bible. Compare the story of Elijah performing a sacrifice to God on Mount Carmel (1 Kings 18:17-40), which also has a test of faithfulness toward God by a sacrifice and a favorable response. In the Elijah story the faith of the Israelites as a nation is tested, whereas in the case of Abraham it is his faith as a person that is tested.

Abraham makes no excuses to avoid God's will. With the knife raised ready to stab his beloved son, God confirms the father's faithfulness: "Do not lay your hand on the boy or do anything to him; for now I know that you fear God, since you have not withheld your son, your only son, from me" (22:12). Can we imagine a Hebrew father, who lived his life for his son to be his heir, obeying a God who demands absolute faithfulness, even to the point of sacrificing that son? The purpose of the story is clear from the written text, but what about implications from what is not written? Biblical writers condemn the sacrifice of children, one of the most abominable practices of the Canaanite religion. The prophets decried it, and it came to be forbidden in Deuteronomic law (Deuteronomy 18:10; see also Ezekiel 23:36-39). It seems, then, that the author of the Abraham story was saying in an indirect way that his God disapproved the sacrifice of children as a proof of faithfulness. Although Abraham was willing to make the ultimate sacrifice, that was not what God wanted as a sign of faithfulness.

### Isaac and Rebekah (24:1-67, J)

The story of Isaac and Rebekah is a romantic interlude between the story of Abraham's life, which was about to end, and that of Jacob, about to begin. The whole story is typical of J, with Yahweh in charge, a unified account, and clever repetitions that emphasize the underlying action of God and of Abraham's servant, Rebekah, and her brother Laban. A trusted servant swears to return to the homeland of Abraham and find, among kin, a wife for Isaac. This assures Abraham that Isaac does not get a wife "from the daughters of the Canaanites," thereby preserving the religion and culture of Abraham and his race. The servant has also sworn that, if the girl should refuse to return with him, he would not take Isaac back to her home. To do so would violate the agreement between Yahweh and Abraham that Abraham's present home – "this land" (24:7) – is to be the land of his offspring.

As the story progresses the readers' admiration for the servant increases, with an appreciation, as well, of Laban's hospitality in acting in the absence of the father. There is no description of Rebekah, except that she was "very fair to look upon, a virgin" (24:16). Her actions as a friendly, hospitable, excited young girl telling her family what just happened, and her unhesitating consent – "I will" – make her a person worthy of the son of Abraham. The climax comes when she became so excited at seeing Isaac coming toward her that "she jumped down from her camel" (*NJB*). This love at first sight resulted in marriage to a wife Isaac loved, and they conceived twin sons, Esau and Jacob.

### *Esau and Jacob, Sons of Isaac and Rebekah (Genesis 25:19-20, 26b, P; 25:21-26, 27-34, J)*

The first-born son of Isaac and Rebekah was red and hairy, so he was named Esau; the second was born gripping the heel of Esau, so he was named Jacob. Isaac loved Esau the hunter because he liked the taste of game, but Rebekah loved Jacob the cook. Coming in famished from the hunt, Esau asked Jacob for "some of that red stuff" Jacob was cooking, so he was called Edom. Jacob took advantage of Esau's hunger, and in return for Esau swearing to give up his birthright, Jacob gave Esau some food. However, going away after he ate and drank, Esau "despised his birthright" (25:34). As with some other Genesis stories, there are parallels with the Gilgamesh Epic. The words that Esau was born with a "body like a hairy mantle" are very similar to ones used of Enkidu in that epic: "shaggy with hair was his whole body." And Esau was an outdoors man like Enkidu (Speiser, *Genesis*, p. 196).

### *Rebekah Deceives Isaac in his Blessings (Genesis 27:1-26, J)*

This story harks back to J's account of the birth and boyhood of Esau and Jacob (25:21-34, J). Just as Jacob swindled Esau out of his birthright, here the likeable young girl who married Isaac becomes an adult deceiver. Due to the craftiness of the eavesdropping Rebekah, Isaac is tricked into bestowing upon Jacob his blessing intended for his older son Esau.

The accounts of the young men Esau and Jacob and the blessings they received from their father Isaac, although both from J, have some important differences. In both the contrast between the two brothers and between the parents is central, the first with the birthright and the second with the blessings. The lifestyles of the two boys are different. In the first, Esau is hairy and a rugged hunter, whom Isaac loved because of a taste for game. Because Jacob is a quiet fellow, living in tents, Rebekah loved him. In the second, Esau is hairy, an outdoors person, and favored by Isaac; Jacob has smooth skin, is a tent dweller, cook, and mother's boy. In the first, Jacob took advantage of Esau and swindled him out of his birthright.

In our present story Esau is an innocent victim of Jacob's lies. Jacob attributes his faked success at hunting to Yahweh. Behind it all is the eavesdropping Rebekah. After rebuking Jacob rightly named as a supplanter, Esau is portrayed as emotionally weeping and begging for a blessing, but then his disappointment turns to a grudging desire to kill Jacob. Many years later Jacob is portrayed as still feeling guilty when Esau welcomes his brother in a most compassionate way, without any evidence of resentment (33:1-17, J).

According to Hurrian law, a father could decide about the birthright and was not bound by the age of the son (see "your firstborn" in 27:19). The statements "the elder shall serve the younger" (25:23) and "you shall serve your brother" (27:40) reflect Hurrian law. While the elder son could claim twice the share of the inheritance as the younger, the one giving the blessing could name any son as elder, irrespective of age. But, in the story of Jacob and Esau, Isaac did not decide about the birthright. Rather, Jacob bribed Esau for it by taking advantage of his hunger. And, with respect to the blessing, Isaac did not choose Jacob over Esau. Rebekah made the choice and, in doing so, swindled Esau out of his blessing. There can be little doubt that ancient laws and customs were the background for the blessings of Isaac, but in the course of transmission some things became somewhat confused.

### *Isaacs' Deathbed Blessings (27:27-40, J)*

The blessing by a man about to die, "the deathbed blessing," was very important in ancient laws and customs. It was introduced sometimes in the Bible by the formula "I have now grown old." Compare Isaac's words to Esau: "See, I am old; I do not know the day of my death." J stresses the old age of Isaac by saying that his eyesight was so bad that he could not see (27:1-2). Isaac's deathbed blessing of Esau and Jacob is reminiscent of their birth and Esau's birthright. The deathbed blessing is a drama played out on two levels, individuals and nations: the brothers Esau and Jacob and the nations of Edom and Israel. In the birth story Yahweh tells Rebekah: "Two nations are in your womb, and two peoples born of you shall be divided; the one shall be stronger than the other, the elder shall serve the younger."

There are several underlying reasons why Esau was not liked, which reflect the tradition that he was the ancestor of the Edomites, a people hated by the Israelites. Esau did not conform to the patriarchal tradition of a nomadic way of life, as Rebekah's reference to "the flock" and "kids" indicates (27:9). Moreover, hunting never became an important part of Hebrew/Israelite culture as it did in some ancient cultures, notably Egyptian. For the Egyptians hunting not only provided food, but it was also symbolic of the strength needed to overcome wild animals, which they thought threatened humans. The Israelites, on the other hand, believed that God gave mankind dominion over all animals.

## Understanding the Blessings Stories

Realizing Israel's hatred for Edom and Edomites, we can now turn back to the story of Isaac's blessings for the climax. That comes with Esau's pleas: "Bless me, me also, father!... Have you not reserved a blessing for me?... Have you only one blessing, father? Bless me, me also, father!" (27:34, 36, 38). Isaac is given every chance to bless Esau, but it is too late because Jacob has acted true to his name: he has supplanted his brother out of both birthright and blessing. Yet, in spite of the fact that it is too late (27:33), Isaac answers Esau with words that are more like a curse than a blessing: "By your sword you shall live, and you shall serve your brother; but when you break loose, you shall break his yoke from your neck" (27:40).

Turn now to the actual blessing of Jacob (27:27-29), where Jacob deceived his blind father into thinking he was Esau. In that blessing the "smell" is "the smell of a field that the Lord has blessed." This and the verse that follows are the blessing of fertility of land, which are indicative of a settled agrarian people. And such fertility is about to be denied Esau in precisely the same words. The phrases "the dew of heaven" and "the fatness of the earth" occur in texts from Ugarit, where it is said of Anat, the consort of Baal, that she bathes herself with those same substances (*ANET*, 136).

Neither a settled agricultural way of life nor living in a house (27:15) reflects the time of the patriarchs, who were primarily a nomadic, tent-dwelling people (18:2-10; 24:67; 26:25; 31:25-34). This is a clear example of the author taking a way of life that appeared centuries later and putting it back into the time of Abraham. Likewise, in 27:29, 40, J speaks of the servitude of Esau, which may allude to the time when David conquered the Edomites and subjected them to his rule. Isaac's blessing of Jacob, with its combination of cursing and blessing absent in the blessing of Esau, reflects Yahweh's words to Abram (12:3, J). Isaac says, "Cursed be everyone who curses you, and blessed be everyone who blesses you!" The same formula occurs in Numbers 24:9, where a blessing also counters a curse on Jacob (Israel; see also 24:5) but in reverse order: blessed/cursed instead of cursed/blessed.

The words in 27:40 about serving his brother and then breaking loose are unique to the words about Esau. They may be an allusion to the revolt of Edom that won its freedom from Judah under King Jehoram (849-842 BCE; 2 Kings 8:20-22). Since J is generally dated before Jehoram's time and perhaps also before David's conquest of Edom, there is serious doubt that the words alluding to those incidents come directly from J. An editor from a later time may have added them to J's account.

*Isaac's Blessings and History*
The blessings of Isaac raise again the question of how much is history and how much legend. Is it predictive prophecy in that the words of Isaac to Jacob and Esau foretell the events of David's conquest of Edom and its subsequent independence? Alternately, are Isaacs's words a record of the past written in the future tense? Or, as suggested above, are the words alluding to the times of David and Jehoram those of a later editor inserted into the context of J's account? At any rate, a lot of legendary aspects of oral traditions were probably written down over a long period of time.

Written long after J, P (27:46–28:9) gives a different impression of the characters in our story in his literary style. P's account contains characteristic words, such as *El Shaddai* for the name of the deity and the place Paddam-aram. There are differences in the motives for actions and in the conception of time. In J, Rebekah sends Jacob away because she feared Esau's anger would lead to his murder of Jacob (27:41-45). In P, Rebekah suggests to Isaac that he send Jacob away so that he won't marry a Hittite woman. In J, Jacob is sent to Rebekah's brother Laban at Haran and is not to return until she sends for him. In P, the place where Esau learned that Isaac had blessed Jacob is Paddam-aram. Esau also saw that Jacob had obeyed his father and mother and gone to Paddam-aram and that the Canaanite women displeased his father Isaac. In P, there is nothing of Esau's hatred for his father or his brother.

In P, Isaac invoking the blessing of Jacob by El Shaddai (28:3-4) has almost nothing in common with the similar blessing in J (27:27-29). It is closer to Yahweh's words to Abraham (12:1-3, J) and especially God's promise to him in 17:4-8, P. In J, Isaac was an old man, blind, and expecting death (27:1-2, 41). In P, there is no sign of Isaacs's feebleness, and he appears very active. He was mentally able to give Jacob orders not to marry a Canaanite woman and to invoke the blessing of God (28:4-8). In P, there is nothing of Esau's hatred of Jacob when he sees that Isaac had blessed him. And when Esau saw that his parents did not want Jacob to marry a Canaanite woman, Esau married one of Ishmael's daughters.

According to J (27:1-2, 7), Isaac was on his deathbed. In P's first account (25:26), Isaac was 60 years old when the twins were born, and in P's second account (26:34), Esau was 40 years old when he married. According to the third account of P (35:28), Isaac was 180 years old when he died, which means he would have had to live 80 years after he was on his deathbed. "The Bible Says So!" These and other differences between J and P show that there are different sources for the lives of the legendary characters who gave rise to the biblical events associated with them, and we are left with many unanswered questions about how much of the accounts is actually historically accurate.

*Morality and Isaac's Blessings*
As with many stories, those of Isaac and Rebekah and their sons Esau and Jacob can pose questions of morality for us. Consider Rebekah's deception of her innocent husband; her favoritism of Jacob over Esau, who was cheated out of something generally seen as rightfully his; Rebekah's demanding nature when Jacob hesitated to obey because his response might bring a curse instead of a blessing; and Jacob's repeated lies to his blind, aged, and dying father. The drama seems to end, though, with compassion for Esau on the part of Rebekah. After she told him to leave because he thought of killing his brother, she questions: "Why should I lose both of you in one day?" But, is this compassion or selfishness?

In seeking insightful answers, we must try to understand these stories in light of the times when they were written. It is important to realize that the authors were not writing about morality, which was a word unknown to biblical writers, including those of the NT (but see 1 Corinthians 15:33). Most of what is written had long been a part of the oral tradition of a people who became known for their greatness and morality. Although Rebekah appears morally unquestioned, readers may have some sympathy for Jacob and Esau as victims of her schemes and the helpless Isaac, also a victim. Jacob himself did not plan the action for the deathbed blessing, in spite of Esau's slur about him being true to his name as supplanter.

Instead of focusing on morality, the patriarchal narratives illustrate how God's promise to Abraham was carried out. Rebekah was, after all, only acting out dramatically the predictions of Yahweh about two nations in her womb. After "the children struggled together within her," she asked, "If it is to be this way, why do I live?" (25:22-23, J; 27:46, P). Rebekah remains free from blame and goes on with a normal life. Jacob goes into exile but finds a wife within the family line of Abraham and Sarah and becomes the father of the Israelite nation. Esau marries a daughter of Ishmael (28:9, P) and becomes the ancestor of the Edomites, enemies of Israel. So, the enmity between Esau and Jacob is continued by their descendants. And, from the writers' points of view, God's promises to Abraham that he would be "a great nation," have a great name (12:2, J), and be "the ancestor of a multitude of nations" (17:4, P) are fulfilled through Jacob.

Although Rebekah is a prominent character in the Genesis narratives, her name is mentioned elsewhere in the Bible only in Romans 9:10. In contrast, the name of Jacob occurs more than 300 times in the OT and 26 times in the NT, and Isaac's name occurs more than 100 times in the OT and about 20 times in the NT. However, Isaac's name is used most often as one of the three patriarchs in the formula "Abraham, Isaac, and Jacob." Thus, Isaac remains a rather insignificant character, as in the Genesis stories.

Perhaps surprisingly, the Deuteronomist gives Esau a place in history. He writes that Moses spoke to the Israelites and said that the children of Esau are their brothers and that God gave Seir (Edom) to them as a possession. Esau is never mentioned in a negative way (Deuteronomy 2:4-29; see also Joshua 24:4). On the other hand, the prophets are bitter toward Esau and Edom, the land of his descendants.

The prophets Hosea and Jeremiah sometimes show a moral sensitivity about Jacob's wrongdoing. Hosea clearly disapproved of his behavior when he wrote: "The Lord...will punish Jacob according to his ways, and repay him according to his deeds. In the womb he tried to supplant his brother" (Hosea 12:2-3). However, there "Jacob" is probably a metaphor for the nation Israel rather than for him (Israel) as a person. Jeremiah warns his readers by alluding to the Jacob/Esau story in a disparaging way that they should not trust their brothers (Hebrew) because they "are supplanters" (Jeremiah 9:4).

## Joseph

The stories of Joseph provide a great literary and dramatic climax to the patriarchal narratives. They are comprised of mostly J and E, with a little from P. J and E are often so closely meshed that it is difficult to distinguish between them. Like the wives of Abraham and Isaac, Rachel, the favorite wife of Jacob, was barren. When Rachel gave birth to a son, she was so happy that she named him Joseph, which means "he adds," and exclaimed, "May the Lord add to me another son!" (Genesis 30:22-24). Benjamin, a second son, was born later, thus fulfilling Rachel's wish and showing the significance of the name Joseph.

The story of Joseph begins with Jacob (Israel) loving Joseph more than his other sons born of his wife Leah, because Joseph was born in Jacob's old age. Because of his love, Jacob made Joseph a robe, popularly known as "a coat of many colors" (37:3). And immediately this raises a question about what "the Bible says." Because the Hebrew in question is so uncertain, the *KJV* and the *ASV* used the translation in the Septuagint, where the words "a coat of many colors" occur. Beginning with the *RSV*, "a long robe with sleeves" or similar words were used, as the following translations show: "a richly ornamented robe," *NIV*; "a tunic of many colors," *NKJV*; "a long robe with sleeves," *REB*; "a long robe with sleeves," *NRSV*; and "a decorated tunic," *NJB*.

The Hebrew phrase occurs elsewhere in the Bible only in 2 Samuel 13:18, where one of David's daughters wore "a long robe with sleeves; for this is how the virgin daughters of the king were clothed in earlier times." So, was Joseph dressed as a woman in order to save him from hard labor, as some have suggested? Paintings in ancient tombs reveal very little difference, though, between the clothing of women and important men. Although no one knows the significance of Joseph's robe, it seems likely that it was meant to show favoritism to a beloved son.

Dreams, a universal phenomenon in the ancient world, play a significant role in the stories of Joseph. They are not only the motivation for actions, but they are also literary devices for showing God at work in saving Joseph and his people in Egypt. Joseph's dreams got him off to a bad start with his brothers when he interpreted them as portraying his brothers as subservient to him. As a result, they not only called him "this dreamer," but they also plotted to kill him. Later in Egypt Joseph became a master at interpreting dreams, no matter what circumstances he was in.

The Joseph stories became a saga about Jacob and his sons (Genesis 37:1–50:26), of which 37, 39–45, and some of 46–50 are most important for Joseph himself. The story begins with Genesis 37:1-36, the sources for which most scholars suggest the following: the sons of Israel (37:3, 13, J) or Jacob (37:24, E) plot against Joseph, who is defended by Judah (J) or Reuben (E).

In 37:21-30 there are inconsistencies, repetitions, and contradictions. In 37:21-24 (E) Reuben ultimately wants to spare Joseph's life and convinced his brothers to throw Joseph into a pit, so that he could later return him to his father. After stripping Joseph of his robe, they threw him into the pit. Then Judah, also wanting to spare Joseph's life, persuaded his brothers to sell him to some passing Ishmaelites (37:25-27, J). However, when some Midianite traders came along (37:28, E), they took Joseph out of the pit and sold him to the Ishmaelites for 20 pieces of silver (37:28, J). Then

Joseph was taken to Egypt, where the Midianites sold him to Potiphar, "one of Pharaoh's officials, the captain of the guard" (37:36, E). Meanwhile, Reuben, unaware of the sale, was shocked at not finding Joseph in the pit: "The boy is gone; and where am I to turn?" These obvious contradictions reflect different sources put together into an account with no regard for consistency.

The brothers soaked Joseph's robe in the blood of a goat, took it to Jacob, and asked if it was the robe of his son. Jacob replied that it was and that a wild animal must have torn Joseph to pieces. Jacob mourns deeply for several days and could not be comforted (37:29-35, E). This part of the dramatic saga about a father and his favorite son and the resultant jealousy and hatred on the part of most of his other sons and love by two of them ends in an unexpected way in that both father and favorite son are alive, but neither knows it.

The incident we have considered may best be understood as two original units: the differences among Israel, Judah, and the Ishmaelites (J) as opposed to Jacob, Reuben, and the Midianites (E). As usual, the story arose in oral tradition and was later put into writing, in which forgotten details were added by a redactor who combined the traditions. Originally, each author had written his own account without knowing the other, and later someone put them together without concern about differences.

In spite of differences in details, there are cohesive likenesses. Most noticeably, up to this point there is no reference to a deity intervening to save Joseph. The brothers hate Joseph and are jealous because he was a favorite son of their father, but another brother intervenes to spare his life. Joseph is sold to traders and gets to Egypt, where he will rise to a high position in the government. The stage is set for Joseph's experiences in Egypt and the continuing drama there among the same characters.

As the saga progresses, dreams are not only the motivation for what happens, but they are also the vehicles for the safety of Joseph and the Israelites in Egypt through the hand of Yahweh. The key for our understanding is Genesis 39:2: "The Lord was with Joseph, and he became a successful man," elaborated in 39:3-6, J. Recognizing Yahweh's favor of Joseph, Joseph's master made him "overseer of his house." However, "the handsome and good-looking" Joseph aroused the sexual desires of his master's wife, who invited Joseph to have sex with her. The moral of the story is in Joseph's words, "How then could I do this great wickedness, and sin against God?" (39:9). Joseph refused the woman's repeated advances and slipped away from her by leaving his coat behind. The wife showed his garment to her husband and lied about Joseph to the master, who put him in prison (39:6-23, J). Twice it is reported that the Lord was with Joseph, and he won the favor of the jailer.

The theme of a wife unfaithful to her husband who then turns against the man who refused her advances was well known in Egypt before the time of Joseph. In a document known as *The Tale of the Two Brothers (ANET,* 23-25), the elder brother had a wife, but the younger, who was "a perfect man," and "a god's virility was in him," did not. The wife saw the virility of the young man, took hold of him, and asked him to spend an hour sleeping with her. The man became angry but said he would tell no one. The woman then faked sickness and told her husband that she had been assaulted by his brother. Moreover, she said that if he did not kill his brother she would kill herself. Her husband became like an Egyptian panther and decided to kill his brother. Waiting in the barn to do so, one cow and then another informed the younger man of the danger, and he fled with the killer in pursuit. The younger man prayed to a god, and the older brother was prevented from approaching his brother by a pond filled with crocodiles. The younger brother appealed to the older, cut off his own penis, and threw it into the water, where it was eaten by a catfish. This so grieved the elder brother that he returned home and killed his wife, and the younger went to live in a separate place.

The similarities in both stories are obvious, but the differences are more important. In the Joseph story the woman told everyone in her household that the Hebrew servant had assaulted her. This racial note is lacking in the story of the two brothers who were, of course, both Egyptians. The Egyptian woman in the Joseph story was never punished, but Joseph was put in prison, a light punishment for the supposed offense. According to Near Eastern and Deuteronomic law, the punishment for adultery was death for both the woman and the man (Deuteronomy 22:22). However, if Joseph had been put to death, the stories about him would have come to an abrupt end. But for Yahweh, who was in control of Hebrew history, Joseph had to live in order to save his people in Egypt.

According to E (40:1-23), while Joseph was in jail he interpreted the dreams of Pharaoh's chief cupbearer and chief baker, favorably for the cupbearer but the baker was to lose his head. At Pharaoh's birthday party the cupbearer was restored to his position, but the baker was hanged. However, the cupbearer forgot to speak favorably of Joseph as he had promised, so Joseph remained in jail. According to E (41:1-57), two years later Pharaoh had a dream, but no magicians or wise men in Egypt could interpret it. Then the cupbearer remembered Joseph, with his interpretations of dreams, so Pharaoh sent for him. The interpretation was that there would be seven years of plenty, followed by seven years of famine, which God was to bring about. Joseph advised Pharaoh to store up grain from the good years for the bad, which Pharaoh did by putting Joseph in charge of all the land of Egypt. As a sign of Joseph's authority as "second-in-command," Pharaoh put his signet ring on the hand of Joseph and a gold chain around his neck (41:41-43).

Jacob comes back into the scene when he learns that there is grain in Egypt (42:1-26, 29-38, E; 42:27-28, J). He sends his sons to Egypt, and they deal with Joseph, who is "governor over the land," but they do not recognize him. Joseph immediately recognizes his brothers, but he treats them harshly as strangers. They tell Joseph of a younger brother who remained in Canaan. He puts them in prison for three days and then demands that Simeon remain as hostage until they bring the boy to Egypt. Put in this situation, the brothers began to feel guilty about what they had done to Joseph. According to J (42:27-28), when the brothers were at a lodging place on the way back to Canaan, they discovered that the money for the grain had been placed in their sacks with the grain, and they became afraid. In E (42:35) the money was discovered when they were unpacking after they got back to Canaan. The brothers report to Jacob, who protests their plan to take the young Benjamin back to Egypt, and he says that Joseph and now Simeon are gone. Reuben offers to have his two sons killed if he does not bring Benjamin back, but Jacob refuses.

The story is continued, mostly in J, with some E and a little P (43:1–48:22). The famine in Canaan becomes severe, so Jacob sends the brothers to Egypt a second time to buy grain. Now Judah offers himself as security for taking Benjamin to Egypt, and the father (Israel) agrees. They take with them the money left in the sacks, along with Benjamin, and are on their way. Upon seeing Benjamin, Joseph has a feast prepared for his brothers, who told him about the money in the sacks. Joseph's steward alleviated their fears by saying: "Rest assured, do not be afraid; your God and the God of your father must have put treasure in your sacks for you; I received your money" (43:23). Joseph inquires about the health of his father and is assured that he is alive and well. Money is again put in the sacks, but this time Joseph's silver cup is also put in Benjamin's sack. When the Egyptians recovered it, Judah intercedes on behalf of all. Joseph finally reveals himself to his brother.

Both J and E think of the famine and Joseph's ascent to power as historical events. Both writers perceive of a divine power in the vindication of Joseph and punishment for his brothers. Both make sure that Benjamin is not harmed, and Joseph's love for Benjamin, the son of his mother Rachel, is never doubted. In mostly J, with some E and a little P, after Joseph reveals his identity, he tells his brothers not to be distressed or angry because of what they had done. It was God's will for him to get to Egypt in order to preserve the life of a remnant. Joseph invites the family to come to Egypt and settle in the land of Goshen, where he will take care of them. Later Pharaoh tells Joseph to have his family brought to Egypt and provides wagons for them to bring their possessions. Jacob is stunned at Joseph being alive and says that he must go to see Joseph before he dies. In Egypt the family is provided land and the necessities for life, and they prosper. Jacob (Israel) blesses Joseph's sons, Ephraim and Manasseh, and then blesses Joseph and his brothers.

According to E (50:15-26), after their father died, the brothers were concerned lest Joseph bear a grudge against them, so they begged forgiveness. Joseph says that although they intended harm to him, "God intended it for good, in order to preserve a numerous people." Not long after Jacob and his family got to Egypt, Joseph and Jacob died, and both were embalmed according to Egyptian custom (50:2-3, 26, E). Embalming is not mentioned anywhere else in the Bible.

While the other patriarchal narratives were influenced by Near Eastern literature and culture, the local color in the Joseph narratives is unique. One example is the temptation of Joseph to have sex with an Egyptian woman and the Egyptian *Tale of the Two Brothers*. The reference to Joseph receiving the signet ring from Pharaoh and being "second-in-command" correspond to the Egyptian Vizier, who was also the king's "Sealbearer" (41:42-43). These titles, in addition to "overseer in the house" (39:4), reflect official positions in Egyptian history. Although not having the title, Joseph served as "superintendent of the granaries," a title known from texts of the times.

In order to keep Joseph from being recognized by his brothers, the writers have thoroughly Egyptianized him. He is given an Egyptian name, "Zaphenath-panesh," and a wife who was in the priestly line (41:45). Joseph's brothers did not know that he understood them, because he spoke through an interpreter (42:23). This indicates that he knew the Egyptian language. All of these things indicate that the writers of the Joseph stories were thoroughly familiar with Egyptian history and customs.

## *The Significance of Names*

Remember that some scholars believe the patriarchs were historical persons who lived in, were influenced by, and shared in the cultures of the ancient

Near East. Others, however, think that they are merely literary figures invented by later authors trying to explain aspects of Israel's prehistory or history and religion. Regardless, there is much significance in the names and places in the Genesis stories.

For most of us a person's name is used only to identify that person as distinct from someone else. In the ancient world, though, there was much more to a name. It was intrinsically linked with the being of an individual in the sense of "self" or "person." Asking someone's name was the same as asking, "What kind of person is she or he?" According to Proverbs 30:4, God knows the answer: "What is the person's name? And what is the name of the person's child? Surely you know."

The idea that the name represents the person is aptly illustrated in the story of David and Abigail (meaning "my father rejoices") and her husband, whose name was Nabal (meaning "fool"). Abigail "was clever and beautiful, but the man was surly and mean." Abigail tells David, "Do not take seriously this ill-natured fellow, Nabal; for as his name is, so is he; Nabal ["fool"] is his name, and folly is with him" (1 Samuel 25:3, 25).

Israelites thought of the name of their God as representative of God, and the "name" commended the same respect and authority as God himself. Invoking or calling upon (Genesis 4:26; 12:8; 13:4; Psalm 16:4, 13), proclaiming (Exodus 34:5), blaspheming (Exodus 20:4; Leviticus 24:16), fearing (Isaiah 59:19; Psalm 102:15), blessing (Job 1:21; Psalm 113:2; Daniel 2:20), or praising (Psalm 7:17) the name of God are the same as doing those things to him. A good example to show that the name is the same as God himself is Psalm 113:1, where the two are in parallel: "Praise the Lord!... praise the name of the Lord." And, Isaiah 30:27 illustrates the name as indicative of the power of God himself: "See, the name of the Lord comes from far away, burning with his anger."

A change in the name of a person usually indicated a change in status or destiny. It is very likely that often a name was changed after a person had already achieved a particular status. As the patriarchal narratives were assembled after a long history of oral tradition, it would be natural for their authors and editors to change names of "great persons" to emphasize their greatness and especially God's role in their achieving it.

### Abraham and Sarah

Abraham was first called "Abram." Even the person untrained in languages can see that there is a linguistic relationship between the two words. The word *abram* is made up of two parts, *ab*, which means "father," and *ram*, meaning "be high" or "exalted," so the name Abraham means "father exalted."

Abram is used instead of Abraham in Genesis 11:26–17:4. According to Genesis 15:1-6, "The word of the Lord" came to Abram in a vision saying that in spite of his childlessness, a member of his own family would be his heir. Then Yahweh took him outside and showed him the heavens and said that his descendants would be as numerous as the stars.

Abram's childlessness reflects not only the ancient idea of a male heir for descendants, but also the longing for a son to assure proper burial of the father. Nuzi law that a son should mourn the death of his father and bury him throws light on Yahweh's promise that Abram will die "in peace" and "be buried in a good old age" (15:15). These examples may illustrate his name as "exalted." According to Genesis 17:1-5, Abram's name was changed to Abraham, which means "father of a multitude" and linked to God's covenant with him (Genesis 12:1-4). So, befitting his name and in a wordplay with it, God tells Abraham he shall be "the ancestor of a multitude of nations" (Genesis 17:5).

As with names of Abraham, the change in the name of his wife Sarai to Sarah is also symbolic. Both names mean "princess," and it is the generally accepted meaning. However, because of Sarai's contempt for Hagar, it has been suggested that the name Sarai is derived from another word with three consonants, meaning "strive" or "contend." Nonetheless, Sarah's destiny as one blessed by God was to be the ancestress of nations, a role befitting her name "princess" (Genesis 17:15-16).

## *Ishmael*

A meaning of the name Ishmael occurs in three sources (J, E, P). In J, the reason for the name is stated: "the Lord (Yahweh) has given heed to ("heard") your affliction" (Genesis 16:11). In E, "God (Elohim) heard the voice of the boy" (Ishmael; 21:17). In P, God (Elohim) heard Abraham's plea for his favor to Ishmael (17:20). The name Ishmael, then, is a combination of the verb "hear" and El, a word for God. Although El does not occur in any of the texts about Ishmael, it is clear from the word itself. El is used very often in Genesis, probably due to its use in the Canaanite religion. So, the word Ishmael means something like "God (El) has heard" or "God hears."

## *Isaac*

The name Isaac is derived from the Hebrew verb *tsachak*, meaning "laugh," and there are several wordplays on the word. However, the laughing is presented in different ways in the sources. In P, Abraham fell on his face laughing when God told him that Sarah was to have a son and mockingly remarked about his age and that of Sarah. God reassures him and says, "You shall name him Isaac," which means "he laughs," a wordplay on the name "Isaac" (Genesis 17:15-19, P), although the meaning is implied, not stated.

In J, one of the strangers who appeared to Abraham announced that Sarah would have a son. Sarah was eavesdropping and "laughed to herself" when she heard what was said (Genesis 18:9-12). Speaking as Yahweh, the stranger asked Abraham why Sarah laughed at the thought of having a son in spite of her old age. And, Sarah asked if she should really bear a son and said, "Is anything too wonderful for the Lord?" Then Sarah denied that she laughed and was afraid. The Lord replied, "Oh yes, you did laugh"(Genesis 18:13-15).

The above account of J differs from that of P in several important ways. Typical of J, Yahweh speaks in human form in a literary dialogue, but with assurance and awe – Sarah "was afraid." And Sarah is also thoroughly human. As an eavesdropper, she laughs in mockery at the words of a man she thought was a passing guest. Her mockery is turned to denial – "I did not laugh." The repeated wordplays on the name "Isaac" make the narrative a better *literary* work than a record of *history*. In E's account of the birth of Isaac, God has brought joy to Sarah, as she says, "God has brought laughter for me; everyone who hears will laugh with me" (Genesis 21:6). "Laughing with" is wordplay on the name "Isaac," "he laughs."

### *Jacob and Esau*
The derivation and original meaning of the name "Jacob" are uncertain. It occurs in the form *Jacob-el* in several ancient texts as the name of a person and of a place. Therefore, the name "Jacob" is not unique to the Bible, but in the course of transmission the *el* was dropped. However, *el* is added to some words to form names of persons and places, for example, "Ishmael" and "Bethel" (meaning "house of God"), a town associated with Jacob. The name of this town reflects that Jacob had seen God there when "he dreamed that there was a ladder set up on the earth, the top of it reaching to heaven; and the angels of God were ascending and descending on it" (Genesis 28:10-12). The words to the familiar African American spiritual, "We are climbing Jacob's ladder...," refer to that passage.

The facts that the name "Jacob" occurs in texts much older than the Bible and that the original meaning of the name is unknown indicate that the biblical authors gave names to Jacob and Esau with meanings that symbolized their circumstances. In the story of the birth of Esau and Jacob there are several wordplays on the name. In 25:25 (J), Jacob was given that name, which means "heel gripper," because he was born "with his hand gripping" the heel of his twin brother Esau. Esau "came out red," the word "red" being *admoni*, a wordplay on "Edom," the name given to him and meaning "red region." The word for "hairy" is *sear*, wordplay on the word Seir, another name for Edom (seyar) meaning "hairy" or "shaggy." In 25:30 (also J), Esau was called Edom ("red region"), because he asked for "some of that red stuff," another wordplay on Edom. And "heel" in 25:26 is *yqb*, a play on *yqb*, Jacob. In Genesis 27:36 (J), "Jacob" is given the meaning "he supplants" (which means "be at the heel") because Esau says: "he has supplanted me these two times," that is, by deceitfully taking away first his birthright and then his father's blessing.

In 32:22-30 (J), after Jacob wrestled with "a man" all night and would not let the man go unless he blessed him, the man changed his name to "Israel," which probably originally meant "may El (God) prevail." But in this context, because of Jacob's striving with God, it means something close to "he strives with God" (El) or "God (El) strives." Then Jacob asked the man his name, but he would not tell him and blessed him instead. Jacob called the name of the place "Peniel," which means "the face of God" (El). In this way the reader becomes certain that the "man" was God, although a hint was given in verse 28 (recall J's story of Abraham not recognizing the strangers).

A change in Jacob's name occurs also in 35:9-12 (P), where God (Elohim) blessed him at Luz and changed his name to Israel. God also tells him that "a nation and a company of nations" shall come from him. Jacob built an altar of stones, made a drink offering, and poured oil on the altar.

## *Chapter Summary*

So, what can we conclude about the patriarchal narratives, including how we understand the meanings of names and places in those stories? It seems that the contexts of the biblical narratives gave rise to the meaning of names as the different authors understood them. If that is true, then the individual stories first circulated orally as legends or sagas in which many of the original names and contexts were lost. Names as they appear now were probably added by editors and compilers of the documents that were assembled and included in the book we know as Genesis. Because name changes occur in different contexts and in different sources, there may have been several versions of the same story. This and all we have learned earlier about the patriarchs raises doubt about the historicity of the narratives.

Perhaps most importantly, we must remember that the stories in the Pentateuch were written primarily for the religious ideas they convey, not as historical fact. The basic viewpoint of the authors is that their God was not separated from the history of the Israelites. He was *making* their history. In the next chapter we look at different gods mentioned in the OT.

Chapter 9

GODS MENTIONED IN THE OLD TESTAMENT

*Introduction*

The subject of this chapter is often included under the titles of "Names for God in the Old Testament" or "The God of Israel." However, both imply that there was only one deity with different names. Our title is more neutral to emphasize a focus on how the Hebrews/Israelites were influenced by the polytheism of the ancient world, what gods they worshiped in their early history, and how they eventually came to believe in a deity of their own and then ultimately became a monotheistic people. As in other aspects of the Hebrew/Israelite religion, the conception of the deity was influenced by the environment in which biblical authors lived.

It was customary for clans and tribes in the ancient world to have their peculiar gods, especially among nomads like the patriarchs. Added to this complexity are the patriarchal narratives themselves, with their intertwining sources from differing dates, which makes the task of trying to determine the truth about their deities confusing and sometimes frustrating.

*Elohim and Yahweh*

Elohim, the favorite of E, is really a grammatical plural in Hebrew. Sometimes it means "gods" (e.g., Exodus 20:3; Deuteronomy 6:14), but when used of Israel's God (about 2,500 times in the OT) it usually has a singular meaning. Exceptions include when God said: "Let us make humankind in our image, according to our likeness" (Genesis 1:26) and "Come, let us go down, and confuse their language" (Genesis 11:7). The plural Elohim and pronouns seem to indicate a carryover from the polytheism of ancient Hebrews. A different example is in Isaiah 6:8, where the prophet heard the Lord (*Adonai*, translated as "the Lord") ask: "Whom shall I send, and who will go for us?" However, by the time the Septuagint was written, the Israelites had become monotheistic, so LXX Isaiah 6:8

reads: "Whom shall I send, and who will go to this people?" The author, therefore, avoids the implication of polytheism by not using "us."

Other passages show awareness of gods besides Yahweh. In Exodus 18:11 Moses' father-in-law, Jethro, says: "Now I know that the Lord (Yahweh) is greater than all gods, because he delivered the people from the Egyptians" (see also Exodus 12:12; 20:3; Deuteronomy 10:17; 1 Samuel 4:8; Psalm 86:8). Joshua exhorts the Israelites: "Revere the Lord...put away the gods that your ancestors served beyond the River [Mesopotamia] and in Egypt, and serve the Lord" (Joshua 24:14).

In the Hebrew Scriptures Yahweh is written with four letters (*YHWH*), and for that reason it is referred to as the tetragrammaton. In English versions it is usually translated as "the Lord," and Yahweh is frequently combined with Elohim as *YHWH Elohim*, "God Yahweh" or "Yahweh God," and translated as "the Lord God" (e.g., Genesis 2:7-9).

*Origin and Meaning of the Term Yahweh*
The origin and meaning of the designation *YHWH* are uncertain. In (J) its origins go back to the time of Enosh, grandson of Adam. "At that time people began to invoke the name of the Lord" (*YHWH*; Genesis 4:26). J consistently uses the name Yahweh from the creation story onward in order to show that the God of Israel was the God of humankind. If you look at Exodus 3:15 (E), you will see that God told Moses to say to the Israelites: "The Lord (*YHWH*), the God (Elohim) of your ancestors, the God (Elohim) of Abraham, the God (Elohim) of Isaac, and the God (Elohim) of Jacob." In P, the latest account, God said to Moses: "I am the Lord...I appeared to Abraham, Isaac, and Jacob as God Almighty," but he did not make his name (*YHWH*) known to them (Exodus 6:2-3). In E and P, then, the designation *YHWH* was not used before the time of Moses. Sometimes the name Yahweh is used in combination with other names of deities: Yahweh and El Shaddai (Genesis 17:1), El and Yahweh (Numbers 23:8), and most often, Yahweh Elohim (Genesis 2:5, 7; Exodus 5:1).

In J, Yahweh called Abram to leave his own country and go to a land he would show him (Genesis 12:1). Therefore, some scholars believe that Yahweh was worshiped by the patriarchs (*4 Maccabees* 7:19; 16:25; John 7:22; Acts 7:8-9; Romans 9:5; 15:8; Hebrews 7:4). In E and P the divine name was revealed to Moses personally, but some scholars question if Moses was even an historical person. Many think, though, that the name does go back to Moses' time.

In the E account of the conversation between God and Moses in Exodus 3:13-14, we get some knowledge about the meaning of the word *YHWH*.

Moses says to God that if the Israelites ask him, "What is his name? What shall I say to them?" God said to Moses, "I am who I am." God then told Moses to say to the Israelites: "I am has sent me to you." It is generally agreed that the name *YHWH* stems from a form of the verb "to be," a view reflected in the *NRSV* footnote to Exodus 3:14: "I AM WHAT I AM or I WILL BE WHAT I WILL BE." For some scholars those meanings are taken to indicate the existence of God contrasted to idols that have no existence (e.g., Isaiah 44:9-20; Wisdom 14:12-14). Others have suggested that, since God as Creator causes what happens, *YHWH* means something like "I cause it to be" or "come into being." As such, Yahweh is responsible for the events in history (Deuteronomy 4:32-40; Isaiah 40:28; 44:24).

Eventually the Israelites came to believe that Yahweh was their peculiar God, a God among other gods, as the Deuteronomist puts it: "The Lord (Yahweh) your God (Elohim) is God (Elohim) of gods (Elohim) and Lord (Adon) of lords (Adonai), the great God (El), mighty and awesome" (Deuteronomy 10:17; see also Psalm 136:2; Daniel 2:47). Notice the different names for the deity. The phrase "the Lord your God" occurs more than 400 times and the phrase "the Lord, the God of Israel" more than 100 times. In Hebrew "Lord God" is *Yahweh Elohim*. By the time of the Deuteronomist, Yahweh had assumed other names.

After the Babylonian exile (sixth-fifth centuries BCE), if not before, the Israelites (Jews) became a monotheistic people. See, for example, "So that all the people of the earth may know that the Lord (*YHWH*) is God (Elohim); there is no other" (1 Kings 8:60; Deuteronomic influence). Does this mean that there is no other God of Israel or no other god at all? Compare Joshua 22:22: "The Lord, God of gods!" and Joshua 22:24: "the Lord, the God of Israel." The authors known as the Second and Third Isaiah (the designation for the unknown authors of parts of Isaiah 40–66) were the monotheists of the OT par excellence: "I am the Lord (*YHWH*), and there is no other; besides me there is no God" (Elohim; Isaiah 45:5-6; see also Isaiah 37:20; 45:14, 18, 22; Deuteronomy 6:4; Psalm 83:18).

The name "Yahweh" is used more often than all other names for the deity combined. In a shorter form it was sometimes used as part of personal names that begin with *je-*, *jeho-* or end with *iah* or *jah*, for example, Jeremiah, Jehoshaphat, Adonijah, Elijah, and Isaiah. In post-exilic Judaism the tetragrammaton was regarded as so sacred that it should not be pronounced when reading the scriptures aloud. Instead, the word *Adonai* (meaning "my Lord") was pronounced whenever *YHWH* occurred, and the vowel points of *Adonai* were used with the consonants *YHWH* to remind the reader to say "*Adonai*," not "Yahweh."

*Yahweh as "Lord of Hosts"*
The name Yahweh was used with the word "hosts" and formed the designation "Yahweh (Lord) of hosts." The designation occurs first in 1 Samuel 1:3, where it is reported that Elkanah went to Shiloh "to worship and to sacrifice to the Lord of Hosts." In 1 Samuel 4:4, the people took "the ark of the covenant of the Lord of hosts" into the battle of the Israelites against the Philistines. Thus, the "hosts" seem to refer to the Israelite armies. The designation occurs some 270 times, often in the prophets, especially in Isaiah, Jeremiah, Amos, Haggai, and Zechariah, but the hosts are not identified. The identity of "hosts" with military forces is further supported in 2 Samuel 5:10: "And David became greater and greater [after capturing Jerusalem], for the Lord, the God of hosts, was with him." That deity is sometimes called "the God of Israel." See "the Lord of hosts, the God of Israel" (2 Samuel 7:26-27) and the more emphatic form, "The Lord of hosts, the God of Israel, is Israel's God" (1 Chronicles 17:24; see also Isaiah 17:16; 17:3).

The top position among gods was eventually given to Yahweh. See, for example, Psalm 89:6-9: "Who in the skies can be compared to the Lord? Who among the heavenly beings is like the Lord...O Lord God of hosts, who is as mighty as you, O Lord?" The parallel of the "Lord of hosts" and "the heavenly beings" is one of the reasons why some scholars think that the "hosts" refer to celestial beings.

## El

In the Semitic language of the Canaanites and Hebrews, El was widely used as a word for deity. As the chief god of the Canaanite pantheon, he was regarded as creator, sometimes with the title "Creator of the Earth." He was also thought of as the father of gods and human beings. El came into the Bible as a name for God and, including words compounded with it, occurs some 200 times. In Job it is a favorite deity. After the Israelites entered Canaan, they worshiped El at Canaanite shrines, and in that way aspects of the cult of El became a part of the Israelite religion. El is sometimes called "the God of Israel." See the footnote to Genesis 33:20 in the *NRSV*: "*God* [El], *the God* [Elohim] *of Israel.*" Influence of El on the Israelites is evident in the names of persons and places, for example, Elijah ("Yahweh is God") and Bethel ("house of god").

As in some other ancient literature, El is frequently combined in the OT with other words for names of tribal or local gods. A good example of this is the angel's remark to Jacob: "I am the God (El) of Bethel, where...you made a vow to me" (Genesis 31:13). In Genesis 28:13-19, Jacob perceived that Yahweh was "in this place" and said, "This is none other than the house of God." He then called the place Bethel, meaning "house of God." Since Yahweh was not known to the patriarchs, the general and vague name "the god of your (our, their) fathers ("ancestors," NRSV) was used for their deity (e.g., Exodus 3:15-16). In some places, though, Yahweh was read back into the time of the patriarchs: "as the Lord (*YHWH*), the God of your ancestors, has promised you" (Deuteronomy 6:3; see also Joshua 18:3).

## *Baal*

While El was the main deity in the Canaanite pantheon, he was much more of a figurehead than Baal (meaning "lord"), who was the main deity of action. He was thought of as the king of the gods, known in the ancient Semitic world as the storm-god Hadad who ruled from a high mountain in the north.

The chief feature of the Canaanite religion was its fertility cult, so male gods had their female consorts. The chief female deities were Anat, consort of Baal; Asherah; and Astarte, also known as Astoreth and Astarat. Asherah appears in the Bible mostly as a cult image (e.g., 1 Kings 15:13; 2 Kings 21:7; 23:6). The best known story about Baal and Asherah is the showdown between the prophet Elijah and the prophets of Baal on Mount Carmel. Another Canaanite goddess was Ashtoreth (plural, Ashtaroth; see 1 Samuel 31:10; 1 Kings 11:5; 2 Kings 23:13). She is mentioned in the Bible in the plural form as the name of a place (e.g., Deuteronomy 1:4; Joshua 9:10; 12:4). Portrayed as prostitutes or pregnant women, the chief function of the Canaanite female deities was their role in the fertility cult. They were at the same time portrayed as delighting in the blood and gore of warfare. Anat's exploits are explicit: Her "heart fills with joy, Anat's liver exults; For she plunges knee-deep in knights' blood, Hip-deep in the gore of heroes" (*ANET*, 136).

Another main feature of the Canaanite religion was the annual celebration of the death and resurrection of Baal, which corresponded with the dying and coming to life again of things in nature. Members of the cult believed that, as in nature, fertility in humans depended upon the interaction of the gods. Worshipers believed that sexual intercourse with male and female prostitutes at religious shrines would provoke the gods and goddesses to do the same thing and thus assure another year of the fertility of soil, crops, animals, and humans.

Baalism, with its fertility cult and all its debauchery, including sacred prostitution and child sacrifice, had made inroads into the religion of Israel, so Israelites sometimes were victims to such practices. The religious reformation under King Josiah of Judah is vividly described in 2 Kings 23:4-7. With Josiah's royal housecleaning in Jerusalem, the vessels made for Baal and Asherah were brought out of the temple of Yahweh and burned. Josiah deposed the idolatrous priests and removed those who sacrificed to Baal, removed the images of Asherah, and destroyed the places of male prostitutes who were in the temple of Yahweh, where the women wove hangings for the Asherah. Many other things were also done to subdue Baalism.

There are many allusions to the fertility cult in the OT with opposition to it. The prophet Micah asks: "Shall I give my firstborn for my transgression, the fruit of my body for the sin of my soul?" (Micah 6:7; see also Ezekiel 23:36-39). Concerning the apostasy (unfaithfulness) of Israel, Jeremiah asks how she can claim she is not defiled and "not gone after the Baals." Israel's way is like "a wild ass at home in the wilderness, in her heat sniffing the wind! Who can restrain her lust?" (Jeremiah 2:23-24; see also Hosea 4:13-14; 9:1). Israel has "played the whore with many lovers… Where have you not been lain with?" (Jeremiah 3:1-2). The writer of 1 Samuel 2:22 reports that the sons of Eli the priest were lying with women at the entrance to the place of worship. Probably as the result of influence from the prophets and Josiah's reformation, laws were passed forbidding child sacrifice, divination, augury, sorcery, and other "abhorrent practices" (Deuteronomy 18:10-14), and temple prostitution by Israelite women and men was outlawed (Deuteronomy 23:17).

*Baalism and Elijah and Yahwism*
In spite of Israel's unfaithfulness, including the cultic practices of the Canaanites, Yahwism triumphed in the end, largely because of the prophets who preached moral reform for individuals and the nation. The most dramatic story of the conflict between Yahweh and Baal is Elijah's showdown with hundreds of prophets of Baal and Asherah on Mount Carmel (1 Kings 18:17-40). The stage is set in the time of King Ahab of Israel (869-850 BCE), who "did more to provoke the anger of the Lord (Yahweh), the God (Elohim) of Israel, than had all the kings of Israel who were before him." His wife Jezebel "was killing off the prophets of the Lord" (1 Kings 16:33; 18:4; see also 16:25, 31). And Ahab had "forsaken the commandments of the Lord and followed the Baals" (1 Kings 18:18), an indication of the Deuteronomist's hand in the story.

Elijah challenges Ahab to bring on the Baalists, which he does (1 Kings 18:17-20). Elijah asks the assembled Israelites how long they will continue in their "limping" between Yahweh and Baal and states the terms of the challenge: "If the Lord is God, follow him; but if Baal, then follow him" (18:21). Baal's prophets are to prepare a sacrifice but put no fire to the wood, and Elijah is to do the same. The Baal prophets are to call upon their god, Elijah on his God, and the god who responds with fire is really God. The people agree to the terms of the contest (18:23-14). The Baal prophets pray all forenoon, but there is no response. Elijah has a good time mocking them with humorous sarcasm. They should pray louder. "Surely he is a god; either he is meditating, or he has wandered away, or he is on a journey, or perhaps he is asleep and must be awakened" (18:27). In spite of crying louder, cutting themselves until they were all bloody, and raving on, Baal did not respond.

Elijah carefully prepared his sacrifice and had everything around it thoroughly soaked with water. Then he prayed to the God of Abraham, Isaac, and Israel (Jacob) to show that Yahweh is God. God responded with fire that consumed everything, including the stones of the altar, "and even licked up the water that was in the trench," which had been built around it (1 Kings 18:36-40). When the people saw what happened, they prostrated themselves and exclaimed: "Yahweh, he is the God; Yahweh, he is the God" (Hebrew). The prophets of Baal are murdered, and that assures the triumph of Yahweh over Baal.

Elijah on Mount Carmel is one of several stories about him that probably was transmitted orally and later written down, perhaps by the Deuteronomist (see 1 Kings 17–19; 21; 2 Kings 1:1–2:15). The people's exclamation that "Yahweh, he is the God" may imply that there is none other in existence but him. Or does it mean that Yahweh, not the Baal of Ahab and Jezebel, is the God of Israel? See 1 Kings 18:36, where Elijah prays, "Let it be known this day that you are God in Israel." The view that Yahweh is the God of Israel coincides with the statement in Deuteronomy 6:4: "Hear, O Israel: The Lord is our God, the Lord alone."

The author or compiler of the story seems to be familiar with some patriarchal narratives, the story of Moses on Mount Sinai, and other traditions. There are close parallels between Moses and Elijah. The Lord responded to Moses in Egypt when "fire came down on the earth" (Exodus 9:23-24); fire from Yahweh "fell and consumed the burnt offering" and everything else (1 Kings 18:38). Moses made an altar of stones (Exodus 20:25); Elijah built an altar of stone in the name of Yahweh (1 Kings 18:30-32).

In the accounts of Elijah and Moses, God reveals himself in fire to an assembly (Exodus 19:18; 1 Kings 18:38). Moses built an altar and set up 12 pillars, one for each of the tribes of Israel (Exodus 24:4); Elijah took 12 stones, one for each tribe, and built an altar in the name of Yahweh (1 Kings 18:30-32). Moses took blood from the sacrificial oxen and dashed it on the altar and the people (Exodus 24:6-8); Elijah cut the sacrificial bull in pieces and then had water poured on the offering and on everything else (1 Kings 18:33-35). Elijah prayed to Yahweh, "God of Abraham, Isaac, and Israel" (1 Kings 18:36); and Moses implored the Lord (Yahweh) to turn from his anger and "Remember Abraham, Isaac, and Israel" (Exodus 32:13). Both accounts have "Israel" for "Jacob."

The person(s) writing about Elijah on Mount Carmel apparently did not notice that the people getting all the water they wanted to wet down everything contradicted the statement that they were in the third year of a severe drought (1 Kings 18:1-2). Or, perhaps he was not concerned about the contradiction. He wanted to stress the confession of Yahweh as the God of Israel and that he sent the rain to end the drought (1 Kings 18:44-45). Israel's faith was restored, at least temporarily. Clearly, this incident of Elijah on Mount Carmel must be understood from a religious, not historical, point of view. The name Elijah may not even be that of a particular person but, instead, a concrete symbol for the abstract belief that "Yahweh, he is the God." The Hebrew word for Elijah, in fact, is *Eliyahu* and means "Yahweh is God."

These are but a few examples that show how the belief in the ascendancy of Yahweh above the Canaanite gods developed and ultimately that he was the only God in existence. But, Baalism had greatly influenced Yahwism, as evident even in some Israelite names. In the LXX of 2 Samuel 2:10 Saul had a son named Ishbaal, meaning "man of Baal" (see also the LXX of 2 Samuel 2:8-15; 3:7-15; 4:1-2). As time passed, Israelites did not want to pronounce the name "baal," so there was a tendency to change names to give them a different meaning. In the Hebrew text the name Ishbaal was either omitted or changed. Ishbaal became Ish-botheth, meaning "man of shame." The son of Jonathan, David's friend, was originally named Merib-baal, meaning "man of" or "hero of" or "beloved of Baal" (1 Chronicles 8:34; 9:40) It became Mephibosheth, "one spreading shame" or "shameful mouth" (2 Samuel 4:4; 9:6).

## Other Gods

Eloah is a feminine form and occurs only in Hebrew in the Semitic languages. It may be a variant of El and Elohim and occurs mostly in Job (42 times) and less frequently in other poetry (e.g., Deuteronomy 32:15, 17; Proverbs 30:5; Isaiah 44:8). Eloah is synonymous with Elohim in Psalm 50:22-23 and with Yahweh in Psalm 18:31. Why poets seemed to prefer Eloah we do not know.

El Shaddai and the names of deities below might represent separate gods or are, perhaps, only descriptive titles for the same god El or Elohim. See, for example, Genesis 31:42, where Jacob says to Laban: "the God (Elohim) of my father, the God (Elohim) of Abraham and the Fear of Isaac" (see also Genesis 31:53). There is also confusion about the meaning of the word translated as "Fear" in the *NRSV* ("Kinsman," *NJB*) and how it relates to the other words used with it. Is the God of Abraham the one Isaac feared (see Genesis 22:7-14)? Or is the "Fear of Isaac" a separate deity and one that Isaac worshiped?

In Exodus 6:2-8, God appeared to Abraham as El Shaddai. There and elsewhere the meaning of "Shaddai" is uncertain. It may mean "mountain," so El Shaddai would be "god of the mountain" or "mountain god." This accords with the ancient belief that gods frequently resided on mountains, often in the north (e.g., Isaiah 14:13 and footnote in the *NRSV*; Psalm 48:1-3).

Moses frequently met with God on a mountain. He left his home with Jethro and "came to Horeb, the mountain of God" (Exodus 3:1). The Lord frequently "summoned Moses to the top of the mountain" (Exodus 19:20; see also 24:12). Moses received the Ten Commandments on Mount Sinai (also called Horeb; Deuteronomy 5:1-5), and Elijah defeated the prophets of Baal and Asherah on Mount Carmel (1 Kings 18:17-40). In the LXX El Shaddai is rendered as *theos pantokrator*, "God Almighty," used in the *NRSV* and some other translations.

With El Elyon, El Olam, El Berith, and El Roi, the deity is El with a qualifying word, and they were worshiped by the patriarchs at shrines or sanctuaries in specific places. El Elyon ("God Most High") was worshiped at Jerusalem before it was captured by David (c. 1000 BCE). In Genesis 14:18-20 (source uncertain) Melchizedek, "priest of God Most High" (El Elyon), blessed Abram "by God Most High" (El Elyon). The deity is called "maker of heaven and earth" who delivered Abram from his enemies. In the P narrative of creation Elohim is the Creator (Genesis 1:1), and in J Yahweh Elohim is Creator (Genesis 2:4b). Is this one god with two names or two gods?

El Olam ("God Forever" or "Everlasting God") occurs only in Genesis 21:33 in the Pentateuch and was apparently a local Canaanite deity worshiped at Beer-sheba. After Abraham made a covenant with Abimelech, he planted a tree in Beer-sheba and "called there on the name of the Lord, the Everlasting God" (Yahweh El Olam). Perhaps the god El Olam was applied to Yahweh to make sure the covenant was everlasting. See Isaiah 40:28: "The Lord is the Everlasting God."

El Berith ("God of the Covenant") was apparently another local Canaanite deity, this one worshiped at Shechem where, as we learn from Judges 9:46, there was "the temple of El-berith." After the Israelites conquered Canaan, Joshua called an assembly of the tribes of Israel for a covenant ceremony. Such covenants or treaties had a long history before the Israelites, and it was fitting to hold a covenant ceremony at Shechem, where the deity of the covenant was worshiped.

In Genesis 16:7-14 an angel of Yahweh appeared to Hagar and told her that she had already conceived and would bear a son. She should call him Ishmael, a name symbolic of the Lord's hearing about Hagar's affliction. Hagar named the Lord (Yahweh) who spoke to her "You are El roi" ("God of Seeing" or "God Who Sees"), because she thought she had seen God. Then Hagar questioned whether she had really seen God and remained alive. This reflects the Israelite view that seeing God meant death (Genesis 32:30; 33:20; Exodus 3:1-6; 19:16-25; Judges 13:22).

The El deities usually appear in connection with religious shrines in Canaan and reflect the religion of ancient Semitic peoples. Therefore, they were probably pre-Israelite in origin. As Israelites got control of Canaan, they took over Canaanite shrines and the religious practices and ideas associated with them. After the Israelites became monotheistic, they read their monotheism back into their earlier history and adapted foreign religious practices to the worship of Yahweh. This is quite clear from the words of Joshua in Joshua 24:14-15, where he tells the Israelites to serve Yahweh and to give up the gods of their ancestors. If they are not willing to serve Yahweh, they should choose between the gods of their ancestors and the gods of the Amorites. Then Joshua says: "But as for me and my household, we will serve the Lord" (Yahweh).

### Further Thoughts about Gods in the Old Testament

Speculative thought originated in the western world, not in the ancient Near East. Unlike some Greco-Roman philosophers, the Hebrews never questioned the existence of a deity or deities. According to a psalmist,

"Fools say in their hearts, 'There is no God'" (Psalm 14:1). The "fools" are described as corrupt, doers of evil, and do not call upon the Lord (Yahweh). In the early history of Israel there is no absolute denial of the existence of gods other than Yahweh. How, then, are we to understand what the Hebrews/Israelites believed about their deity or deities?

The Deuteronomist writes emphatically about the God for Israel when he has Moses, speaking for Yahweh, say to the Israelites: "I am the Lord (Yahweh) your God (Elohim)... You shall have no other gods besides me" (Deuteronomy 5:6-7). Now consider again Deuteronomy 6:4, which may be taken in at least two ways: "Yahweh is our God, Yahweh alone" (*NRSV*) or "Yahweh our God is the one, the only Yahweh" (*NJB*). The first is to be understood in opposition to the many deities of Baalism; the second emphasizes the oneness of Yahweh and is to be understood in light of the many different traditions and shrines of Yahweh. In contrast to the gods of other peoples, Yahweh was to be recognized as a living God and, therefore, real. The making of images or idols of Yahweh was strictly prohibited (e.g., Exodus 20:4; Deuteronomy 5:8; 1 Kings 23:4-6). Yahweh and Elohim were both gods of the Israelites, but Yahweh gradually replaced Elohim as the *only* God for Israel.

### Household Gods

So, what about the household gods (Hebrew, *teraphim*) of Laban that Rachel stole when she left home with Jacob (Genesis 31:19-35)? They were family gods, perhaps in the form of humans (see 1 Samuel 19:13, 16; Judges 17:1-5; 18:14-20). They may have been cult objects, but their origin and significance are uncertain. In Ezekiel 21:21-23 (see also Hosea 3:4; Zechariah 10:2), household gods were consulted in the use of divination, the practice of foretelling future events. But, what was the significance of Rachel taking them (Genesis 31:19, 30-32)? Several customs practiced in the vicinity of Haran may help us understand her action. In Nuzi law, a son-in-law was entitled to a certain share of a father-in-law's estate confirmed by the transfer of the household gods. Because Laban had tricked Jacob into marrying Leah instead of Rachel, whom he loved, Laban could not be trusted to make such a transfer. That would explain his anger about the disappearance of the gods (Genesis 31:30-35).

We must remember that the details of the story of Laban and his daughters may not be historical. The authors (J+E) and Rachel, a farmer's daughter, even more so, probably were not familiar with Nuzi law. The authors likely took the story from some ancient tradition and added it to their stories about the patriarchs. The significant point is that the household gods were not images of Yahweh.

## Henotheism and Monotheism

Although some scholars do not agree, it seems most accurate to say that after the polytheism of the patriarchs, the proper designation for the early religion of Israel is henotheism (Greek, "*hen*," "one," plus *theos*, "god"). It is the name for the religion of a particular people who worship one deity without denying the existence of other deities. Besides passages already mentioned, see, for example, what Jethro says to Moses: "Now I know that the Lord is greater than all gods, because he delivered the people from the Egyptians" (Exodus 18:11) and Yahweh's words: "You shall have no other gods besides me" (Exodus 20:3; see also Deuteronomy 10:17; 1 Samuel 4:5-8; Psalm 86:8).

The Israelites probably did not become a monotheistic people until the time of the Second Isaiah (sixth century BCE). For that writer, Yahweh is Elohim and there is no other god. His convictions are expressed in beautiful poetry: "I am the Lord, and there is no other; besides me there is no god" (Isaiah 45:5). "God is with you alone, and there is no other; there is no god besides him" (45:14; see also Isaiah 43:11; 44:6, 8, 14-21; 47:8, 10).

The prohibition of images of Yahweh goes back to early Israelite civilization. This prohibition is confirmed by archaeology, which has proven the existence of idols in all other ancient civilizations. Insofar as I know, however, there has never been a fragment of an image of Yahweh discovered among innumerable fragments of images of pagan gods.

Second Isaiah regarded the making of images as buffoonery. If the Israelites thought their God was the only living one, it was natural for them to think of pagan images (idols) as merely wood or stone (Deuteronomy 5:26; Joshua 3:10; 1 Samuel 17:26, 36; 2 Kings 19:4; Psalms 42:2; 84.2; Jeremiah 10:10; 23:36; Daniel 6:20, 26). Read the beautiful passage on the folly of idolatry in Isaiah 44:9-20. Here is a summary with some quotations: All idols are a mockery because they are made by humans, not god. Ironsmiths and carpenters take great care in fashioning their productions. After cutting a tree from the forest, they take some of it for fuel to warm themselves and do their cooking and boast about what they have done. The rest of the wood the carpenter "makes into a god, his idol, bows down to it and worships it; he prays to it and says, 'Save me, for you are my god.'" Idols do not comprehend or understand, nor can they see. The carpenter cannot discern that with half of the wood he kept warm and ate his food, nor can he ask, "Now shall I make the rest of it an abomination? Shall I fall down before a block of wood?"

Israelites came to ascribe many attributes to their God, such as Creator (Isaiah 40:28; 43:15) and Deliverer or Savior (2 Samuel 22:2-3; Psalms 17:7; 40:17; 140:17; 106:21; Jeremiah 14:8; Hosea 13:4). The Second Isaiah has three favorite attributes of God: Savior (Isaiah 43:11; 45:15, 21; 49:26; see also Isaiah 60:16; 53:8); Redeemer (41:14–55:8; see also Isaiah 59:20; 60:16; 63:16; Jeremiah 50:34; Job 19:25; Psalms 19:14; 78:35); and Holy One, often with the qualifying phrase "of Israel" (40:25–55:5). The concept of the holiness of Israel's God goes back to the time of the prophet Isaiah himself (eighth century BCE), who was probably responsible for most of the material from Isaiah 1–39. "The Holy One" occurs only twice in Isaiah 56–66, sometimes regarded as the Third Isaiah (see also 1 Samuel 2:2; 2 Kings 19:22; Job 6:10; Psalms 71:22; 78:41; Jeremiah 50:29; 51:5; Hosea 11:9; Habakkuk 1:12).

The concept of God's holiness is extensive and emphatic in much of the OT. Holiness meant being set apart from anything profane or evil, so holiness set the Hebrew deity, whether Yahweh, El, or Elohim, apart from all other gods. In one of the oldest pieces of Hebrew literature (about thirteenth century BCE), a beautiful poem attributed to Moses, the poet, asks: "Who is like you, O Lord (Yahweh) among the gods [*elim*, plural of *el*]? Who is like you, majestic in holiness...?" (Exodus 15:1-18). Earlier, the poet says that Yahweh is his God (El; 15:2). The holiness of God is expressed in many ways, but here are just a few examples. "There is no Holy One like the Lord (Yahweh), no one besides you; there is no Rock like our God" (Elohim; 1 Samuel 2:2). People who forsake Yahweh for other gods cannot serve him, "for he is a holy God (Elohim). He is a jealous God" (Joshua 24:19). A psalmist sings: "Extol the Lord our God... Holy is he" (Psalm 99:5; see also Psalm 99:9). Holiness is the attribute of God par excellence.

## *The Gender of the Deity*

In answer to a question about the Hebrew concepts of God, a student of mine once wrote: "It is a wonder how God could survive through all that he has gone. He has been kicked around like a football." For faithful readers of the Bible God has survived, and an insightful understanding shows how faithful biblical writers helped their God survive, under many names, over many other gods long gone. But were there female deities among the gods mentioned in the Bible? That question is the final subject of this chapter.

I think it was John A. T. Robinson, a bishop in the Church of England and NT scholar, who in the mid-1960s first suggested that it was time to equalize the masculine representations of the deity with feminine ones. About the same time, the influence of the feminist movement brought attention to gender equality or inclusiveness in the secular world. These ideas have also been applied to the Bible, with the usual diversity of opinions. While the *REB* and the *NRSV* most often use inclusive language with respect to gender, neither translation is entirely consistent.

Whenever "brothers" is used generically, *NRSV* almost always has "brothers and sisters." For "fathers," especially with "our fathers," it uses "ancestors." In Acts 1:15-16 "brothers" is "believers" and "men brothers" (Greek, *andres adelphoi*) becomes "friends" in *NRSV*. For the former, *REB* reads "assembled brotherhood" and, for the latter, "my friends." In Acts 2:29 the Greek "men brothers" is "fellow Israelites" in *NRSV* and "my friends" in *REB*. In Acts 1:15-16 *NJB* reads "brothers" both times, and in Acts 2:29 it also has "brothers." In Joshua 1:14 the Hebrew "brothers" is given as "kindred" in *NRSV*, "kinsmen" in the *REB*, and "brothers" in *NJB*.

In Genesis 15:15 "fathers" is "ancestors" in *NRSV* and *NJB* and "forefathers" in *REB*. In Exodus 3:15 "sons of Israel...fathers" is "Israelites...ancestors" in both *NRSV* and *NJB* and, in *REB*, "Israelites...forefathers." In Romans 1:13 "brothers" is "brothers and sisters" in *NRSV* and *REB* and "brothers" in *NJB*. In Romans 7:1 "brothers" is "brothers and sisters" in *NRSV*, "my friends" in *REB*, and "brothers" in *NJB* (so also in Romans 8:12). However, in 1 Corinthians 6:8 "brothers" is "believers" in *NRSV*, "fellow-Christians" in *REB*, and "your own brothers" in *NJB*.

Most scholars have no difficulty with such language to convey inclusiveness or gender neutrality. However, there are different opinions concerning the Hebrew deity as female and female deities in general. Most scholars still think there is insufficient evidence to show that the Hebrews/Israelites thought of their deity as female. Some scholars have argued that the Hebrew deity transcends humanity and, therefore, is without gender, as several passages seem to indicate. According to Numbers 23:19, Balak, king of Moab, summoned Balaam to curse the Israelites before they entered Canaan. Speaking for the deity, Balaam says, "God is not a human being, that he should lie, or a mortal, that he should change his mind."

The words translated as "a human being" and "a mortal" are two different Hebrew words for "man." The first is *ish* and means "man" in contrast to an animal, a woman, and the deity. The second is *ben adam*, literally "son of man," and it is the same as "man" in the sense of "a human being" or "a mortal." The same combination of words occurs in Psalm 8:4 (Hebrew):

"What are human beings that you are mindful of them, mortals that you care for them?" Both passages imply the mortality of humans as opposed to the immortality of the deity. The words that follow the quotation tell in what ways the deity is not human. The deity has promised that, having brought the Israelites out of Egypt, he intends to keep his promise to deliver them into Canaan. Moreover, Yahweh, not Balaam, is responsible for Balaam uttering blessings upon Israel instead of curses.

Another passage thought by some persons to imply a sexless deity is 1 Samuel 15:29: "The Glory of Israel [that is, Yahweh of the previous verse] will not recant [Hebrew, "deceive"] or change his mind; for he is not a mortal (*adam*), that he should change his mind." The words are those of Samuel who tells King Saul that Yahweh will not change his mind about taking the kingdom from him because of his sins. In that way the deity is not a mortal.

In Hosea 11:9 the prophet speaks about the deity not going to destroy Israel again: "For I am God (El) and no mortal (*ish*), the Holy One in your midst, and I will not come in wrath." Like the prophets in general, Hosea believed that the fall of Israel was due to its apostasy. Because the deity is not human he will not act in human fashion by showing vengeance. The deity's love for Israel is greater than his wrath (see also Hosea 11:1-8).

Among the first things we learned about the Hebrew deity were his human traits. He speaks ("God said"; Genesis 1:3; often); "created/formed man" (Genesis 1:27; 2:7); "The Lord God took the man and put him in the garden" (Genesis 2:15); "planted a garden" and "walked" in it (Genesis 2:8; 3:8); "formed every animal" (Genesis 2:19); "made a woman" and "brought her to the man" (Genesis 2:22; and "made garments" for the couple (Genesis 3:21). We also learned that some biblical writers stress such anthropomorphisms of God, while others try to avoid them.

I think it was Mark Twain who said that God first created man in his own image and that humans have created him in their image ever since. In studying the Bible insightfully we must resist making ideas from it conform to current thinking, but concentrate, instead, on understanding them given the times when they were written.

Some persons who argue for the femininity of the Hebrew deity use the designation "Mother." The most significant passages supporting this view occur in the book of Isaiah, such as Isaiah 42:14. There, after a long time of silence and restraint, Yahweh says, "Now I will cry out like a woman in labor, I will gasp and pant." Here the figure is simile, "like a woman," not metaphor. In the context of this passage, "The Lord goes forth like a soldier, like a warrior he stirs up his fury," and he will destroy mountains and all their growth. Can it be argued any more or any less that the deity is a mother than a soldier?

In Isaiah 49:14-15, Zion (Jerusalem) says, "The Lord (Yahweh) has forsaken me, my Lord (Adonai) has forgotten me. Can a woman forget her nursing child, or show no compassion for the child of her womb?" Although such a woman may forget Yahweh, he will not forget Jerusalem. Again, Yahweh is not called "Mother" but is portrayed as showing maternal love (see Isaiah 45:9-11). It is probably no more likely or unlikely that the deity would be a woman than that the city of Jerusalem would speak as a human.

Isaiah 66:12-13 is also thought to be a passage in support of the deity as Mother. The prophet is writing about the coming glory of the restored Jerusalem, which will happen as though the conception and birth of inhabitants of Jerusalem occurred on the same day. They will be nursed, carried, and held as a mother does her children. "As a mother comforts her child," so will Yahweh comfort the people in Jerusalem. Again, the figure is simile, not metaphor, and it hardly indicates the femininity of the deity but the caring and compassionate nature of it. Compare Psalm 103:13: "As a father has compassion for his children, so the Lord has compassion for those who fear him." Does the father who shows motherly compassion become a mother in doing so? Is a deity with feminine traits the same thing as a feminine deity?

Think about what Paul says to the members of his church in Thessalonica: "We were gentle among you, like a nurse tenderly caring for her own children" (1 Thessalonians 2:7). Do we think of Paul as a woman or mother because he writes so affectionately? Moreover, the word for nurse is feminine (*trophos*), so should we think of the simile associated with it as indicating a female writer? In Romans 16:13 the author (probably not Paul) writes, "Greet Rufus...and greet his mother – a mother to me also." The woman was obviously not the mother of Paul. In Galatians 4:26 Paul writes allegorically of Jerusalem and says, "She is our mother." Surely this is allegorical, as is Hosea 2:2, 5; 4:5.

In Deuteronomy 32:18 it is reported that Moses spoke poetically to the Israelites: "You were unmindful of the Rock that bore you; you forgot the God (El) who gave you birth." The deity is characterized as "the Rock," an ancient designation used in Canaanite texts, where it symbolizes might or power. Rock is used five times in parallel with the deity in Deuteronomy 32:1-43, so would we think of "Rock" as having feminine traits in the same way we think of the imagery of the deity giving birth as a sign of a female deity? When the Israelites thought of their deity as giving birth, they did not think of the process as the result of sexual intercourse as the Canaanites did.

On the other hand, the figure of simile instead of metaphor cannot always be used against the femininity of the deity. We have learned that in Isaiah 42:13 Yahweh goes out "like a soldier" and "like a warrior" but that "like" does not mean "he was." However, in Exodus 15:3-4, 8, "The Lord is a warrior; the Lord is his name." In the following verses Yahweh acts the part of a warrior: "Pharaoh's chariots and his army he cast into the sea... At the blast of your nostrils the waters piled up." As with the Rock, such imagery shows influence from the Canaanite religion. The poem or song in Exodus 15:1-18 shows influence from Canaanite texts. However, the phrases "in the greatness of your majesty," "majestic in holiness," and "in your steadfast love" show unique aspects of the deity absent in the other texts.

It was probably easier for the Hebrews/Israelites to think of their deity as a warrior than as a woman or, more specifically, as a mother. The point to remember is that Semitic peoples, including the Hebrews, thought of their gods in concrete living images of simile and metaphor, not in abstract philosophical or theological thought. Even metaphors were attempts to convey experiences of faith and life. When a psalmist wrote, "The Lord is my shepherd" and "The Lord is my rock...my God, my rock" (Psalms 23:1; 18:2), he did not actually think that Yahweh was a shepherd or a stone.

## Chapter Summary

How shall we understand what the Bible says about various deities? Biblical writers wrote down their ideas of the deities long after the Hebrews/Israelites had come into contact with the gods of the polytheistic world. It seems plausible that during the time of the patriarchs (second millennium BCE) the Hebrews were polytheistic. They observed the worship of many gods, found it convenient to worship at Canaanite shrines, and adopted pagan gods, most importantly El. Eventually the Israelites came to believe in a God of their own that they called Yahweh. During the time of the Judges and Kings of Israel and Judah (1200-586 BCE), the Israelites were probably a henotheistic people. As the peculiar God of Israel, Yahweh was worshiped by devotees who did not deny the existence of other gods.

During the time of the Babylonian Exile (sixth/fifth centuries BCE), the Israelites became a monotheistic people. The Second Isaiah was probably the first Israelite to proclaim Yahweh as the only God in existence, and that name was sometimes combined with Elohim to become "the Lord God." The gods of the pagans were only manufactured objects of wood or stone, not living gods. The highest attribute ascribed to Yahweh was holiness, and the holy God demanded ritual and ethical/moral holiness on the part of all who believed in and worshiped him.

The unique aspect of the Israelite/Jewish religion was its ethical monotheism, which set the standard of morality/ethics for much of the Western and some of the Eastern world for centuries. Any discussion that overlooks that point ignores what most distinguished the Hebrew/Israelite religion, with its deity or deities – female, male, or without gender – from those of the paganistic world in which it originated. As we turn our attention now to the NT, the influence of the Israelite/Jewish religion will continue to be very clear. Indeed, many authors of the NT wrote about Jesus and the early church in an effort to show how the prophecies of the OT were fulfilled through Jesus as Messiah, his followers, and the religion that developed, and eventually separated, from its roots in Judaism.

Part III

THE NEW TESTAMENT

Chapter 10

BACKGROUND OF THE CHRIST MOVEMENT

## Introduction

Although the NT begins with the gospels, they were not the earliest NT literature. Paul's letters are, dating from about 50 to 65 CE. And, while Matthew is the first gospel in the Bible, Mark was actually the first gospel to be written. Written at the earliest in 70 CE, Mark was a primary source for Matthew and Luke, which were written about 80 and 90 CE, respectively. The gospel of John was written about 100 CE. Some gospels were probably not written by the persons whose names are ascribed to them, but for convenience we use the names of the gospels as their authors. The author of Luke also wrote the book of Acts, so for that reason we sometimes use "Luke" for the author of Acts.

All NT writers belonged to groups of persons who were devoted followers of Christ and committed to faith in him. Eventually such groups were given various names, the best known being church or churches, which is the topic of the next chapter. The first uses of those names are in Paul's letters and Acts, from which we learn other names for Jesus' first followers and beliefs about him. Although Acts was not written before 90-100 CE, it contains information for early followers of Jesus several decades before.

We begin our study of the NT with the Epistles of Paul, as the earliest NT literature, and the book of Acts, with its information for Jesus' early followers. We only consider the seven letters of Paul that are universally regarded as genuine: 1 Thessalonians, 1 and 2 Corinthians, Galatians, Romans, Philippians, and Philemon. Sometimes, when referring to something in those letters, I may simply use "in Paul" or "Paul."

## New Testament Manuscripts

There are about 3,000 manuscripts of the NT, but four uncial codices are generally regarded as the most important. The oldest, from mid-fourth century, is *Codex Vaticanus*, which is called B. Containing the whole Bible in Greek, with some lacunae (missing sections) both in the OT and NT, B includes most of the LXX, apocryphal writings, and NT. *Codex Sinaiticus*, designated *aleph* and represented by the first letter of the Hebrew alphabet, is also from the fourth century. Known as S, its text generally agrees with that of B, but there are some variants. S is the work of at least two scribes, with corrections by others. It includes the Greek OT and NT, plus two non-canonical Christian writings, and it is the only one of the most important codices to have the whole NT.

*Codex Alexandrinus*, from the early fifth century, is known as A. It contains the Christian non-canonical writings of 1 and 2 Clement and the Jewish Psalms of Solomon. But, A is missing 30 psalms, several other sections of the OT, and also the first 24 chapters of Matthew, most of John 7–8, and 1 Corinthians 4–12. *Codex Beza*, designated D, is also from the fifth century. D has no OT writings and only the gospels, Acts, and a few verses of the post-Pauline epistles. Written in Greek and Latin on opposite pages, it is the oldest manuscript of the NT in two languages. The text is generally different from that of the other three codices, but sometimes it is useful in determining what some scholars believe to be more accurate readings.

An author's words were often dictated to and written by a person who might be a better writer, usually a scribe. As a title for one specially trained in writing and the study of the law, "scribe" was probably not used before the time of Ezra and Nehemiah (fifth century BCE). Ezra, a priest, was also known as "the scribe, a scholar of the text of the commandments of the Lord" (Ezra 7:11; see also Ezra 7:6; Nehemiah 8:1-8).

At the end of 1 Corinthians, after someone had finished writing the body of the letter, Paul writes: "I, Paul, write this greeting with my own hand" (1 Corinthians 16:21). The person who wrote the body of the letter from dictation may have been an amanuensis (from Latin, "by hand"). Such a person usually served as secretary or was hired to write from dictation. The amanuensis gives his name in Paul's letter to the Romans: "I Tertius, the writer of this letter, greet you in the Lord" (Romans 16:22). Tertius might have been a convert who may or may not have been paid for his work. These two examples do not mean that Paul did not or could not write. However, he may have had difficulty in doing so, perhaps because of bad eyes (see Galatians 4:12-15). He says to the converts at Galatia: "See what large letters I make when I am writing in my own hand!" (Galatians 6:11).

## Jesus as Messiah, Lord, Son of God, and Son of David

Just as the OT originated from the religious beliefs of those who wrote its various narratives and books, the NT is also a collection of religious literature written by persons expressing their beliefs that Jesus of Nazareth was unique because he transcended the mortality of humans. The first followers of Jesus were all Jews who believed that he was the long-awaited Messiah and that God raised him from the dead. Jesus' followers also believed that their Messiah and his resurrection had been predicted in the OT (Acts 2:29-36; see also Acts 3:17-26; 4:25-26; 5:42; 8:5). All the writings of the NT were written within a hundred years after Jesus' death.

In Acts Paul first preached in the synagogues that Jesus was "the Son of God" and that "he was the Messiah," as proven in the scriptures (Acts 9:19-22). Later Mark takes the Messiahship of Jesus back to Peter's confession, "You are the Messiah" (Mark 6:29); Matthew adds, "the Son of the living God" (Matthew 16:15); and Luke writes, "the Messiah of God" (Luke 9:20). But, the background for the belief in the Messiahship of Jesus is Judaism. The author of the *Psalms of Solomon* (mid-second century BCE) says that the messianic ruler will be "a righteous king" and that he will be "the Lord Messiah" (17:32; 18:7). In the Qumran Scrolls the religious leader of the Qumran Community was called "the teacher of righteousness" or "righteous teacher" (e.g., 1QpHab 1:13; 2:2; 5:10; 7:4-5; 8:3). "Righteous One" is a title for Jesus in Acts 3:14, where Peter accuses the Jews who do not believe in Jesus of rejecting "the Holy and Righteous One" (see also Acts 7:52; 22:14).

In the *Psalms of Solomon* the titles "Messiah" and "Lord" are combined as "the Lord Messiah" (17:32; 18:7). In Acts 2:36 Peter preaches that God made Jesus "both Lord and Messiah" (see also Acts 11:17; 15:26; 20:21). Paul uses a combination of "Jesus," "Messiah," and "Lord" in every letter, for example, "the Lord Jesus Christ" (1 Thessalonians 1:1), "Jesus Christ our Lord" (1 Corinthians 1:9), and "Christ Jesus our Lord" (1 Corinthians 15:31).

Genesis begins with a statement of faith: "In the beginning God" (Genesis 1:1). Paul writes that Jesus became "Son of God...by resurrection from the dead" (Romans 1:4). Mark begins with a confession of faith: "The beginning of the good news [gospel] of Jesus Christ, the Son of God" (Mark 1:1). Although "Son of God" does not occur as a title in the OT, the background for it is 2 Samuel 7:14. God says of a son to be born of David: "I will be a father to him, and he shall be a son to me." In a Jewish work known as 2 Esdras (end of first century CE), the writer uses "my son the Messiah" for the ruler to come and says that at the final judgment "my Son will be revealed" (2 Esdras 7:28; 13:32). Compare Paul's statement: "to wait for his Son from heaven" (1 Thessalonians 1:10; see also 1 Corinthians 15:28).

Although the Israelites believed that a special person was coming to free them from foreign rule and restore the kingdom to Israel, the designation "Messiah" is not applied to him in the OT. However, it was widely thought that this special person would be a descendant (son) of David (Isaiah 7:12-17; 11:1-9; Jeremiah 23:5-6; 33:14-22; Ezekiel 34:23). In the *Psalms of Solomon* and the Qumran Scrolls, the special ruler to come was referred to as "messiah," "son of David," and "lord messiah" (*Psalms of Solomon* 17:21–18:12). Jews at Qumran thought of themselves as a messianic community that should separate themselves to live in the desert as in Isaiah 40:3 and "prepare there the way of the Lord. As it is written, 'In the desert prepare the way of the Lord; make straight in the desert a highway for our God'" (1QS 8:12-16; 9;20; see also Mark 1:2-3; Matthew 3:3; Luke 3:4-5; John 1:23).

The earliest followers of Jesus also ascribed the title "Son of David" to Jesus, and Paul must have learned about it from them, because he says that Jesus "descended from David according to the flesh" (Romans 1:3). Matthew begins with "the genealogy of Jesus the Messiah, the son of David" (Matthew 1:1) and goes on at length to try to prove it (Matthew 1:2-17). "Son of David" is a favorite expression of Matthew (10 times; Mark, 3 times; Luke, 4 times).

## *The Messiah (Christ) Movement*

It was natural for Jews who believed that Jesus was the Messiah to think of him also as Son of David and Son of God. Just as naturally, they wanted to persuade other Jews to believe the same things, so they became missionaries for what they believed. An inclusive name for early followers of Jesus the Messiah is "the Christ movement," which included not only Jesus' first disciples but all who later joined the movement, known by various names. For information about the Christ movement, we depend primarily on Acts and Paul's letters, especially Galatians. Church, although in a primitive stage, is used in Acts and Paul's letters for this movement and later became the prevailing name.

According to Acts, Paul began his preaching in the synagogues of Damascus (Acts 9:19-20) and then in other cities during his travels (Acts 13-19). He sometimes spoke elsewhere to persons who may have heard a rumor that an interesting person was wandering around. He spoke to the crowd at Lystra (14:13-18), in the market place at Athens (17:17-21) and at the Areopagus there (17:22), in the house of Titius Justus, "a worshiper of God" (18:7), and in the lecture hall of Tyrannus (19:9). At first Paul had most success in synagogues, where he found other Greek-speaking Jews, Gentile converts to Judaism, worshipers of God who did not become full converts because they did not submit to circumcision, and curious visitors. In Acts 13:42-49; 14:1-2; and 17:1-4, 10-12, Paul was respected and persuasive enough to win followers among Jews and Gentiles.

Until some Jews began to persecute converts to the Christ movement, members met in synagogues (see John 9:22; 12:42-43). Eventually, the movement separated from Judaism and converts then met in houses of members, who were mostly Gentiles. Paul, the Greek-speaking Jew, appeared at just the right time to spread the Christ movement among Gentiles. Undoubtedly he made converts through his occupation of tentmaker or leather worker (Acts 18:1-3). He would first teach prospective converts "the word of God" (Acts 18:11), which occurs 12 times elsewhere in Acts and in 1 Thessalonians 2:13; 1 Corinthians 14:36; 2 Corinthians 2:17; 4:2; Romans 9:6; and Philippians 1:14. Paul would also teach about Jesus as "Son of God" and "Lord," terms that would get the attention of Gentiles that "Messiah" would not, because, unlike Jews, they were not expecting a Messiah.

## Names for Members of the Christ Movement in Paul and Acts

### Identifying Different Groups

In the earliest history of the Christ movement it is sometimes difficult to distinguish among its various groups. Names for members of ancient groups and their religions usually did not come by choice; they arose spontaneously and sometimes evolved over a long period of time, as Christians and Christianity did. Members of one religious group may not have intended to separate themselves completely from their origin but became separated by unintended circumstances. Sometimes adversaries of one group may have exaggerated differences and given that group a name.

Acts 6:1-2 is a clear example of this. There the names "disciples," "Hellenists," "Hebrews," "the Twelve," and "the whole community of the disciples" occur. We cannot tell who was included among the "disciples," but within them the Hellenists and Hebrews were probably separate groups. The Hellenists may have been Greek-speaking Jews who lived outside Palestine, or they may have been converted Gentiles who spoke Greek. "Hebrews" likely were Jews by race and language who spoke only Aramaic or Hebrew. However, they may have been Jews who were members of the

Christ movement and may or may not have spoken Greek. Paul was a Hebrew (2 Corinthians 11:22; Philippians 3:5) who spoke and wrote Greek.

"The Twelve" is used in Acts only in 6:1-2. It includes the eleven original disciples of Jesus plus Mathias, who was chosen by lot to replace Judas after he hanged himself (Matthew 27:3-10; Acts 1:21-23). In the phrase translated as "the whole community of the disciples" the words "whole community" is the Greek word *plêthos*, meaning "a great number," "multitude," or "crowd" (Acts 2:6). Because Luke liked to increase numbers, *plêthos* is a favorite word and occurs 31 times in the NT, 8 in the gospel of Luke and 16 in Acts. In Acts 6:2 the question is if *plêthos* is the same group as the "the disciples" in 6:1.

## Christian

If Christians today were asked what the name for the first followers of Jesus was and what their religion was called, they would probably respond "Christians" and "Christianity." The term Christian, however, occurs only three times in the NT, twice in Acts (11:26; 26:28) and in 1 Peter 4:16. First Peter was written to Christians who were living somewhere in Asia Minor and were suffering persecution about the end of the first century CE. The author encourages them by saying that, if they suffer for the name of Christ, they are blessed. They must not be immoral in any way nor think it is a disgrace to suffer for the name Christian they bear (1 Peter 4:14-16). In fact, Christians were set apart by their unique moral behavior. For that reason, "Christian" was used as a word of scorn or ridicule, as in pagan literature and on the lips of Agrippa in Acts 26:28: "Are you so quickly persuading me to become a Christian?"

Luke probably wrote Acts about the same time as 1 Peter was written and, therefore, was familiar with the designation. But, there is no evidence in either Paul or Acts that early converts used the name Christian to refer to themselves. Nor is there any evidence that, in the conflict with the Jews, either the Jews or the converts used that term. Even in the gospel of John, where antagonism between Jews who believed in Jesus and those who did not was at a breaking point, Christian does not occur. Those Jews who confessed Jesus as the Messiah were to be put out of the synagogue (John 9:22; 12:42). John was written about 100 CE or a little later, and after that the name Christian was more widely used.

## Christianity

Christianity originated within Judaism and did not become a separate religion until after the gospel of John was written. The name Christianity occurs nowhere in the NT. Judaism as a name for the life and religion of the Jews arose during the Maccabean Era in the second century BCE. The writer of 2 Maccabees 2:21 refers to those "Jews who fought bravely for Judaism" (*Ioudaismos*) against despotic Greek rulers (see also 2 Maccabees 8:1; 14:38; 4 *Maccabees* 4:26). Paul uses *Ioudaismos* when writing to the Galatians about his growth in and zeal for his own religion (Galatians 1:13-14). If Paul had thought of himself as a Christian and his religion as Christianity, would he not have used the designations in his controversies with his Jewish adversaries? That question would also apply for the author of John.

The name Christianity (*Christianismos*) for the religion of Christ's devotees was first used by Ignatius, a bishop in the church at Antioch, about the end of the first century. Christianity had become a religion separate from Judaism, and his writing reveals antagonism toward Judaism.

### Designations for Followers of Christ

"Believers" is not used as often as we might suppose from its use in the *NRSV*, where it is sometimes substituted for other designations. In Greek, "believing" is expressed three ways: "faithful" or "believing," "the faithful ones" or "believers," and "the believing ones" or "believers." In 2 Corinthians 6:14-16 Paul places "believers" in antithesis to non-believers and links the former with righteousness, light, and Christ and the latter with wickedness, darkness, and Beliar (the devil). Here, as in 1 Peter, moral conduct of believers is stressed.

In pagan society "brothers" was used for members of religious associations. And, Acts 22:5 and 28:17, 21 imply that the name was used by Jews when referring to other Jews. Paul also uses it that way in Romans 9:3, and it occurs in every letter. Because "brothers" is used in Acts 1:15 and often thereafter, the name did not originate with Paul when referring to members of the Christ movement. The name would have appealed to Jews and non-Jews, and, therefore, may have been one of the earliest names, along with "disciples," for members of the Christ movement.

As in pagan society, "disciple" was used to distinguish a pupil or student from his teacher. See Matthew 10:24, "A disciple is not above the teacher" (see also Luke 6:40). "Disciples" occurs in Acts 6:1 and is not limited to the first followers of Jesus. They are "the Twelve" in 6:2 and "the Eleven" in 2:14 (see Luke 24:9, 33). Paul does not mention "disciples," but he uses "apostles" as a comparable designation (see 1 Corinthians 9:5; 15:7; Galatians 1:17). Besides Acts, "disciples" occurs in the NT only in the four gospels, where the same Greek word (*mathetai*) refers to disciples of John the Baptist (Mark 2:18; Matthew 9:14; Luke 5:53; 7:18; John 1:35; 3:25) and of the Pharisees (Mark 2:18; Luke 5:33).

The Greek *hoi hagioi* means "the holy ones," which is translated, for example, as "saints" in Romans 1:7 (*NRSV*), "his people" (*REB*), or "his holy people" (*NJB*). "Holy ones" is one of the earliest names for followers of Christ, and its background is thoroughly Jewish, beginning with the OT. The basic meaning of holiness in the Bible is "dedicated," "separated," "set apart" (for God). With respect to human behavior, Leviticus 19:2 became the basic text for Jews: "You shall be holy, for I the Lord your God am holy."

Holy persons were thought to be set apart as members of a community of holy people. See LXX Leviticus 20:26: "You shall be holy to me, because I the Lord your God am holy, the one who separated you from all the nations to be mine." Thus, holiness was associated with God's people. See Deuteronomy 7:6, "You are a people holy to the Lord your God" (also Exodus 22:31; Psalm 16:3; LXX Psalm 37:28). This is precisely the basis for the Qumran Community, and it is reflected in Acts 20:32 put on the lips of Paul. He commends the elders from the church in Ephesus to the grace of God "to give you the inheritance among all who are sanctified [made holy]" (from *hagiazô*, "make holy"; see Isaiah 4:3; 6:3). As "holy ones" members of the Qumran Community are to seek God, do what is right, refrain from evil and maintain the good, and live perfectly before God (1QS 1:1-10). Their holiness is described in 1QS 8:4-11. God's chosen ones are to inherit the lot of the "holy ones" (1QS 11:5-8; see also 1 QM 3:4; 8:4-11).

"Holy ones" is Paul's most distinctive name for members of the Christ movement, and he uses it in every letter except 1 Thessalonians (his first letter) and Galatians. When Paul wrote Galatians, he was probably so angry with the converts who were being persuaded to follow one of his adversaries that he thought they did not deserve that name. However, Paul does use the term "holiness," as in 1 Thessalonians 3:13 when he prays that God might strengthen the converts' hearts in holiness so that they might be blameless at the coming of Jesus "with all his holy ones" (*NRSV*, "saints"). In 1 Thessalonians 4:4 Paul also exhorts the converts to control their bodies in holiness. In 4:7 he reminds them that he had strongly warned them that God did not call them for immorality but to live in holiness. These thoughts became the basis for his later designation of converts as "holy ones."

Paul uses words for holiness some 60 times, and each time the basic meaning is set apart for holiness of life, or righteousness. Already when he wrote 1 Thessalonians 4:7, Paul thought of his converts as called by God for holiness of life. He addresses the Roman converts: "to all God's beloved in Rome, who are called to be holy ones" (Romans 1:7; see also 1 Corinthians 1:2). Paul says the Corinthian converts are a community of righteous persons who should be capable of settling disputes among themselves rather than by a court of unrighteous persons (1 Corinthians 6:1-11). As "holy ones," the converts are set apart from pagans, who are not holy because they do not believe in God and live accordingly.

In Acts the use of "holy ones" is confined to accounts of Paul's "conversion" and adjoining narratives (9:13, 32, 41; 26:10). The first members of the Christ movement in Jerusalem were called "holy ones." This fact, together with Paul's characteristic use of that name for his converts, indicates that "holy ones" was one of the earliest names for members of the Christ movement. Moreover, the emphasis on holiness is continued after they became known as Christians. Recall that in 1 Peter 4:14-18, the author exhorts his readers to refrain from wrongdoing and not to feel disgraced because they bear the name Christian.

"The Way" is closely related to "holy ones" because it means a moral way of life by obeying God's commands. It occurs first in Genesis 18:19, the oldest source of the Pentateuch. God chose Abraham to charge his descendants "to keep the way of the Lord by doing righteousness and justice" (see also Judges 2:16-22; 2 Kings 21:20-22; Psalm 18:2). "Way" is often used metaphorically with the verb "walk" in the ethical sense of "conduct one's life" or "live." Samuel will instruct the Israelites "in the good and the right way" (1 Samuel 12:23; see also Psalm 119:27; Proverbs 8:20). In Jeremiah 10:2 "the way" is used negatively of non-Jews when Jeremiah exhorts the Israelites: "Do not learn the way of the nations."

Members of the Qumran Community pledged to do what is good and right before the Lord, to abstain from all evil and to practice truth and righteousness, to live perfectly before the Lord, and to conduct their lives perfectly in all the ways of God (1QS 1:1-12; 3:9-10; see also 1QS 4:20-23; 9:17-18). In Acts 2:28 "the ways of life," a phrase from LXX Psalm 16:11, is put on the lips of Peter. Paul sent Timothy to remind the converts at Corinth of his "ways in Christ Jesus" (1 Corinthians 4:17). Love is "a more excellent way," even than "all faith" (1 Corinthians 12:31).

Acts first uses "Way" for those converts Saul (Paul) sought out to persecute (9:2). Apollos, an eloquent Jew from Alexandria who knew the scriptures, "had been instructed in the Way of the Lord" and "taught accurately the things concerning Jesus" (18:24-25). Acts has "Way" five times elsewhere, and each time it is associated with Paul (19:9, 23; 22:4;

24:14, 22). In light of the usage in the OT, Qumran, and related information in Acts and Paul, "The Way," understood as a way of life, was also one of the earliest names for members of the Christ movement.

In Acts 24:14 "Way" is called a "sect." In his defense against charges by the Jews, Paul admits "that according to the Way, which they [the Jews] call a sect, I worship the God of our ancestors" (Acts 24:2-8). Tertullus, the spokesman for the Jews, accuses Paul of being "a pestilent fellow" and "a ringleader of the sect of the Nazarenes."

Although the Greek word *hairesis* is often translated as "sect," it is not the best understanding of the word, which comes from the verb meaning "choose." Members of a *hairesis* have made choices of particular principles or ideas from several options. It does not imply separation as "sect" does. Paul uses it twice (1 Corinthians 11:19; Galatians 5:20), where it is translated as "factions" both times in the *NRSV*, but it does not imply separation either time. "Party" would be the best choice, for example, "party of the Pharisees" (Acts 15:5, *REB*, *NJB*). Members of the parties of the Pharisees and Sadducees were both Jews by faith and life, although with different opinions. "The Sadducees say that there is no resurrection, or angel, or spirit; but the Pharisees acknowledge all three" (Acts 23:8).

Religious assemblies of Jews and pagans were sometimes represented with the Greek *plêthos*, meaning "a large number," "multitude," or "crowd"; sometimes "people" is its equivalent. In Acts 14:1 "a great number (*plêthos*) of both Jews and Greeks (Gentiles) became believers." *Plêthos* is sometimes the equivalent of *ekklēsia*, meaning "assembly." See, for example, Acts 4:32, where it is said of all who held their possessions in common, "The whole group (*plêthos*) of those who believed were of one heart and soul" (see also Acts 6:2). The meaning of *plêthos* has to be understood in light of its contexts. In Acts 4:32 the group was probably limited to those who had things in common, but in Acts 6:2; 6:5 "the whole community (*plêthos*) of the disciples" may be all the believers other than the Twelve.

At Antioch the apostles gathered the congregation (*plêthos*) together, where *plêthos* is the equivalent of *ekklēsia* (Acts 15:30). In Acts 19:9-10 "congregation" (*plêthos*) refers to the disbelieving Jews in a synagogue meeting, in contrast to the disciples. In Acts 25:24 "the whole Jewish community" is also *plêthos*, as is "the whole assembly of the people" (Jews) in Luke 1:10. Thus, Luke can use *ekklēsia* and *plêthos* in various ways, both with respect to members of the Christ movement and unbelievers.

"The faith" may have been a synonym for "the Way" or for "the brothers." It is used as a synonym for the former in Galatians 1:23, where "the faith" is the same as "the Way" that Paul sought to persecute (Acts 9:1-2; see also

Galatians 3:23-25). See also Acts 13:8, where the magician Elymas opposed the apostles "and tried to turn the proconsul away from the faith." Acts 6:7; 14:22; 16:5; 1 Corinthians 16:13; and 2 Corinthians 13:5 belong to the same category.

It is important to understand that "the faith" does not yet have the same connotation as in some later NT literature. In the Pastoral Epistles (about 100-120 CE), "the faith" sometimes is the orthodoxy of the church in contrast to unorthodox beliefs that were threatening it. With respect to the resurrection, false teachers were "upsetting the faith of some" (2 Timothy 2:17-18; see also 1 Timothy 1:19; 3:9, 13; 4:1, 6; 5:8; 6:10, 12, 21; 2 Timothy 2:18; 3:8; 4:7; Titus 1:13; Jude 1:3). By the time of these writings, church organization was being established, hymns and creeds were known (1 Timothy 2:4-5; 3:16; 2 Timothy 2:10-13), and some doctrines had become fixed. Church officials were "not to teach any different doctrine" (1 Timothy 1:3-5) and "preach with sound doctrine" (Titus 1:9; 2:1). There is also an emphasis on sound moral character for both church officials and members. "A bishop, as God's servant, must be blameless" (Titus 1:7). It appears that women were active in the churches, and like the men, they were to be of upright character (e.g., Titus 2:1-10).

## The Book of Acts

Although Luke has been called "the first church historian," he did not write about things as they actually happened. He was as much a theologian and literary figure as historian, and he uses literary devices that make it difficult to separate facts from his own religious beliefs. For example, as with ancient historians, Luke composes speeches that present his views and puts them on the lips of other persons.

Luke also uses the literary techniques of repetition and variation. Paul's so-called "conversion" is narrated three times: 9:1-19 (in Luke's words), 22:1-16 (in Paul's words before Jews), and 26:12-18 (in Paul's words before Agrippa), each with obvious differences. This makes it difficult to distinguish fact from fiction, especially since Paul says nothing specifically about it in his letters. The vision of Cornelius, the Roman centurion, is told twice, first in Luke's words (10:3-8) and then in the words of Cornelius (10:30-33). In between scenes Luke narrates a vision Peter has about clean and unclean foods (10:9-16), with Peter then alluding to that vision and changing the subject from foods to people. Peter says that God told him not to call anyone common or unclean (10:28-29). Cornelius's virtues of reverencing God, charitable gifts, and prayer are stressed twice, first in

Luke's words ((10:1-2), then by Cornelius' reply to Peter about his own vision (10:30-32).

Thus, Luke justifies the association of Peter the Jew with Gentiles and the conversion of Cornelius, a Gentile, to the Christ movement. At Cornelius' suggestion, Peter begins a speech with the statement that God does not show partiality. Anyone who reverences God and does what is right is accepted by him. Then Peter's words are a summary of Luke's theology, followed by Luke's words that the Holy Spirit (a favorite emphasis of Luke) was responsible for the Gentiles being receptive to the apostles' preaching (Acts 10:34–11:1). In reality, the attempt by the apostles to convert many Jews to the Christ movement failed, so the movement turned to Gentiles. And this raised the problem of circumcision for converted Gentiles.

Remember that God promised Abraham that his descendants would be a great nation. In turn, Abraham promised that his male offspring would be circumcised (Genesis 17:1-27). Jews believed that they were God's people and that any male Gentile who wanted to become a member of the Christ movement had to be circumcised and obey certain Jewish laws. This view is stated clearly in the conference at Jerusalem, where Peter and James were the leaders, but easily resolved by Luke (Acts 15:5-35) with the letter from the conference to the church at Antioch, where Paul, Barnabas, and others were the leaders. According to that letter, Gentiles were to abstain from eating meat of an animal sacrificed to idols, from the blood of strangled animals, and from illicit sexual activity (Acts 15:19-21, 28-29). The commands in that letter were accepted with rejoicing, and Paul and his companions resumed their mission activity.

Luke too easily resolves the factions of Peter and Paul, apparently wanting to present the church of his time in a favorable light by showing a united front. However, according to Paul in Galatians and Romans, circumcision for Gentile converts was still the main problem between Paul and his Jewish adversaries. Paul never mentions the assembly at Jerusalem in his letters.

Indeed, it is difficult to determine the difference between history and religion in Acts. When Acts and Paul disagree, we should probably choose Paul over Acts, because his letters are in his own words. Paul and Luke, like other biblical writers, were concerned with their own beliefs, not history. For Paul, those beliefs were primarily about God and the morality of converts in his churches and, secondarily, about Jesus. At least with Paul's letters, though, we hear his beliefs directly, whereas in Acts Luke's theology and literary style create dilemmas for us in trying to differentiate his own ideas from those of Paul.

## Chapter Summary

All the writings of the NT were written within a hundred years after Jesus' death, and Paul's letters, the earliest NT literature, were written from about 50 to 65 CE. Since the letters of Paul are the earliest NT writings and Acts contains information for the followers of Jesus decades before it was written, they provide a logical starting point for NT study. As with the OT, there are no simple answers that provide insightful understanding about the NT or about Jesus and his life and teachings. NT writers in general believed that Jesus taught as a human, was crucified, and rose from the dead, and each author wrote from his own religious convictions, not from a historical perspective. While the NT certainly provides insight into the early followers of Jesus and what they believed, differing accounts and discrepancies leave us with many unanswered questions.

Jesus' first followers were Jews who thought he was the Messiah prophesied in the OT, and Jesus came to be known as Lord, Son of God, and Son of David. Early followers of his were part of the Christ movement and were referred to by a number of different names, some of which had their origins in Judaism. While we often think of these early followers of Jesus as the first Christians and their religion as Christianity, that term never appears in the NT, nor does the designation "Christian Church." In the next chapter we consider "church" and "churches" as names for groups of members belonging to the Christ movement.

Chapter 11

CHURCH AND CHURCHES

*Introduction*

The Greek word generally translated as "church" is *ekklēsia*, which means "a calling out" and then what is called out – "assembly," "congregation," or "community." In Greek society the word was used of regularly convened assemblies or town meetings. In the LXX *ekklēsia* is used to translate Hebrew words with the same meaning.

There is a difference of opinion and general uncertainty about the origin of the name "church." The position of the Roman Catholic Church is that it goes back to the time of Jesus and that Peter was its foundation (see Matthew 16:13-19). Since *ekklēsia* is a Greek term, it may have originated after the Christ movement came to include Greek-speaking Gentiles. First used by Paul, no other name for members of the Christ movement has endured as long as "church." Referring to both particular communities of Christians and to a universal group, the church today is a much more formalized and highly organized institution than in the NT.

*Understanding Church and Churches in Paul*

*Paul's Use of Church*

Paul uses "church" in three ways. The first refers to a local group or groups of converts, for example, "the church of God that is in Corinth" (1 Corinthians 1:1) and "the churches of Galatia" (Galatians 1:2). Paul's second use of "church" is for converts everywhere as a body, for example, Paul was "persecuting the church of God and was trying to destroy it" (Galatians 1:13). Within these first two categories, it is sometimes difficult to tell what Paul means. He reminds the converts of his "ways in Christ Jesus" as he teaches "them everywhere in every church" (1 Corinthians 4:17). Here he addresses the church at Corinth, but what about "everywhere in every church"? Are just the churches that Paul established intended, or are churches founded by other apostles also included? The same questions apply for "in all the churches" (1 Corinthians 7:17; 14:33-34) and for women not speaking "in the churches" (1 Corinthians 14:35).

In 1 Corinthians 6:1-6 Paul distinguishes between church members and persons outside the church and also between unbelievers and believers. And the words "who have no standing in the church" indicate distinctions among members. Such distinctions coincide with Paul's statement, "God has appointed in the church first apostles, second prophets, third teachers" (1 Corinthians 12:28). Although writing to the church at Corinth, "the church" is probably the universal body of believers.

Paul's third use of "church" refers to the assembly of converts at worship, for example, "when you come together as a church" (1 Corinthians 11:18). He speaks of all members of a local group meeting together to observe the Lord's Supper (1 Corinthians 11:18-22) and for other worship (1 Corinthians 14:1-37), which promoted the spiritual and moral well-being of the members (14:26).

The background of *ekklēsia* for Paul is Jewish, especially in the way he associates God with it. This is a unique aspect of his thought and distinguishes it from the use of *ekklēsia* in the pagan world. See, for example, "assembly for the Lord your God" (Deuteronomy 16:8), "the assembly of the people of God," (Judges 20:2), and "the assembly of God" (Nehemiah 13:1). Similar expressions are frequent, such as "the whole congregation of Israel" (Exodus 12:3; Numbers 14:5-7) and "the whole congregation of Israelites" (Sirach 50:20; see also 1 Maccabees 4:59). In the Qumran Scrolls there are several synonyms meaning "congregation" or "community." Members shall bring their possessions into "the Community of God" (1QS 1:12; 2:22). See also "the congregation of Israel," "in the congregation," and "all the congregation" (1QSa 1:20-23). As with the usages in the OT and Qumran, "church" was not just the assembly as a meeting but the people themselves. This is another difference between churches and pagan assemblies.

Paul uses "the church of God" (e.g., 1 Corinthians 1:2; 2 Corinthians 1:1; Galatians 1:13), "the churches of God" (e.g., 1 Corinthians 11:16), and "all the churches of Christ" (Romans 16:16), the latter unique to Paul. At times churches other than the local one are specifically mentioned, for example, "the churches of Galatia" (1 Corinthians 16:1; Galatians 1:2). Sometimes the local congregation as an independent church is meant; sometimes unity with other local assemblies as a universal body is also intended. Paul prefers "the church of God" (see "the Israel of God" in Galatians 6:16), in keeping with his theology. He never uses "the church of Christ," and his "churches of Christ" (Romans 16:16, if from Paul) distinguishes them from other assemblies, both pagan and the synagogues.

*House Churches*

Converts to the Christ movement, at first mostly Jews, probably met in synagogues. Then, as Gentiles joined the movement, converts met in the houses of members for the celebration of the Lord's Supper and for other worship. Such assemblies came to be known as "house churches." See "the church in their house" (1 Corinthians 16:19; Romans 16:5; see also Philemon 1:2). Most houses were probably too small to accommodate many people, especially if unbelievers were also present (1 Corinthians 14:22-25). Therefore, "the whole church" coming together in 1 Corinthians 14:23 must be the local "church" meeting in someone's house, not the universal body or a church building. Such house assemblies would be the best situation for making a convert or two (14:23-25), but it is also plausible that local church members met in some public place. See Acts 19:8-10 about Paul speaking in the synagogue and then in the lecture hall of Tyrannus.

As in 1 Corinthians 11:1-16, women were present at worship, yet Paul says in 1 Corinthians 14:33-35 that "as in all the churches women should be silent." On that issue, how many persons today agree to do so because "The Bible Says So"? And, this certainly seems to contradict Paul's words other places, as in 1 Corinthians 7:2-5, where he makes the wife equal with the husband in marital relationships. Worshipers were to judge for themselves about women praying with heads unveiled and the length of women's and men's hair (1 Corinthians 11:4-16).

It could be that Paul, as a Jew, thought women should not speak in the churches since they did not do so in the synagogues. He alludes to the passage in Genesis 3:16 about the man ruling over the woman, but nothing is said there about her silence. Recall that Adam got into trouble with God because he listened to the woman talking to him and ate the forbidden fruit. Had some women become so influential in the church at Corinth that Paul was afraid men would get into trouble with the authorities in the church if they listened to their wives speak? If you think Paul's words are stringent, those of the author of 1 Timothy 2:8-12 are more so: women should dress modestly in appropriate and inexpensive clothing, have no braided hair, jewelry, "but with good works, as is proper for women who profess reverence for God," learn in silence, and be completely submissive. No woman is permitted "to teach or to have authority over a man; she is to keep silent." Again, although "The Bible Says So," these are beliefs understandable in biblical times but not in ours.

In one of the churches where I frequently taught church groups and Sunday School teachers, I usually raised the question about believing all the Bible says. Session after session, one woman kept saying, "Well, *I do* believe everything the Bible says." Finally, I said, "Mrs Tracy [name changed], if you believed everything the Bible says, you would not tell me that because Paul says that women should keep silent in the churches." I don't know if she still believed everything or not, but she stopped saying so, at least!

*Understanding Church and Churches in Acts*
In Acts the treatment of "church" is vague and inconsistent. It is especially difficult to distinguish between "church" as a local group and the generalized meaning. For example, in Acts 5:11 "great fear seized the whole church," probably a local group, as in "the church in Jerusalem" (Acts 8:1). Both may imply other churches. Churches as local ones and the generalized "church" are combined in "the church throughout Judea, Galilee, and Samaria" and "it increased in numbers" (Acts 9:31).

Acts 8:1-3, about Paul persecuting the converts in Jerusalem, raises a question. That Paul persecuted "the church of God" in a universal sense is confirmed in his letters (Galatians 1:13, 22-23; Philippians 3:6). His statements mean that he persecuted followers of Jesus wherever he could find them. However, Paul nowhere mentions doing so in Jerusalem. Moreover, in Galatians 1:22-23 Paul says that after many years he "was still unknown by sight to the churches in Judea." They had only heard reports about him. Paul may have been hated as a persecutor; but if he had entered "house after house" and dragged away men and women and imprisoned them, he would hardly have been unknown or forgotten. Therefore, Acts 8:1-3 is not to be taken as history but attributed, instead, to Luke's special interest in the church in Jerusalem.

In Acts "the church of God" occurs only in 20:28, part of a speech of Paul to the elders of the church at Ephesus that is highly Christianized. "All the flock," "overseers," "shepherd the church," and "the blood of his own" ("Son," added in *NRSV*) indicate a more advanced church in general. Paul does not use any of those metaphors in the same way, but later in the gospels Jesus has become a shepherd and his followers are the flock (Matthew 26:31; Luke 12:32; John 10:12-16). Titles for church officials not part of the church of Paul's time are also mentioned in later epistles. A bishop (overseer) must know how to take "care of the church of God" (1 Timothy 3:5), and elders are "to tend the flock of God" (1 Peter 5:2). "Overseers,"

Luke's word in Acts 20:28, occurs in 1 Timothy 3:2: "an overseer must be above reproach" (see also Titus 1:7). See also "overseers and servers" (Greek) in Philippians 1:1. The metaphors and terms of later times were undoubtedly put into Paul's speech by Luke.

Luke was very adept at adapting words about persons and events to the situation at hand. While in Acts 20:28 he thinks of "church" as a divine institution, he had previously used *ekklēsia* with reference to a pagan assembly in the context of pagan gods and goddesses in Ephesus: "the assembly was in confusion," "in the regular assembly," and "he dismissed the assembly" (Acts 19:32, 39, 41). In Acts 7:38 *ekklēsia* is correctly used in the Hebrew understanding when Stephen, in a speech (composed by Luke), says of Moses: [He] "was in the congregation (*ekklēsia*) in the wilderness."

## Luke as "Historian"

Although Luke was a kind of "historian," he was not writing about events as they actually happened. This is clear in his portrayal of the "church," which is oversimplified, because the conflict between Jews and members of the Christ movement is evident in most NT writings, including the gospel of Luke. Similarly, Paul's travels surely did not take place in three journeys so systematically as Luke presents them (Acts 13:2–14:28; 15:36–18:22; 18:23–21:17), with a trying trip to Rome at the end (27:1–28:16).

### The Role of the Spirit in Luke's "History"

The (Holy) Spirit is the motivating force behind Luke's "history," both with respect to persons and events. Peter says that the death of Judas fulfilled the scripture that the Holy Spirit had foretold (Acts 1:15-16; Psalm 41:9). For an excellent example of how difficult it is to give a simple answer about what "the Bible says," compare the death of Judas by hanging (Matthew 27:5) with gory details of his death in Acts 1:18. In Luke 24:49 Luke says that The Father promised the Spirit's coming and has it predicted in Acts 1:8 and fulfilled at Pentecost, when all present "were filled with the Holy Spirit" (2:4).

Many of Luke's characters are filled with or received the Spirit, including Peter (Acts 4:8), Stephen (6:5), and others (10:47; 13:52; see also 5:3, 9; 8:17, 29; 9:17, 31; 11:12). "In the comfort of the Holy Spirit" the church "increased in numbers" (9:31). The Spirit sometimes caused negative reactions: "filled with the Holy Spirit," Paul struck the magician blind (13:8-11), forbade the apostles "to speak the word in Asia," and did not allow them to go into Bithynia (16:6-7).

Acts ends as it began – with activity of the Holy Spirit. Paul tells the Jews in Rome that the Holy Spirit was right in predicting (LXX Isaiah 6:9-10) that they would reject the apostles' preaching. So, the message of salvation "has been sent to the Gentiles; they will listen" (Acts 28:25-29), a theme often repeated in Acts (9:15; 11:18; 13:46-48; 14:1-5, 27; ch. 15; 18:6; 21:11-25; 22:21; 26:17-23). The prophecy of the Spirit being effective in the lives of witnesses "to the ends of the earth" (1:8) is fulfilled with the arrival of Paul in Rome, the hub of the Roman Empire.

*The Role of Angels and Visions in Luke's "History"*
Luke surely thought that the Holy Spirit shaped the "history" of the "church." An equally compelling force behind Luke's "history" is his belief in angels and visions. The Greek word for "angel" is *aggelos*, which means "messenger," and that is the role angels play in Acts. We deal with them only as they appear in the visions. The word *aggelos* occurs 176 times in the NT, of which 25 are in the gospel of Luke, 21 in Acts, and 67 in Revelation, the classic biblical work on angels and visions.

Luke interrupts the account of the early mission activity of the Christ movement among Jews to report Paul's visionary experience on the road to Damascus, where he was going to persecute "any who belonged to the Way." Although this incident, with the vision of Ananias, is probably the best known (Acts 9:1-19), read about other interesting visions in Acts 2:17; 9:1-12; 10:3-8; 11:5-17; 12:6-11; and 16:9-10.

Luke uses images of angels and visions in Acts to give credibility to his main characters. In doing so he reflects the time when belief in angels, demons, spirits, visions, and miracles was universal. We have learned how literary style and personal interests and beliefs affected what Luke wrote in his "history." At the same time, it also shows how difficult it is to understand insightfully what "the Bible says."

## *Final Thoughts about the Early Church*

All authors of NT writings were faithful church members, but their beliefs were personal and proclaimed to others in the hope of winning converts to the Christ movement. However, there is very little specific evidence of what beliefs were required for admission to early churches. This is in strong contrast to the beliefs in the creeds and catechisms that are taught in churches today for persons wanting to join "the church." This is true even for the statements about the founding of the church on Peter ("this rock"). Peter confesses that Jesus is the Messiah (Mark 8:29). Matthew adds, "the

Son of the living God" (Matthew 15:15), and Luke has "The Messiah of God" (Luke 9:20). In the three passages "Messiah" is the point.

In the only other reference to "church" in Matthew, the point is not a matter of faith but of moral conduct. If a brother sins against another, the two should try to settle the issue in private. If that fails, and the guilty person refuses to listen to two or three witnesses, and if he is still not convinced, the matter is to be told to the church. If the offender refuses to listen to the church, he is to be to the offended "as a Gentile and a tax collector," that is, an outcast (Matthew 18:15-17). No specific offense is stated, but Matthew's words about the offender amount to expulsion from the church. Paul says that the Corinthians should have removed the immoral man from among them (1 Corinthians 5:1-2) and that members should "drive out the wicked person from among" them, a direct quotation from Deuteronomy 17:7. Notice that offenders are put out because of immoral conduct, not because they did not believe something the church was teaching about Jesus.

*Chapter Summary*

In trying to learn about Jesus and his early followers, we could turn to the gospels, as the first books in the NT. However, the letters of Paul were written before any other book in the NT, and Acts contains information for early followers of Jesus several decades before it was written. In Paul's letters and in Acts, written by the author of the gospel of Luke, we learn about the early "church" and "churches" of the followers of Jesus. Paul's letters were written by him and probably provide a more accurate account of the early "church" than does Luke. Athough sometimes called the first church "historian," Luke's theology and literary style provide challenges in trying to determine actual history.

The focus of the next chapter is Paul and his thought. By closely examining the seven letters of Paul that are considered to be genuine and the book of Acts, we can gain further understanding about the early churches that eventually became institutions separate from the Jewish synagogues. Like them, the churches struggled for survival in a pagan world.

## Chapter 12

### PAUL AND HIS THOUGHT

*Introduction*

If Christians today were asked what "the Bible says" about Paul and his thought, most would probably mention the story of his "conversion" on the road to Damascus and his change of name from Saul to Paul, the letters (epistles) he wrote to churches, and his teachings about baptism. They might also identify him as the first Christian. And, more than likely, they would also be familiar with his doctrine of justification by faith in Christ.

Christians, ever since Martin Luther (1483–1546) opposed the Catholic doctrine that good works were essential for salvation, have generally been taught that being justified by faith is the same as being saved. That has been a major dispute between Catholic and Protestant theologians. Scholars on both sides of the issue have tried to reach a compromise in order to bring the two groups closer to unity. The Roman Catholic Church and the Lutheran World Federation are about to sign a *Joint Declaration on the Doctrine of Justification*, and some Methodists may also sign.

In this chapter, we will examine closely Paul and his thought in search of insightful understanding and in an attempt to determine the meaning of Paul's writings. We will seek answers to questions such as whether or not Paul can be called the first Christian and if he actually was converted to Christianity. Perhaps most importantly, our study of some of the Greek words Paul used will reveal whether or not the joint declaration, mentioned above and quoted later, expresses accurately Paul's concept of justification by faith. The simple answer would be that Christians are saved through faith in Jesus, not good works. "The Bible Says So!" But the real question here is whether or not that's what the Bible really says and, more specifically, what Paul actually said and intended. Before tackling that issue, we start with his religious experience on the road to Damascus.

## Paul's Special Religious Experience on the Road to Damascus

*According to Acts*

The subject of endless speculation, Paul's experience on the way to Damascus in Acts 9:3-8 (1); 22:6-11 (2), and 26:9-18 (3) is confusing because of its three different accounts. After studying the accounts, represented by the numbers in parentheses, we will consider what Paul says or does not say in his letters about his supernatural experiences.

All three accounts agree that Paul was on the way to Damascus with the authority of the Jews to persecute those of "the Way" (1, 2) or "the saints" (3). All agree on a light from heaven, but (1) adds flashed around Paul, (2) has "a great light," and in (3) it was brighter than the sun and shone around Paul and his companions. In (1, 2) Paul fell to the ground, but in (3) "We had all fallen to the ground." The voice saying, "Saul, Saul, why do you persecute me?" is in all accounts, but (3) adds "in the Hebrew language" before the voice, "It hurts you to kick against the goads," after it, Saul's question, "Who are you, Lord?" is the same in all three, and all have "Jesus" as the response, but (2) adds, "of Nazareth." In (1) the voice also tells Paul to "get up and enter the city," for which (2) has "Damascus; there you will be told everything that has been assigned to you to do." These words of (2) imply a divine plan not so apparent in the others.

In (1) the men "traveling with" Paul "stood speechless because they heard the voice but saw no one." In (2) the men who "were with" Paul "saw the light but did not hear the voice of the one who was speaking to" him, an outright contradiction of (1). In (1) Saul got up without being told to do so, but in (2) Paul asked, "What am I to do, Lord," and the Lord told him to "get up and go to Damascus."

The order of words in the narratives is sometimes arranged differently, obviously a stylistic trait of Luke. In (3) the words to get up are a part of the Lord's answer to Paul's question, "Who are you, Lord?" And, the words "I am Jesus..." are followed with "But get up and stand on your feet; for I have appeared to you for this purpose, to appoint you to serve and testify to the things in which you have seen me, and to those in which I will appear to you." The Lord continues by saying that he will save Paul from the Jews and the Gentiles to whom he is being sent to fulfill several OT predictions. This is "so that they may receive forgiveness of sins and a place among those who are sanctified [made holy; that is, "holy ones"] by faith in me."

In (3) Paul's words to Agrippa (Acts 26:19-23) illustrate how the words the Lord had said are a part of Luke's theology. The passage seems to replace the story of Ananias and his vision in (1) and (2), again with variations and additions. In (1) Ananias lays his hand on Paul, who is filled with the Holy Spirit and baptized, but there is neither a reference to his sins being forgiven as in (2) nor a reference to his baptism in (3).

The words of Ananias (2) that Paul is to see "the Righteous One" occur only there in the three stories. However, in a speech at Jerusalem, Peter accuses the Jews of rejecting "the Holy and Righteous One" (Acts 3:14), and Stephen, also in a speech, accuses the Jews of killing "those who foretold the coming of the Righteous One" (7:52), an allusion to an OT prophecy. In (1) after the vision, although Paul's "eyes were open, he could see nothing," so they led him by the hand into Damascus. In (2) Paul says, "Since I could not see because of the brightness of that light," those who were with him took his hand and led him to Damascus.

Now, let's think a bit more about the Ananias scenes. In (1), because Saul is the Lord's chosen instrument, he sent Ananias to see Saul. Ananias "laid his hands on him and said, 'Brother Saul, the Lord Jesus, who appeared to you on your way here, has sent me so that you may regain your sight and be filled with the Holy Spirit.' And immediately something like scales fell from his eyes, and his sight was restored." In (2) Paul tells the story of Ananias, a disciple, who was "a devout man according to the law and well spoken of by all the Jews." Instead of being sent by the Lord, Saul says of Ananias, "He came to me; and standing beside me, he said, 'Brother Saul, regain your sight!' In that very hour I regained my sight and saw him."

In (3) there is nothing about Ananias and Paul's blindness and being led into Damascus. Rather, Luke uses those ideas symbolically in (3) as a summation of his theology. In (1) Saul had been blinded, but the scales fell from his eyes and he saw, and in (2) he was baptized and his sins washed away. In (3) Paul says that he is being sent to the Gentiles (referred to three times) "to open their eyes so that they may turn from darkness to light and from the power of Satan to God, so that they may receive forgiveness of sins and a place among those who are sanctified by faith in me" (Acts 26:17-23). And he is to proclaim light to both Jews and Gentiles. Saul is about to fulfill the promise God made to him (2) in Acts 22:14-15 that he is to be God's "witness to all the world of what you have seen and heard."

We are certainly left with some questions with Luke's reports of Paul's special religious experience. How did Luke get the information he reports, especially the details, which increase as the story is retold? And why are there differences in the accounts? One answer is that Luke was a traveling companion of Paul on some of his journeys and would have gotten his information directly from him. This view is based on certain passages in Acts known as "we sections" (16:10-18; 20:5-16; 21:1-18; 27:1–28:16), because in them Luke suddenly shifts from "he," "they," and "them" to "we" and "us." See, for example, "When he had seen the vision, we immediately tried to cross" (Acts 16:10) and "They went ahead and were waiting for us" (20:5). But, if Luke received his information from Paul, why would he report the experience in three such different and sometimes conflicting ways, even in the speeches put on Paul's lips?

*According to Paul*
There is no doubt that Paul believed he had special religious experiences that involved the supernatural. In the order he mentions them in his letters, let's see what he says. In 1 Corinthians 9:1-3 Paul is defending himself against his adversaries. Some, perhaps Peter among them, were claiming better authority because they had been with Jesus in person. Paul asks some rhetorical questions for which the assumed answer is "Yes." 'Am I not free?" that is, to do the things he wants, and "Am I not an apostle?" "Have I not seen Jesus our Lord?"

The Corinthians themselves are Paul's work in the Lord and the proof of his apostleship. That is his defense against those who question his authority. In the last question, the verb for "see" is *horaō*, which may mean "see with the eye" or "see" in the sense of "see with the mind" or "perceive" or "experience." There is no evidence that Paul ever saw Jesus in person, so he makes a strong defense to compensate. "Perceive" or "experience" is probably the best way to understand what Paul says.

As evidence for Jesus' resurrection, Paul lists persons to whom the resurrected Jesus appeared. Then he says, "Last of all, as to one untimely born, he appeared also to me" (1 Corinthians 15:8). He defends himself by saying that he is the least of the apostles because he persecuted the church of God, by whose grace he is what he is, and by that grace he worked harder than all the apostles (1 Corinthians 15:9-10). Commentators generally take the appearing to Paul here as a reference to his experience on the Damascus road mentioned in Acts 26:16. There the Lord says to Paul, "I have appeared to you," and "I will appear to you," that is, for a mission to Gentiles. However, neither in Acts nor in 1 Corinthians 15:9-10 does it say that Paul himself "saw" the Lord who appeared to him.

The next passage (2 Corinthians 12:1-4) is somewhat textually uncertain, and that is one of the reasons why it is hard to understand. Paul begins by saying, "It is necessary to boast; nothing is to be gained by it, but I will go on to visions and revelations of the Lord." Here "Lord" is to be taken as the initiator of the phenomena, not the object of them. Paul says, "I know a person in Christ...caught up to the third heaven – whether in the body or out of the body I do not know; God knows." Then Paul says that he knows that "such a person" – repeating what he had just said about the body – "was caught up into Paradise and heard things that are not to be told, that no mortal is permitted to repeat."

If only God knows what Paul is talking about and no mortal is to repeat it, how are we to understand what he is saying? It is generally thought that the "person in Christ" is Paul himself. However, "in Christ" is a favorite phrase for the new existence of converts, and it occurs about 54 times in his undisputed letters. "If anyone is in Christ, there is a new creation: everything old has passed away" (2 Corinthians 5:17).

Do you see why it is hard to understand the passage being considered? Not long after Paul's letters were published, the author of 2 Peter said that "our beloved brother Paul wrote...according to the wisdom given him... There are some things in them [Paul's letters] hard to understand, which the ignorant [false teachers] and unstable [in their faith] twist to their own destruction" (2 Peter 3:15-16). Perhaps it is good that the things the person heard in Paradise were left untold, because we would not be able to understand them, anyway! Then we do not have to fear for our destruction (2 Corinthians 12:2-4; 2 Peter 3:16).

Without fearing destruction, let's try to understand what Paul has written about his supernatural experiences in light of his discussion of worship in 1 Corinthians 14:6, 26. The purpose of worship is to promote the moral and spiritual growth of worshipers (1 Corinthians 14:3-5). They cannot benefit in that way if they do not understand what is going on.

In 1 Corinthians 14:6 Paul asks how it will benefit the Corinthians if he comes to them speaking in tongues unless he speaks "in some revelation or knowledge or prophecy or teaching." Is the meaning of what he says here any clearer than what he says about those "speaking mysteries in the Spirit" (14:2), which he discourages? Perhaps the most likely answer is that the people to whom Paul was writing had already been taught about the phenomena of worship that he is mentioning. Commentators often do not comment on 1 Corinthians 14:6, perhaps because Paul is something of a mystic and a mystery combined. He is a mystic in the sense of having "a direct subjective communion with the Deity." Paul seems to have had that kind of experience with both God and Christ, as stated in the last passage dealing with his supernatural experiences (Galatians 1:15-17).

Paul is on the defensive because some Jewish believers were insisting that Gentile converts had to be circumcised and obey some Jewish laws, especially not eating with Gentiles. Paul accuses Peter of eating with Gentiles at Antioch until some Jews from the circumcision faction of Jews appeared on the scene. Paul accuses Peter and some others of hypocrisy. If they lived like Gentiles, how could they force Gentiles "to live like Jews" (Galatians 2:11-14)?

With anger Paul writes of his astonishment at the Galatian converts so quickly deserting God who called them in Christ's grace and turning to a gospel different from the one preached by him and his companions. Twice Paul says that they should be accursed. His gospel did not originate with humans, nor was he taught it, which implies that the gospel of his adversaries was of human origin. He "received it through a revelation of Jesus Christ" (Galatians 1:6-12). Is this an allusion to the Damascus road experience? If so, we should recall that in the accounts of that experience in Acts Jesus is revealed as "the Lord," not Jesus as the Messiah (Christ). "Lord" is Luke's favorite designation for Jesus.

Paul writes that the Galatians had probably heard of his zeal for Judaism and his persecuting "the church of God." Then comes the crucial passage about Paul's supernatural experience (Galatians 1:15-17, literally):

> But when it pleased the one [God] who set me apart from my mother's womb, and called me through his grace, to reveal his Son in me, in order that I might preach him among the Gentiles, I did not immediately consult with flesh and blood [humans], nor did I go up to Jerusalem to those who were apostles before me, but went away into Arabia and returned again to Damascus.

Since Paul mentions returning to Damascus, perhaps he is alluding to the place where, according to Acts, his mission began. However, there is no reference to Ananias or any other human being involved in the outcome of Paul's experience. Despite major differences between Paul and Acts, God is the initiator of Paul's mission in both (Galatians 1:15; Acts 9:15). The Christ movement among Jews has failed, and the conflict between Paul and his adversaries over the question of circumcision of Gentile converts is serious. Since the persons in Paul's churches were mostly Gentiles, the conflict was threatening Paul's work. Like the prophet Jeremiah (Jeremiah 1:5), he now believes, in retrospect, that God had set him apart, before he was born, for a Gentile mission.

There is no reference to the risen Jesus as Lord in Galatians so prominent in the accounts in Acts. Jesus is revealed as "Son," and that coincides with Paul's first preaching about Jesus as the Son of God in Acts 9:19-20. In Galatians 2:16 Paul says that he and other Jews came to believe in Christ Jesus. Believing in Christ fits well with Paul's preaching in Acts 9:22 that Jesus was the Messiah.

Paul does not mention Jesus as Lord in his discussion of his supernatural experience in Galatians 1:15-17, and that seems to indicate that he came to that belief after he began preaching to Gentiles. According to Acts, Paul's special religious experience was objective, that is, it came to him from the outside. But in Paul it was subjective, that is, it happened within him. He says, God revealed "his Son in me," not "to me" (*NRSV*; Galatians 1:16). No matter how we think of Paul's experience, it should not be seen as transforming him from being a Jew to a Christian and from Judaism to Christianity. To call it a "conversion," therefore, is misleading, because the verb "convert" means "to bring over from one belief, view, or party to another." Paul never gave up his faithfulness toward the one living and true God of his Jewish faith (1 Thessalonians 1:8-9).

Another misconception that many people have is that Paul's name was changed from Saul to Paul as a result of his "conversion." Actually, many Jews living outside of Palestine had two names, one Hebrew (Saul) and one Roman (Paul). For example, one of Paul's friends, John, had a second name, Mark (Acts 12:12). Since Paul never uses the name Saul in his letters, it is probably fiction created by Luke when he focuses on Paul's missionary activity to the Gentiles. This avoided the use of a Jewish name, but it had absolutely nothing to do with his special religious experience on the road to Damascus, which we learned was not really a true "conversion."

### *Understanding Paul's Supernatural Experiences*

Paul's beliefs about Jesus as the Messiah, Son of God, and Lord probably did not all happen through a sudden flash of light. Paul had seen followers of Jesus suffering persecution from Jews like himself. According to Acts, Paul had watched the stoning of Stephen, kept the coats of his killers, and approved of his death (Acts 7:58–8:1). That may or may not be historical. However, Paul writes that he had violently persecuted the church and tried to destroy it (Galatians 1:13). Persecutions of Jesus' followers had gotten to his sensitive being.

It is difficult to determine the basis for the accounts in Acts and if anything in them is related to what Paul says about his supernatural experiences in his letters. In both Acts and in Paul's letters, Paul speaks of his life in Judaism, which he stresses in Galatians: "my earlier life in Judaism... I advanced in Judaism beyond many among my people...for I was far more zealous for the traditions of my ancestors" (Galatians 1:13-14). On this evidence, it is hard to believe that Paul would have thought he was completely converted in any sense of the term. He neither completely changed from no religion to religion nor from one religion to another. He did not forsake Judaism, because he never gave up his basic belief about God and the moral convictions stemming from Jewish law. His beliefs about Jesus were simply added to his Judaism, regardless of the nature of his supernatural experiences.

Although Paul's letters indicate that he never completely forsook his Judaism, they sometimes reveal an inner struggle concerning his old ways of Jewish life under the law and his life in Christ under the Spirit. It is probably better, therefore, to think about the phenomenon reported in Acts – if, indeed, it occurred as reported – as a special religious experience rather than as a conversion.

To his adversaries in the church at Corinth Paul writes: "Are they Hebrews? So am I. Are they Israelites? So am I. Are they descendants of Abraham? So am I" (2 Corinthians 11:22). But then Paul also asks, "Are they ministers of Christ?... I am a better one" (11:23). He gives as evidence numerous hardships, including imprisonments, floggings, lashings five times by the Jews, three times being beaten with rods, a stoning, and other sufferings. At the end of the passage he exclaims: "The God and Father of the Lord Jesus (blessed be he forever!) knows that I do not lie" (2 Corinthians 11:31). The hardships Paul lists, especially the lashings and stoning, and his invocation of God as witness to the truth of what he says, indicate that he was still under the rules of the synagogue, not the church.

The following passages also support the view that Paul never forsook his Judaism, with its belief in the one God and the morality of Jewish law. He calls the Jews who subjected him to some of the perils he mentions as "my own people" (2 Corinthians 11:26; see also Galatians 1:14). In Romans 9–11 Paul wrestles with the problem of God and his people who have rejected Christ. He refers to them as "my own people, my brothers" (Romans 9:3), although he has "great sorrow and increasing anguish" for them (Romans 9:2).

Often some things not said help to confirm things said. This becomes clear when we compare what the author of the gospel of John says about the Jews and what Paul does not say. This has a bearing also on the question of Christian and Christianity.

## *Paul and the Author of the Fourth Gospel*

It is plausible to think of the author of the fourth gospel as a "Jewish Christian." Although he was a Jew by race, by religion he was a Christian. Like Paul, John was a very creative thinker. However, believing in Jesus was the primary reason for belonging to the group of Jesus' followers, as John himself did, whereas for Paul it was faithfulness toward God (see, e.g., John 3:16-21; 6:27-59; 8:12-59). There were "the Jews who had believed in him" (Jesus; John 8:31; see also 2:23; 7:31; 8:30; 10:42). Those who did not believe are called "the Jews" (John 2:18; 5:10-18; 7:1-52; 8:48), and John's adversaries were "the Jews" who rejected Jesus, as distinct from other Jews who believed in him. Jews who believed in Jesus as John understood him may appropriately be thought of as "Christians." The Christ movement began among Jews who accepted Jesus as the long-expected Messiah, in contrast to those Jews who refused to do so (see John 1:20-41; 3:28; 7:25-42; 9:22; 11:27; 20:30-31; Galatians 2:16).

As with Paul (Romans 9–11), John thinks that some Jews rejected Jesus, a frequently repeated theme in his gospel. "He came to what was his own, and his own people did not accept him" (John 1:11). According to Paul, some Jews were apostate, but that apostasy opened the way to salvation for Gentiles. Eventually "the full number of the Gentiles" will come in, and then "all Israel will be saved" (Romans 11:25-26). And Paul quotes from Isaiah 59:20-21 (see also Psalm 14:7) to show that a deliverer will come from Zion (Jerusalem). And this is his covenant with them when he takes away their sins (Romans 11:26-27).

Paul, in contrast to John, did not think the religion he was espousing superseded or replaced Judaism. This becomes clear if we look again at some statements in the gospel of John. As with Paul, John says that some Jews believed concerning Jesus, but John's language and thought are quite different from Paul's. At the Passover Feast, many Jews believed in Jesus when they saw the signs he did, but Jesus did not trust himself to them (John 2:23-24; see also 5:37-47). John writes that Jesus said the Jews would seek him but not find him and "where I am you cannot come" (John 7:34; see also 8:31-59; 11:45-57). Unlike Paul, who was concerned with Jews who did not accept Jesus as the Messiah (1 Corinthians 9:19-20; Romans 9–11), John ignored them. According to John, those Jews who did not believe would die in their sins (John 8:24) and their guilt remains (John 9:41). The devil, not God, was the father of such Jews (John 8:39-47).

The religion John was espousing was something separate from Judaism. "The Jews had already agreed that anyone who confessed Jesus to be the Messiah would be put out of the synagogue" (John 9:22). Many Jews among the authorities believed in Jesus, but they did not confess it lest they be put out of the synagogue (John 12:42). What came to be known as Christianity was still authentic Judaism for Paul because of Jesus' faithfulness, as a Jew himself, to God. Although Paul was probably unaware of it, his Judaism was in a state of transition into a religion separate from Judaism. It is appropriate, therefore, to think of the religion Paul was espousing as that of some persons within Judaism as it was in transition to Christianity. The seat of that religion was no longer in the synagogues, but in the churches.

John states his theme at the end of his work: "These [signs] are written so that you may come to believe that Jesus is the Messiah, the Son of God, and that through believing you may have life in his name" (John 20:31). Although Paul came to believe that Jesus was the Messiah and Son of God before John did, Paul did not turn against his people and their religion.

So, was Paul the first Christian? If we compare what Paul says about his people the Jews with what John says, the answer is "No." Paul did not have to forsake his Judaism for his beliefs in Jesus, but, on the other hand, John and his followers did. The religion they were espousing became known as Christianity, and the author of John and his followers may be regarded as the first Christians. Nevertheless, that designation was still not widely used, although it was known by Luke when he wrote Acts and by the author of 1 Peter.

## *Justification by Faith*

Because of Paul's controversy with his adversaries, we learn about the supernatural experiences reported in his letters and his conviction about his mission to Gentiles. Because of that controversy, we also learn of his belief about being justified by faith.

For an insightful understanding of Paul's concept of justification by faith, it is necessary to consider the passage where he first mentions it (Galatians 2:15-21: "We ourselves [including Peter and other Jews] are Jews by birth and not Gentile sinners." What follows is Paul's attempt to reconcile his differences with other Jews who insisted that converts to the Christ movement be circumcised and obey Jewish dietary laws. Paul says that Peter and others were hypocritical when they disregarded Jewish dietary laws and ate with Gentiles: "If you, though a Jew, live like a Gentile and not like a Jew, how can you compel the Gentiles to live like Jews?" (Galatians 2:13-14). Then come Paul's words about justification: "We have believed with respect to Christ Jesus, in order that we might be justified by the faith of Christ and not by works of the law" (Greek).

Paul's phrase *pisteōs Iēsou Christou* in Galatians 2:16 and related passages is generally translated "faith in Christ." The *KJV* reads "faith of Jesus" in every instance but Romans 3:26, where it becomes "believeth in Jesus." Other translations have "faith in," but the *NRSV* has "faith of" in a note. It's interesting to observe that the oldest translation, the *KJV*, has "faith of Jesus." In a similar way, most translations render Paul's verb *dikaioō* as "to be justified," but the *NRSV* has a note at Galatians 2:15: "or *reckoned as righteous*," as elsewhere. The *NJB* reads "be reckoned as upright" in Galatians 2:16a and "be found upright" in Galatians 2:16b.

In my book, *The Morality of Paul's Converts*, I argued that Paul's Greek phrase *pisteōs Iēsou Christou* should be understood as "the faith of Christ," not as "faith in Christ." This means, then, that the faithfulness is that of Christ, not that of the ones being made righteous. Paul believed that Christ was faithful to God to his death, which made it possible for sinners to become righteous: "God proves his love for us in that while we still were sinners Christ died for us" (Romans 5:8).

In that book, I also gave evidence that Paul's word *dikaioō* should be translated "make righteous" for two reasons. First, it has strong support in the OT; second, most Christians today other than individuals trained in theology would probably not be able to explain what "justified by faith" means, but they would understand "make righteous." With respect to the first point, *dikaioō* in the LXX translates the Hebrew *sdq* and may be translated as "pronounce" or "treat as righteous," "declare" or "make righteous," "acquit," "vindicate." The offense toward which the verb *dikaioō* is directed is generally some form of wrongdoing, as some examples illustrate.

"What shall we say, or how should we be made righteous (*dikaioō*)? God has discovered the unrighteousness (*adikia*) of your servants" (Genesis 44:16). "You shall not make the ungodly righteous for the sake of gifts" (Exodus 23:7). Paul's words in Romans 4:5 that God makes the ungodly righteous are the same as in Exodus. Isaiah says, "Woe to those...who pronounce the ungodly righteous for the sake of gifts and take away the righteousness (*dikaiosynē*) of the righteous (*dikaioi*)" (Isaiah 5:23; see also Deuteronomy 25:1; Isaiah 53:11).

## How Converts Are Made Righteous

With respect to being made righteous and righteousness, Paul uses mostly *dikaiosynē*, the noun from *dikaioō*, for which the correct understanding is "righteousness," not "justification." So, how does Paul think that converts are made righteous? Here 1 Corinthians 6:9-11 and Romans 6:1-23 are the keys to our understanding.

*1 Corinthians 6:9-11*
After listing the kinds of unrighteous persons who will not get into the kingdom of God, Paul says bluntly (Greek): "And such were some of you." Then he continues: "But you were washed (*apolouō*), but you were made holy (*hagiazō*), but you were made righteous (*dikaioō*)." The word "washed" refers to baptism and is synonymous with the other two verbs in the sentence in that all have the same effect: a new existence for persons freed from sin after baptism.

Baptized persons were thought to be separated or set apart as made holy so as to be included in the company of those who are holy, a Hebrew idea. Recall "holy ones" as Paul's favorite name for members of his churches. See LXX Leviticus 20:26: "You shall be holy to me, because I the Lord your God am holy, the one who separated you from all the nations to be mine." Acts 20:32 (Greek) is another example of this idea. The message of God's grace is to build converts up (edify) and give them "the inheritance among all those who are sanctified" (that is, "made holy"; see also Acts 26:18).

Sirach says that in his understanding the Lord makes people different: "Some of them he has blessed and exalted; some he has made holy (*hagiazō*) and brought near to himself; others he has cursed and made low and turned them away from their place" ("status"; Sirach 33:12). There are two groups of persons, those made holy and brought to God and those cursed and turned away. Of Moses Sirach says, "For his faithfulness and meekness God made him holy and chose him from all humans" (Sirach 45:4; see also Exodus 31:13; Isaiah 49:7; Ephesians 1:7). Now Romans 6:1-23 becomes important.

*Romans 6:1-23*
Some converts at Rome clearly did not understand the significance of their baptism, with the forgiveness of past sins and their being made righteous that came with it. No one had instructed them as Paul did the Corinthians: "Be thoroughly sober in mind righteously (*dikaiōs*; adverb) and do not continue to sin" (1 Corinthians 15:34; Greek).

The Roman converts had heard about Paul and his co-workers being supercharged with the Spirit and living under its power, not under the law. Some mistook Paul's freedom from Jewish law as license to sin and even said slanderously that he had said, "Why not do evil in order that good may come?" (Romans 3:8, Greek). Such converts thought that, if God's grace was so effective for the forgiveness of sins, they could continue to sin and be forgiven all over again. If a little grace was good, more would only be better.

## The Symbolism of Baptism

That the Roman converts misunderstood Paul's teachings about the moral implications of baptism is clear by studying Paul's words. The Greek word *baptizō* means "dip" or "submerge." When converts are immersed, according to Paul, they share symbolically in Christ's death and thereby die to past sins. When they emerge from the water, they share symbolically in his resurrection. Just as Christ died and was raised, "we too might walk (conduct our lives) in newness of life." Converts who have died in baptism are "freed from (*dikaioō*) sin... So you also must consider yourselves dead to sin and alive to God in Christ Jesus" (Romans 6:4-11). "Freed from sin" is a translation for Paul's word *dikaioō*, that is, "make righteous."

The experience in baptism is to be lived out the rest of life. Paul exhorts the converts: "Therefore, do not let sin exercise dominion in your mortal bodies, to make you obey their passions. No longer present your members to sin as weapons of wickedness, but present yourselves to God...and present your members to God as weapons of righteousness" (Romans 6:12-13).

Here again Paul was greatly influenced by the Septuagint in what he says about not sinning. One of the things that grieves Sirach's heart is a man "who turns away from righteousness to sin" (26:27). Sirach constantly admonishes his readers not to sin: "Do not say, 'I have sinned and what has happened to me? for the Lord is patient. Concerning forgiveness do not be fearless, adding sin to sin,' and do not say, 'His mercy is great, the multitude of my sins he will forgive'" (5:4-6). "My child, have you sinned? Do not continue to do so any longer, but for your former sins ask forgiveness" (21:1; see also Sirach 10:29; 20:21; Wisdom 15:2; Romans 3:25; 7:8; James 4:13-17).

These passages mean that being made righteous and the forgiveness of sins are the same thing for some writers of the Septuagint and for Paul. Paul twice states the same idea by using the verb "set free": "you, having been set free from sin, have become slaves of righteousness" (Romans 6:18) and "you have been freed from sin and enslaved to God" (Romans 6:22; see also Romans 8:2, 21; Galatians 5:1; see 1 Corinthians 15:34, quoted above).

## Paul on Baptism and Christians Today

Just as Christians today may have difficulty accepting Paul's concept of converts not sinning after baptism, that also seems to be true already for Paul's immediate successors. In the disputed letters of Paul baptism is mentioned only in Ephesians 4:5 and Colossians 2:12. In Ephesians 4.5 the writer simply says, "one baptism," which may be part of a creedal confession. In Colossians 2:12-14 the writer echoes the symbolism of Paul in Romans

6:4 about being buried with Christ in baptism and raised with him and the forgiveness of trespasses (*paraptōmata*). But the writer of Colossians says nothing about remaining free from sin afterward. In fact, he uses Paul's noun "sin" (*hamartia*) only in Colossians 1:14, and he never uses the verb "to sin" (*hamartanō*).

The writer of Ephesians echoes Paul's idea of not sinning after baptism in his exhortations about readers clothing themselves with "the new self, created according to the likeness of God in true righteousness and holiness" (Ephesians 4:24). He includes the exhortation, "Be angry but do not sin" (4:26), a quotation from LXX Psalm 4:5. The writer of the Pastoral Epistles never mentions baptism. And, as if to counter Paul's idea of remaining free from sin after baptism, the writer of those letters says in the name of Paul: "sinners – of whom I am the foremost" (1 Timothy 1:15-16).

While many Christians today, especially Catholics and Lutherans, were baptized as infants, most if not all persons in Paul's churches were adults who had only recently been baptized or were being instructed in preparation for baptism. Moreover, Paul and the converts in his churches were the first generation of persons belonging to the Christ movement. None was born into a Christian family where Christian faithfulness and life were assumed, much less practiced. Indeed, many converts formerly worshiped Greco-Roman deities or belonged to a mystery cult and practiced lifestyles quite different from those advocated by Paul, with his strict Jewish monotheism and moral upbringing.

In Romans 6:17 Paul thanks God that those, "having once been slaves of sin, have become obedient from the heart to the form (*typos*, "model") of teaching to which you were entrusted." The word Paul uses for teaching is *didachē*, which is instruction in morality to prepare converts for baptism. It was conveyed through the lives of teachers, who also were models to be imitated. Paul exhorts the Corinthian converts to be imitators of him and sends Timothy to remind them of his "ways in Christ" as he teaches them in every church (1 Corinthians 4:14-17; see also 1 Thessalonians 1:6; 1 Corinthians 11:1). Paul writes to the "brothers" at Philippi: "Join in imitating me, and observe those who live according to the example [*typos*, "model"] you have in us" (Philippians 3:17).

Now, keep in mind Paul's concept of "justification by faith," as explained by his use of the word "justify" and its meaning and how converts were made righteous, as we examine critically the *Declaration* by Catholics and Protestants mentioned in the introduction to this chapter.

## Joint Declaration on the Doctrine of Justification

According to the *Declaration*, Catholics and Protestants agree: "Together we confess: By grace alone, in faith in Christ's saving work and not because of any merit on our part, we are accepted by God and receive the Holy Spirit, who renews our hearts while equipping and calling us to good works." If we go back earlier than Martin Luther to Paul, we gain a different insight about being saved and works. The following discussion provides some "food for thought" about what "the Bible says" with respect to Paul's thought about justification by faith.

The *Declaration's* words "not because of any merit on our part" and "calling us to good works" are an attempt to reconcile the Catholic view of good works as essential to salvation and the Lutheran doctrine that persons are saved by faith alone. According to the latter, salvation comes only through faith in Christ, not good works. Paul, though, says that the judgment and ultimate salvation lie in the future and are dependent upon works: "For we will all stand before the judgment seat of God... So then, each of us will be accountable to God" (Romans 14:10-12). The goal for converts is not having their faith in Christ "justified" before God, but their deeds: "For all of us must appear before the judgment seat of Christ, so that each may receive recompense for what has been done in the body, whether good or evil" (2 Corinthians 5:10). Also see Romans 2:6: "When God's righteous judgment will be revealed...he will repay according to each one's deeds" (works; *erga*). For Paul the Jewish law with respect to works is summed up in a single commandment, "You shall love your neighbor as yourself" (see Leviticus 19:18).

The very phrase "works righteousness" occurs in Acts 10:35: "In every nation anyone who fears God and works righteousness (*ergazomenos dikaiosunēn*) is acceptable to him" (Greek). Some of Paul's equivalents are: "See that none of you repays evil for evil, but always seek to do good to one another and to all...hold fast to what is good; abstain from every form of evil" (1 Thessalonians 5:15, 21-22). "So then, whenever we have an opportunity, let us work for the good of all" (Galatians 6:10; see also Romans 2:10; 13:1-10).

The words of the *Declaration* about being accepted by God and receiving the Holy Spirit can be supported by Paul. The key passages are 1 Thessalonians 1:4-9 and 4:8. There Paul says that God "has chosen" the converts and that Paul's message came to them "in power and in the Holy Spirit." The converts became aware of the Spirit's power when they became members of the church in Thessalonica. Later Paul reminds them that it is "God, who also gives us his Holy Spirit" (1 Thessalonians 4:8).

Baptism, to Paul, meant dying to sin and rising to newness of life (Romans 6:3), which also meant living by the Spirit, not gratifying "the desires of the flesh." And "the fruit of the Spirit is love, joy, peace, patience, kindness, generosity, faithfulness, gentleness, and self-control" (Galatians 5:16, 22-23). These are virtues that are to be lived (works) in opposing "the works of the flesh" listed in Galatians 5:17-21.

In the *Declaration* the writers refer to the Holy Spirit as "who": "The Holy Spirit, who renews our hearts." The Spirit (*pneuma*) is a neuter noun, but in some translations it is understood as "who" instead of "it" or "which." As in those translations, the "who" in the *Declaration* is influenced by the Christian doctrine of the Trinity, the idea of "God in Three Persons," that is, Father, Son, and Holy Spirit.

## Chapter Summary

Most people in the Greco-Roman world were polytheistic, so they believed in the existence of many gods and goddesses. Images of the deities as objects of worship were present everywhere, even in Palestine, and polytheism was even more widespread than the mystery (secret) religions that were so prominent in certain localities. With its indifference to morality, polytheism, more than anything else, set Greco-Roman religions apart from Judaism, the Christ movement, and the religion that later became known as Christianity.

Paul retained his strict monotheism even after becoming a member of the Christ movement. When his mission to Jews failed, he turned to the Gentiles. For them, heroes were thought to be sons of gods, lords, saviors, even gods; therefore, Paul's message of Jesus as the *Messiah* had no appeal to Gentiles whatsoever. For that reason Paul preached about Jesus as the *Son of God* and *Lord*. His message is summed up in 1 Corinthians 8:4-5: "There is no God but one...in fact there are many gods and many lords – yet for us there is one God, the Father...and one Lord, Jesus Christ." However, God was foremost in Paul's thought throughout his letters.

Converts who had received the Holy Spirit when they became members of a church were subjected to an intense period of training in righteousness or moral/ethical instruction, to which they had committed themselves (Romans 6:17). Then they would be forgiven for their past sins and made righteous through baptism. This indicates, therefore, that the first stage in becoming a member of a church, especially for Gentiles, but also for apostate

Jews, was a profession of faithfulness toward God (1 Thessalonians 1:5-10). Such persons were set apart to become holy or righteous before God. Paul makes this clear to his first converts of record: God has not called them for immorality but for holiness (1 Thessalonians 4:7). And God, who calls them "into his own kingdom," exhorts them to lead lives worthy of it (1 Thessalonians 2:12).

Converts were certainly also taught certain beliefs about Jesus. But what beliefs Paul received from earlier tradition and how much he himself was responsible for the beliefs he transmitted is a matter of debate. From earlier tradition Paul received the belief that Jesus was the Messiah (see, e.g., Galatians 2:16-21; Acts 2:31; 3:18; 9:22), that he was crucified and rose from the dead (1 Thessalonians 4:14; 5:9-10; 1 Corinthians 15:1-19), that he would come again (1 Thessalonians 1:10; 4:14), and perhaps also that Jesus was the Son of God (Acts 9:20; Galatians 1:15-16; Romans 1:3) and Lord (Romans 10:5-13). He learned the tradition of the Lord's Supper, as well (1 Corinthians 11:23-26). To overemphasize these things, however, to the neglect of Paul's emphasis on moral probity, would fail to show an insightful understanding of Paul and his thought.

Chapter 13

THE FIRST THREE GOSPELS

*Introduction*

While writings of Paul were the first literature of the NT, the NT actually begins with four books known as the gospels. Matthew, Mark, and Luke, the first three of these gospels, are known as the synoptic gospels and provide accounts of the life and teachings of Jesus. Incorporating material from both oral and written sources, the synoptic gospels show evidence of a literary relationship that suggests that Mark was the first gospel to be written. In this chapter, we will explore the kinds of stories about Jesus that were handed down orally and theories about the written sources used by the authors of the first three gospels.

Our examination in this chapter of the particular literary styles and special interests of Matthew, Mark, and Luke will provide background understanding for later study of the differences, including contradictions and discrepancies, among the synoptic gospels. This is especially important when trying to gain insight about Jesus, his life, and his teachings. It will also provide a basis for comparisons of the synoptic gospels with the gospel of John, the last gospel to be written.

*Oral Transmission or Oral Tradition*

Just as the earliest stories in the OT were first transmitted orally and later written down and eventually incorporated into the Bible, there is evidence of oral transmission in the letters of Paul, as well. In dealing with problems in relationships between the sexes in Corinth Paul writes: "To the married I give this command – not I but the Lord – that the wife should not separate from her husband...and that the husband should not divorce his wife" (1 Corinthians 7:10-11). When Paul says "not I but the Lord," he refers to Jesus' teaching on divorce that he had learned through oral tradition and that was written down later in different ways in the first three gospels (Mark 10:1-12; Matthew 5:32; Luke 16:18). That tradition was as valid for Paul as if he had learned it directly from the historical Jesus.

The earliest written account of the Lord's Supper or Eucharist is in 1 Corinthians 11:23-26: "I received from the Lord what I also handed on to you." The verbs "receive" and "hand on" mean to do so verbally. Paul had learned about the Supper through oral tradition, as though directly from Jesus himself. And Paul, in turn, handed on the tradition to the church members at Corinth. Interestingly, this tradition probably never would have been preserved in Paul (see 1 Corinthians 11:17-34) if there had not been problems, such as drunkenness, among church members at the Supper.

Paul praises the Corinthian converts because they remember him "in everything and maintain the [oral] traditions just as I handed them on to you" (1 Corinthians 11:2). Paul exhorts the converts in the church at Philippi: "Keep on doing the things that you have learned and received and heard [by word of mouth] and seen in me" (Philippians 4:9; see also 1 Thessalonians 4:1; Romans 16:17). In every letter Paul mentions "the gospel," and in every instance it is the oral gospel, the distinctive message that was proclaimed orally.

Legends and myths had developed around famous persons like Deborah, Ruth, David, and Solomon, and the same was true for Jesus of Nazareth, the teacher in Galilee, for whom a few fishermen "immediately left their nets and followed him" (Mark 1:18; Matthew 4:20). Sayings of and about Jesus and stories of his deeds were preserved by oral tradition long before they were written down. Memory and oral transmission, usually called "oral tradition," and writing each played important roles in the teachings and beliefs in the early church. We learn this, of course, from the written documents that have survived.

Through a technique known as Form Criticism, scholars are able to identify forms of material from and about Jesus that circulated orally. Among them are legends, that is, stories about persons inspired by God (young Jesus in the temple; Luke 2:41-52). In contrast to legends, myths deal with actions of the gods (Jesus' birth, baptism, transfiguration). Miracle stories include two types: paradigms (healing of the paralyzed man; Mark 2:1-12) and tales (healing of the leper; Mark 1:40-45; feeding of 5000; Mark 6:36-44). There are short sayings of Jesus, such as proverbs (Matthew 12:34b; Luke 5:39), exhortations (Matthew 5:44; Luke 6:27-28), and beatitudes (Matthew 5:3-11; Luke 6:20-22), and longer sayings, called parables.

All of these types of stories and sayings were eventually written down to be preserved, and Christian writings became more significant with each decade. Gradually they were used in worship, and during the second century

CE some of them came to be regarded with the same authority as the Hebrew scriptures, the "Bible" of the early church (see 2 Peter 3:14-16; 2 Timothy 3:14-17).

## Synoptic Gospels and their Sources

The first three gospels are known as the synoptic gospels (Greek, *synoptikos*, "seeing with," "seeing the whole together"), because they present Jesus' life and work in essentially the same way. Beginning with his birth (lacking in Mark), they proceed with his baptism and temptation, teaching and healing in Galilee, journey to Jerusalem, arrest, trial, death, and resurrection. The word "gospel" (*euangelion*) is derived from the verb *euangelizō*, which means "proclaim" or "bring good news," and it is used in the Septuagint with reference to the deliverance or salvation of God's people (Isaiah 40:9; 52:7; 61:1; Psalm 95:2). The noun *euangelion* means "good" or "glad tidings" (2 Samuel 4:10; 18:22, 25). It has that meaning on a Greek inscription of about 9 BCE, where Augustus is called a god, and it is said that his birthday brought "tidings of joy."

The first verse of Mark, "The beginning of the gospel of Jesus Christ, the Son of God," is loaded with theological meaning, immediately casting doubt about his gospel as biography. Although Jesus was a historical person, the gospels are not records of sayings or events exactly as stated. They were modified in transmission by linguistic styles, special interests, religious convictions, and even biases, of their authors. The gospel writers also adapted their material about Jesus to the peculiar circumstances of the communities of their readers.

As with the Pentateuch, there are theories about sources for the gospels. If you compare the gospels, you will learn that some material is in only one gospel, some in only two gospels, and some in all three. This suggests a literary relationship among the three gospels in that one of them was used as a source by the other two. It is generally accepted that Mark was the first gospel to be written and that it was used by Matthew and Luke.

## The Priority of Mark

The view that Mark was the first gospel is known as "The Priority of Mark." One fact that supports this view is that Matthew reproduces 90 percent of Mark's material with most of the same words. Luke reproduces only a little more than half, and he has a special section (Luke 9:51–18:14), most of which is not in Mark. Matthew and Luke generally follow the order of incidents in Mark and do not agree on an order different from Mark. If the order of Mark and Luke differs, Matthew follows Mark, and if the order of Mark and Matthew differs, Luke agrees with Mark. Sometimes Matthew and Luke copy Mark word for word, and sometimes they change, add, or omit as each chooses.

Mark is not written in Classical Greek but in *Koinē*, which means "common" and was a dialect that Greek-speaking people in the ancient Near East used after the rule of Alexander the Great (336–323 BCE). Mark's language is more primitive than that of the other gospel writers in that he uses words from the Aramaic language, which was spoken by most Jews of Jesus' time. His style is rough and his grammar crude, and both are sometimes refined by Matthew and/or Luke. His style is monotonous and repetitious: compare "that evening, at sundown" (Mark 1:32) with "that evening" (Matthew 8:16) and "as the sun was setting" (Luke 4:40), a rephrasing of Mark's words. Similarly, "hungry and in need of food" (Mark 2:25) becomes "hungry" (Matthew 12:3; Luke 6:3). It is unlikely that the refined language of Matthew and Luke would be changed to cruder phrasing, thereby confirming the Priority of Mark.

Likewise, Mark's language is sometimes toned down to make it less offensive or to avoid misunderstanding. Mark states (6:5) that Jesus, in his hometown, "could do no deed of power"; Matthew changes this to "he did not do many deeds of power there" (Matthew 13:58), and Luke omits the passage. The people's remark, "He has gone out of his mind" (Mark 3:21) is omitted by Matthew and Luke. Human traits of Jesus are omitted or lessened, and Jesus' "anger," "amazement," and "love" for the rich man (Mark 3:5; 6:6; 10:21) are omitted.

Another observation that confirms the Priority of Mark is that the divine powers of Jesus are intensified in Matthew and Luke. Mark's "fever" (1:30), for example, is retained in Matthew 8:14 but becomes "high fever" in Luke 4:38. In Jesus' curing the woman, Mark says that Jesus "took her by the hand and lifted her up" (1:31), whereas in Matthew 8:15 Jesus "touched her hand." In Luke 4:38 Jesus "stood over her and rebuked the fever." The divine power of Jesus progressively increased, as it does in the number healed in Mark 1:32-34; Matthew 16:16-17; and Luke 4:40-41. There is also an increasing emphasis on Jesus as "Lord." Taking all uses of *kyrios* ("Lord") together, it occurs 18 times in Mark, 90 in Matthew, and 104 in Luke.

## The Two-Source and Four-Source Theories

Once the Priority of Mark was established, it was observed that Matthew and Luke had some material in common that is not in Mark. They must, therefore, have used a source in addition to Mark. That source was named Q from the German word *Quelle*, meaning "the source." This was the origin of the two-source theory, that is, that Matthew and Luke, in the composition of their gospels, each used two sources, Mark and Q.

It was also noticed that Matthew and Luke each have material not in the other gospels. The material used only by Matthew was designated as M and that by Luke as L. That gave rise to the four-source theory, namely, that Matthew and Luke together used four sources: Mark, Q, M, and L. Preceding Mark was oral tradition, which may also have been used by Matthew and Luke. And, both Matthew and Luke have peculiar stories of Jesus' birth. The conventional chart below shows the literary relationships among the synoptic gospels.

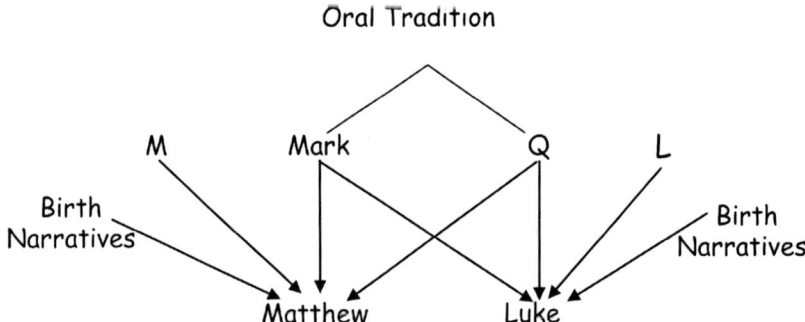

There is very little material only in Mark, notably the parable of the seed growing secretly (4:26-29), the healing of the blind man of Bethsaida (8:22-26), and some of the material in the passage on keeping alert (13:33-37). This shows that Mark also had a source either unknown or not used by Matthew or Luke, and he probably had other sources that are unknown, perhaps one for miracle stories, for example, since he reports so many of them.

The following material is only in Matthew (M): Jesus on prayer (6:5-8), parable of the weeds and its interpretation (13:36-43), unmerciful servant (18:23-35), laborers in the vineyard (20:11-16), ten bridesmaids (25:1-13), the last judgment (25:31-46), and the death of Judas (27:3-10).

Material only in Luke includes the miraculous catch of fish (5:1-11), centurion's slave (7:1-10), widow's son at Nain (7:11-17), woman with the ointment (7:36-50), the good Samaritan (10:29-37), Martha and Mary (10:38-42), rich fool (12:13-21), repentance or destruction (13:1-9), healing a crippled woman (13:10-17), prodigal son (15:11-32), unjust manager (16:1-13), rich man and Lazarus (16:19-31), healing of ten lepers (17:11-19), widow and unjust judge (18:1-8), Pharisee and tax collector (18:9-14), Zacchaeus (19:1-10), Jesus before Herod (23:6-16), road to Emmaus (24:13-35), and Jesus' appearance to the disciples (24:36-49).

## Literary Style of Mark

As with other gospel writers, Mark uses special words and phrases characteristic of his linguistic style. These include (with their meanings): *euthys*, "straightway," "immediately," or "at once" (11 times in only Mark 1:10-43, with a total of 41, compared with 5 in Matthew and 1 in Luke); *archō*, a verb meaning "begin" followed by "to"; *akathartos*, "impure" or "unclean"; *legō*, "say," "speak," or "tell"; and *palin*, "again." Mark also likes to use diminutives, words indicating something small or little, as, for example, *thugatrion*, "little daughter," instead of *thugatēr*, "daughter." Sometimes he uses Aramaic expressions, which he transliterates into Greek and then gives their meaning. Mark repeatedly uses the third person plural indicated in the Greek verb form but left unstated. For example, "They were astounded" in Mark 1:22 has no specified subject, nor does it in Luke 4:32, but "the crowds" is added as subject in Matthew 7:28.

## Special Interests of Mark

Along with characteristics of style, each gospel writer has special religious interests. Mark has an emphasis on the passion of Jesus, that is, his suffering and death, for which he prepares the reader early in his gospel. The Pharisees and Herodians (only in Mark) are out to destroy Jesus (3:6), and there are three predictions of the Passion, beginning with the one after Peter's confession of Jesus as the Messiah (8:27-33; 9:30-32; 10:32-34). The theme reaches its climax on the way into Jerusalem when Jesus says that the Son of Man must "give his life a ransom for many" (10:45), repeated in Matthew 20:28.

If you page through the gospel of Mark, you will discover that the author has more to say about Jesus' miracles than about his teachings. The supernatural – including demons and unclean spirits – was ubiquitous in the NT world. Lacking modern philosophy and science, followers of Jesus believed that demons and spirits could speak and act like humans. But such powers were no match for Jesus as the supernatural Son of God. Sickness and demon possession were both considered as diseases, and Jesus could heal both. By a simple command (1:21-28) or the touch of his clothing (5:24-34), persons were healed or even restored to life (5:35-43). Such supernatural powers were taken as proof of Jesus' divine nature.

Mark is especially interested in keeping Jesus' divine nature secret, but it is gradually revealed in his gospel. Only in Mark does the voice from heaven at Jesus' baptism speak personally to Jesus, saying, "You are my Son" (1:11). Jesus rebukes the unclean spirit that cried out that Jesus is "the Holy One of God" by telling him, "Be silent" (1:21-28). Because they knew him, Jesus would not permit the demons to speak (1:34), and he often tells persons healed not to tell (1:40-44; 3:11-12; 5:42-43; 7:31-37). After Peter's confession of Jesus as the Messiah, which Jesus does not deny, he tells the disciples not to tell anyone (8:29-30; see also 9:9-10). Then, before the Sanhedrin (the Jewish high court), the high priest asks Jesus, "Are you the Messiah, the Son of the Blessed One?" Only in Mark does Jesus reveal his divine nature by replying, "I am" (14:61-62), and, finally, the gradual revelation of Jesus' divine nature reaches its climax with the exclamation at Jesus' death, "Truly this man was God's Son!" (15:39). Mark ends as it began – Jesus is the Son of God (1:1).

Mark wants his readers to know that Jesus' suffering and death do more to confirm his uniqueness as Messiah and Son of God than his teachings or even his miracles. Mark was equally interested in telling his readers that Jesus was also the Son of Man. "Son of Man" was a part of Jewish eschatology (the word about things that are to happen at the end of the world) that began with the author of the book of Daniel (Daniel 7:13). Whether the Son of Man of the gospel writers was Jesus or another figure to come is still debated. Mark's Son of Man has authority to forgive sins (2:10) and is master of the Sabbath (2:27-28). He must suffer, die, and rise again (8:31; 9:9, 31; 10:32-34), and he will return with power and glory at the end of time (13:24-27).

Mark portrays Jesus and his disciples as a secret clique and uses favorite words and phrases in doing so. He uses *parakaleomai*, meaning "call to oneself," as, for example, in 3:13: "He called to him those whom he wanted" (see also 3:23; 8:1, 34; 10:42). Jesus explained everything about his parables "in private to his disciples" (4:33-34). Jesus "was alone, with those who were around him along with the twelve" (4:10). And, he told the apostles, "Come away to a deserted place all by yourselves" (6:30-31).

## Literary Style of Matthew

In general, Matthew's Greek is more refined than that of Mark and more influenced by Septuagint Greek. As with Mark, Matthew has a favorite vocabulary of words and phrases. Here are a few of the most noticeable (from Greek; order is Matthew, Mark, Luke): "he answered and said" (45, 14, 34); "withdraw," "depart" (10, 1, 0); "throw," "cast" (11, 5, 5); "Baptist" (7, 2, 3); "kingdom of heaven" (32, 0, 0); "beget," "bear" (45, 1, 4); "scribes and Pharisees" (10, 0, 3); "take," "lay hold of," "receive" (57, 21, 22); "swear," "take an oath" (13, 2, 1); "heaven" (82, 18, 34); "approach," "draw near" (52, 5, 10); "bring together" (24, 5, 6); "hypocrite" (13, 1, 3); "righteousness" (7, 0, 1); "truly I say to you" (31, 13, 6).

Matthew prefers to state things in threes: teaching, preaching, and healing (4:23); almsgiving, prayer, and fasting (6:1, 18); three negative (6:19–7:6) and three positive commands (7:7-20); and three parables of sowing (13:1-32). He also likes to repeat the same or similar expressions: "You have heard that it was said...but I say to you" (e.g., 5:21-22, 27-28, 38-39). Matthew introduces parables in different ways: "the kingdom of heaven may be compared to" (13:24; 18:23; 22:2) and "the kingdom of heaven is like" (13:31, 33, 34, 45, 47; 20:1). Sometimes this same formula is preceded with "He put before them another parable" (13:24, 31) or "He told them another parable" (13:33).

Other repetitions of Matthew are "when Jesus had finished" (5, 0, 0; e.g., 7:28; 11:1; 13:53), weeping and gnashing of teeth (6, 0, 1; e.g., 8:12; 13:42), and going to hell (7, 3, 1; e.g., 5:22, 29; 18:9). "Hell" (*NRSV*) represents the Greek *gehenna*, which represents the Hebrew *gehinnom*, a valley south of Jerusalem where pagans burned children in sacrifice to their gods. That is why Matthew sometimes says "hell of fire" (5:22; see also 2 Kings 23:10; Jeremiah 7:31-34).

## Special Interests of Matthew

Of the synoptic writers, Matthew is the most Jewish and most interested in things Jewish. Although Peter is the most popular disciple in the synoptic gospels, only Matthew mentions the church and its foundation on Peter, who was well known among Jewish followers of Jesus. By making Peter preeminent, Matthew gives his gospel appeal to Jews both inside and outside his church.

Matthew shares the view of Mark that Jesus was the legitimate Messiah because he was the Son of David. In order to prove it, he begins his gospel with "the genealogy of Jesus the Messiah, the Son of David." Compare this with the beginning of Luke's genealogy (Luke 3:23). Matthew presents evidence not in the other gospels to support what he says. According to Matthew, two blind men address Jesus as "Son of David" and ask him to have mercy on them (9:27-31), and others address Jesus in the same way (12:23; 15:22; 21:9, 15).

Matthew has a special interest in the Jewish law and teachings of Jesus as a new law. Jews regarded Moses as the greatest lawgiver, and the scribes were the authorities on the law. Matthew did not think Jesus wanted to abolish Jewish law, as is clear from Matthew 5:17-18: "Do not think that I have come to abolish the law or the prophets." Matthew's use, both of "the law or the prophets" and "the law and the prophets" (Matthew 7:12), did not come from Mark, because Mark never uses those expressions.

Some scholars believe that Matthew, who saw Jesus' teachings as a new law, arranged them in five discourses comparable to the five books of the Pentateuch and inserted them into the framework of Mark. The first of these discourses is the Sermon on the Mount (Matthew 5:1–7:29). Like Moses (Exodus 19:20), Jesus went up the mountain and sat down (Matthew 5:1), whereas in Luke 6:17 Jesus came down from the mountain and "stood on a level place" to deliver the Sermon. When finished with the Sermon, Jesus "came down from the mountain" (Matthew 8:1), as did Moses (Exodus 19:14, 21). For Matthew the new law demanded righteousness greater that that of the scribes and Pharisees (5:20), and the antithesis in the Sermon only in Matthew stresses the point: "You have heard that it was said... But I say to you" (5:21-44).

Perhaps the most prominent of Matthew's special interests is his use of the OT. All gospel writers believed that the teachings and work of Jesus were the fulfillment of OT prophecy. However, from beginning to end Matthew has more quotations to prove it. Because of this, it has been suggested that he used a special collection of OT quotations known as *Testimonia* as evidence for promoting the belief that Jesus was the Messiah. Matthew's special formula for introducing formal quotations is that things happened "to fulfill the prophecy of." Events in his birth narratives, including Herod's killing of children, the flight to Egypt, and the move to Nazareth, took place for that purpose. For the same reason Jesus left Nazareth to live in Capernaum (4:12-16). Did Matthew use the phrase "Galilee of the Gentiles" (4:15) to support a mission to Gentiles and then say that Jesus moved to Capernaum, the only place where it is said that Jesus lived, to support that mission? Jesus healing the sick (8:16-17) and teaching in parables (13:34-35), as well as "the potter's field," burial place of Judas (27:3-10; Acts 1:15-20), all fulfill OT prophecies.

So, what came first? Did Matthew's familiarity with the OT motivate him to invent incidents to fit the texts? Or, aware of incidents in Jesus' life, did he believe that they fulfilled OT prophecy? And how do we explain the fact that most of the quotations do not occur in Mark or Luke?

### Literary Style of Luke

Luke was probably the best educated of the synoptic writers, and his Greek is among the most polished and classical of NT writers. In ways that do not appear in translations, he changes Hebrew or Aramaic words in his sources to Greek terms. Statistics show the extent and uniqueness of Luke's vocabulary. Of the 2,055 words in the gospel, 971 occur only once and 352 only twice. Of the total words, 47 are repeated more than 50 times in the gospel. Of words and phrases that are considered "characteristic of Luke," 151 occur in Luke, 95 in Matthew, and 41 in Mark.

Mark prefers the historic present tense, which narrates past events as though taking place in the present. Of Mark's 151 present tenses, Luke changes all but one of them to past tenses or substitutes a participle, which he generally prefers. Here are some examples (from Greek): "were approaching" (Mark 11:1), "came near" (Luke 19:29); "were coming" (Mark 5:35), "came" (Luke 8:49). See J. A. Fitzmyer, *The Gospel According to Luke* (Anchor Bible, 28; Garden City, NY: Doubleday, 1981), pp. 107, 109.

In his gospel, as in Acts, Luke sometimes exaggerates things, but in the gospel he sometimes also tones down or omits something that is in his source. Mark 4:37, "a great windstorm arose, and the waves beat into the boat, so that the boat was already being swamped," becomes in Luke 8:23, "a windstorm swept down on the lake, and the boat was filling with water, and they were in danger."

In spite of Luke's excellent Greek, sometimes he translates Hebrew phrases literally as in the Septuagint. All who heard the things talked about "laid them up in their hearts" (Luke 1:66, *RSV*; "pondered them," *NRSV*; "treasured it in their hearts," *NJB*). "They were afraid with a great fear" (Luke 2:9; "were sore afraid," *ASV*; "were terrified," *NRSV*, *NJB*). "He added to send another slave" (Luke 20:11; "he sent another slave," *NRSV*; "he sent another slave," Mark 12:4; "he sent other slaves," Matthew 21:36).

## Special Interests of Luke

According to Acts and Paul's letters, women were important in early churches. Compared with Mark (17) and Matthew (29), Luke uses *gynē* ("woman," "wife") 41 times in the gospel and 19 times in Acts. Women are prominent throughout the gospel. In the birth narratives Mary is the protagonist instead of Joseph, as in Matthew's account, and Luke also has Elizabeth and Anna (2:36-38). In the rest of the gospel only Luke reports the widow's son at Nain (7:11-17), women healed (8:2-3), Mary and Martha (10:38-42), the woman asking a blessing for Jesus (11:27-28), the crippled woman (13:10-17), the widow and the judge (18:1-8), and women mentioned by the men on the road to Emmaus (24:22-24).

Luke also has a special concern for people of all races and social classes, not only for Jews. Already in the birth narratives with Simeon's words that God's salvation is for all people, Gentiles as well as Jews (2:27-32), Luke prepares his readers for the universality of Jesus' mission. This theme is reiterated in Luke 3:4-6 when Luke continues the quotation from Isaiah 40:3 (in Mark 1:3; Matthew 3:3) to include the words "and all flesh shall see the salvation of God." Luke presents Jesus as the fulfillment of Isaiah 61:1-2; 58:6 in proclaiming good news of release for captives, sight for the blind, and freedom of the oppressed.

Only Luke has the Baptist preaching to tax collectors and soldiers, who are to be honest in their dealings with others. Only Luke has the parables of the rich fool (12:13-21), the rich man and Lazarus (16:19-31), and the story of rich Zacchaeus (19:1-10). All show Luke's favor of the poor and disfavor of the rich. Finally, only Luke has the criminal on the cross admit his crimes and receive forgiveness by Jesus (23:39-43).

Luke has a special interest in Samaria and Samaritans, not mentioned in Mark. In Acts he includes Samaria in his theme (1:8) and as one of the lands where the church was spreading (8:1-14; 9:31; 15:3). Only Luke has the parable of the Good Samaritan (10:29-37). In contrast to Luke, Matthew uses Samaritans only in 10:5-6, where Jesus instructs his disciples to go nowhere among the Gentiles and the Samaritans, but only to the lost sheep of Israel. Luke omits that passage. So, was Luke simply showing a bias toward the Samaritans, or was Matthew using Jesus to convey his prejudice against the Samaritans?

Luke's special interest in the Holy Spirit is evident in the gospel as it is in Acts. In the birth stories, the Baptist will be filled with the Holy Spirit before his birth (1:15), and Elizabeth, Mary, Zachariah, and Simeon are motivated by the Spirit (1:35, 41, 67; 2:25-27). Following his baptism, Jesus was "full of the Holy Spirit" and "led by the Spirit in the wilderness," and "filled with the power of the Spirit" Jesus returned to Galilee (4:1, 14).

Luke also has a special interest in Jesus praying and in his followers praying. In the birth narratives the people outside the temple were praying, and Zechariah's prayer was heard (1:10-13). Jesus prayed after his baptism (3:21), in deserted places (5:16), before he called the Twelve (6:12), before he teaches his disciples to pray (11:1), before he asks the disciples who people say he is (9:18), and before he dies on the cross (23:46). Only in Luke does Jesus' transfiguration occur when he was praying (9:29). Two parables only in Luke deal with aspects of prayer: the friend at midnight – persistence brings an answer to prayer (11:5-10), and the Pharisee and tax collector – humility in prayer (18:9-14).

Although eschatology plays a prominent role in all the synoptic gospels, Luke uses it in a conflicting way. He associates the coming of the kingdom of God with it, but not always in the same manner. At times he deeschatologizes it, that is, he eliminates its eschatological nature from a saying in another gospel. Regarding Jesus' preaching in Galilee in Mark 1:14-15, "The time is fulfilled, and the kingdom of God has come near," Luke says simply that Jesus "began to teach in their synagogues" (Luke 4:14-15). In Luke 4:16-21 Jesus read in the synagogue from Isaiah 61:1-2 about good news for the poor, release of captives, and sight for the blind and "to proclaim the year of the Lord's favor." Having finished reading, he says, "Today this scripture has been fulfilled in your hearing." This implies that the end is already present in Jesus' work of teaching and healing if people accept it (see Luke 4:22-30), showing Luke's inconsistency.

The statement in Mark 9:1 that some present will not die "until they see that the kingdom of God has come with power" and Matthew's statement in 16:28 that they will not die "before they see the Son of Man coming in his kingdom" become in Luke 9:27, "before they see the kingdom of God." Here the kingdom of God is a matter of personal experience apart from eschatological signs. This coincides with Jesus' words only in Luke 17:20-21 that the kingdom of God is not coming with observable signs or with exclamations, "Look, here it is!" or "There it is!" "For in fact," says Jesus, "the kingdom of God is among you." Here the Greek words taken as "among you" may equally be rendered as "in your midst" or "within you."

In Luke 10:9 and 10:11 Luke retains the saying that the kingdom of God has come near, although he had omitted it at Mark 1:15 and Matthew 10:7. In Luke 21:25-31 Luke retains the saying in Mark 13:24-29 and Matthew 24:29-33 about seeing signs that the Son of Man is coming. But only Luke concludes with Jesus saying, "When you see these things taking place, you will know that the kingdom of God is near." This is a contradiction of what he had said about the kingdom not coming with signs to be observed in 17:20-21.

## *Chapter Summary*

It is clear when comparing the synoptic gospels, that is, Matthew, Mark, and Luke, that a literary relationship exists among them. The gospels include different types of stories about Jesus that were passed down orally and material from a number of different written sources. The Priority of Mark is the theory that Mark was the first gospel to be written and that it was used as a source by other gospel writers. Because Matthew and Luke contain material unique to each, some shared material not found in Mark, and two different accounts of Jesus' birth, scholars in general accept a four-source theory. Some material found only in Mark and the large number of miracles stories only in that gospel also suggest that Mark had one or more sources not used by Matthew and Luke.

Mark's literary style is characterized by his use of diminutives and certain special words and phrases. His special interest in Jesus' suffering and death, his gradual revelation of the divine nature of Jesus, and his focus on Jesus' miracles rather than teachings are key ways in which the gospel of Mark is different from the other two synoptic gospels.

Matthew also has specific words and phrases that he favors, but his Greek is more refined and influenced by Septuagint Greek than that of Mark. Stating things in threes and repetitions of the same or similar expressions are also typical of Matthew. Matthew is more Jewish than either Mark or Luke, and he has a special interest in Jewish law and Jesus' teachings as a new law. And, his emphasis on Jesus as the fulfillment of OT prophecy is even stronger than that of Mark and Luke and is foremost among his special interests.

Finally, Luke stands out as the most educated synoptic author, with his polished Classical Greek and extensive vocabulary. Luke sometimes exaggerates things, other times tones down or omits things from a source, and includes literal translations of Hebrew phrases. Perhaps what most sets Luke apart from the other synoptic writers is his interest in women and in people of all races and social classes. Luke is also characterized by a special interest in Samaria and Samaritans, the Holy Spirit, and praying, and his conflicting use of eschatology is also unique.

Being aware of the typical literary styles and special interests of Matthew, Mark, and Luke prepares us to consider in an insightful manner what each gospel says about the life and teachings of Jesus and to compare the synoptic gospels with the gospel of John. We focus on these things in the next chapter in an attempt to discover what "the Bible says" about Jesus. Most importantly, we try to determine what Jesus actually said and did, an interesting and challenging task, to say the least.

Chapter 14

JESUS, MATTHEW, MARK, LUKE, OR JOHN?

*Introduction*

In this chapter we examine in more detail selected passages that illustrate the synoptic gospel writers' literary styles and special interests and how these influenced what they wrote. By comparing specific accounts in Matthew, Mark, and Luke, it becomes evident how each gospel writer's particular characteristics resulted in differences among their accounts. In turn, what we learn about Jesus, his life, and his teachings also varies from gospel to gospel. And, of course, that causes uncertainty about what Jesus really did and what he actually said. How much of each gospel is an accurate representation of Jesus, and how much is actually a reflection of a gospel writer's motives for writing, religious beliefs and faith, literary style, or interests?

To complicate the situation, we find additional differences within the gospels and other unanswered questions when we compare the synoptic gospels with the gospel of John. This makes it even more difficult to answer simply that "The Bible Says So" with regard to Jesus. What did Jesus *really* say? What did Jesus *really* do? What did Jesus *really* teach? In this chapter, we strive to gain insightful understanding about the historical Jesus as we more fully explore similarities and differences within and among the four gospels.

*John the Baptist*

Please turn now to Mark 1:1-6; Matthew 3:1-6; and Luke 3:1-6 as we study carefully these passages about John the Baptist. Mark does not introduce John at the beginning of his narrative, but Matthew and Luke do. Matthew has the indefinite "In those days." Luke mentions a specific year in the rule of Tiberius (14–37 CE), with Pilate as governor (26–36 CE) and other rulers in the time of Jesus. In harmony with John's birth by the will of God (Luke

1:5-25, 57-80), the Baptist is called "John son of Zechariah" (Luke 3:2). Luke never calls him "the one baptizing" (verb form) of Mark or "the Baptist" (noun form) of Matthew.

In his own way, each writer gives the subject of John's preaching as repentance and forgiveness, but only Matthew associates the kingdom of heaven with it (3:2). Each writer has an OT quotation from Isaiah 40:3, beginning with "the voice." However, Mark, in introducing John the Baptist, mistakenly attributes to Isaiah his quotation from Malachi 3:1: "I am sending my messenger ahead of you, who will prepare your way." Matthew and Luke compensate for Mark's error by omitting the quotation from Malachi. Because of Luke's special concern for all social classes and races, he continues the quotation to conclude with "all flesh shall see the salvation of God." Luke omits the life of John in the wilderness in Mark and Matthew, probably because he is generally interested in the city rather than the country.

The words in the Q passage in Matthew 3:7-10 and Luke 3:7-9 are almost the same, but there is a peculiar introductory sentence by each writer. In Matthew's introductory statement, John calls the Pharisees and Sadducees vipers, but in Luke it is "the crowds" who are the "brood of vipers" (Luke 3:10-14). This reflects Matthew's antagonism toward the Pharisees and Sadducees and Luke's desire to avoid what could be offensive to Jews. Matthew sometimes speaks disparagingly of the Pharisees separately, and sometimes he links them with the scribes and Sadducees (e.g., 9:11, 34; 22:15).

Only Matthew has a long section on Jesus pronouncing woes on them: "Woe to you, scribes and Pharisees, hypocrites!" (Matthew 23:1-36). We cannot account for Matthew's attitude, but perhaps he had been a Pharisee or even a scribe and was angry because they did not accept his Jesus, the Messiah. It is also difficult to tell how many, if any, of such passages go back to Jesus and how many are actually evidence of the controversy between members of the Christ movement and the Jews (see, e.g., Acts 6:7–7:60; 14:1-7; 15:1-35).

In contrast to Matthew, Luke mentions Sadducees only in 20:27, where he retains the words in Mark 12:18 (Matthew 22:23) in a passage on a question of the Sadducees about the resurrection of the dead, because they did not believe in it. In Acts 23:8 Luke also says, "The Sadducees say that there is no resurrection, or angel, or spirit; but the Pharisees acknowledge all three."

Following John's preaching to special classes of people, he preaches about the one coming after him (Mark 1:7-8; Matthew 3:11-12; Luke 3:15-18). All three gospels agree that John baptizes with water, but only Matthew adds "for repentance"; all agree that John is inferior to Jesus. Jesus will baptize with the Holy Spirit, but only Matthew and Luke add "with fire." Only Matthew and Luke have the winnowing fork, a tool used to separate the wheat from the chaff, which will be burned "with unquenchable fire." As in Isaiah 30:24, the fork is used figuratively for the destruction of the wicked as chaff and the salvation of the righteous as grain. And then Luke adds: "With many other exhortations, he [John] proclaimed the good news to the people." If that was good news, what was bad news?

Only Luke reports that "all" were wondering if John might be the Messiah (3:15). This is significant because it shows that the Baptist had a strong enough following among some Jews to challenge the belief in the Messiahship of Jesus. By the time Luke wrote Acts, there was to be no questioning about John being the Messiah, as Paul's speech indicates: "As John was finishing his work, he said, 'What do you suppose that I am? I am not he. No, but one is coming after me; I am not worthy...'" (Acts 13:25).

By the time the gospel of John was written, the author has the Baptist repeat emphatically that he is not the Messiah and that Jesus is superior (1:20-23, 27-28; 3:3, 28). According to John, the Baptist only bears witness to the light, is just a voice crying in the wilderness, and testifies that Jesus is the Son of God. The gospel of John also shows the preeminence of Jesus over John the Baptist when two of his disciples leave him to follow Jesus and one confesses that Jesus is the Messiah. Jesus was making and baptizing more disciples than the Baptist, and John the Baptist did no miracles. John, the gospel writer, ends his discussion of John the Baptist by saying that the Baptist's followers declared that all he said about Jesus was true (John 1:32, 37-41; 4:1; 10:40-41). This is the ultimate proof of Jesus' superiority over John the Baptist.

## The Rejection of Jesus at Nazareth

According to Luke, the people of Jesus' hometown rejected him, saying skeptically, "Do here also in your hometown the things that we have heard you did at Capernaum" (Luke 4:23). However, up to this point Luke has not reported that Jesus performed any miraculous deeds at Capernaum and does not do so until immediately after the hometown incident (4:31). People from Nazareth drove Jesus out of town and wanted to throw him over a cliff, but he passed through them and went on his way to Capernaum (Luke 4:29-30). At Capernaum the people were immediately amazed at his authoritative teaching and his casting out of demons, and a report about him spread throughout the region.

So, how are we to understand these conflicting stories of events and accounts? Luke was probably aware of some earlier tradition about Jesus' work at Capernaum that he inserted in the Nazareth story without realizing the inconsistency.

### Jairus's Daughter and the Woman's Faith

The intertwining stories in Mark 5:21-43; Matthew 9:18-26; and Luke 8:40-56 are good for illustrating in some detail the sources and literary relationships of the first three gospels. They also illustrate how difficult it is to determine the original words in an incident dealing with Jesus. Matthew's account, which is much shorter that the other two, appears earlier in his gospel, and Luke's order characteristically follows that of Mark. The italicized words in the different accounts below are transliterations of the Greek, that is, the English equivalents of the Greek letters. They are used to show differences in meaning. *"Thugatrion"* (little daughter) in Mark is *"thugatēr"* (daughter) in Matthew and *"thugatēr monogenēs"* (only daughter) in Luke.

Mark 5:21-24

When Jesus had crossed again in the boat to the other side, a great crowd gathered around him; and he was by the sea. Then one of the leaders of the synagogue named Jairus came and, when he saw him, fell at his feet and begged him repeatedly, "My little daughter (*thugatrion*) is at the point of death. Come and lay your hands on her, so that she may be made well, and live." So he went with him.

Matthew 9:18-19

While he was saying these things to them, suddenly a leader [unnamed] of the synagogue came in and knelt before him, saying, "My daughter (*thugatēr*) has just died; but come and lay your hand on her, and she will live." And Jesus got up and followed him, with his disciples.

Luke 8:40-42

Now when Jesus returned, the crowd welcomed him, for they were all waiting for him. Just then there came a man named Jairus, a leader of the synagogue. He fell at Jesus' feet and begged him to come to his house, for he had an only daughter (*thugatēr monogenēs*), about twelve years old, who was dying.

Notice the differences, especially Luke's insertion of "Jesus," which adds clarity. Luke puts the name Jairus before the leader. While the story is a dialogue in Mark and Matthew, Luke changes it to a narrative. Observe that "my little daughter" is an example of Mark's use of diminutives, and Luke's "only daughter" is also different. Matthew has no reference to a crowd or the sea, nor does he give Jairus's name. Just in Matthew is the girl already dead.

At this point the story is interrupted with that of the healing of the woman with the hemorrhages. The passages quoted below are at the end of that story.

Mark 5:34

"Your faith has made you well (*sōzō*); go in peace, and be healed [literally, "be in sound health"] of your disease."

Matthew 9:22

"Take heart, daughter; your faith has made you well" (*sōzō*). And immediately the woman [notice "woman"] was made well.

Luke 8:48

"Your faith has made you well (*sōzō*); go in peace."

Here the verb *sōzō* is translated as "made well," whereas in Luke 8:50 it is "be saved." Luke liked to combine believing with being saved [*sōzō*], as he did back in 8:12. The ideas of being saved and being healed are obviously synonymous for the gospel writers. The reason is that in much of Jesus' time illness was thought to be the result of sin, so being healed was the same as being forgiven of sins. See Luke 17:19: "Your faith has made you well" or "saved you" (*sōzō*) and John 5:14: "See, you have been made well! Do not sin any more."

The story of Jairus's daughter continues with the following part only in Mark and Luke.

Mark 5:35-37

While he [Jesus] was still speaking, some people came from the leader's house to say, "Your daughter is dead. Why trouble the teacher any further?" But hearing what they said, Jesus said to the leader of the synagogue, "Do not fear, only believe." He allowed no one to follow him except Peter, James, and John, the brother of James.

Luke 8:49-51

While he [Jesus] was still speaking, someone came from the leader's house, to say, "Your daughter is dead; do not trouble the teacher any longer." When Jesus heard this, he replied, "Do not fear. Only believe, and she will be saved" (*sōzō*). When he came to the house, he did not allow anyone to enter with him, except Peter, John, and James, and the child's (*pais*) father and mother.

Observe that Luke changes the question to a negative command. Jesus is at the house when he forbids people to follow, whereas in Mark this occurs before getting to the house. Luke changes the order of disciples and adds the father and mother of the child. And then the story continues in all three gospels.

Mark 5:38-40

When they came to the house of the leader of the synagogue, he saw a commotion, people weeping and wailing loudly. When he had entered he said to them, "Why do you make a commotion and weep? The child (*paidion*) is not dead but sleeping." And they laughed at him.

Matthew 9:23-24

When Jesus came to the leader's house and saw the flute players and the crowd making a commotion, he said, "Go away; for the girl (*korasion*) is not dead but sleeping." And they laughed at him.

Luke 8:52-53

[Luke mentions the house earlier and continues]

They were all weeping and wailing for her; but he said, "Do not weep; for she is not dead but sleeping." And they laughed at him [to which only Luke adds] knowing that she was dead.

Perhaps the most noticeable difference here is Matthew's flute players, an indication of his Jewish background. Even poor families hired flute players and a special female to weep at funerals, apparently to stress the loss of the family member. Again, Mark has the diminutive *paidaion*, for which Matthew also has a diminutive (*korasion*) of a different word, which is more colloquial. In 8:51 Luke uses the basic word *pais*, not its diminutive as in Mark. Mark's *paidaion* is more affectionate than Matthew's *korasion* and refers to a child from birth on. Mark uses *paidaion* also in 5:40 with the father and mother and then *korasion* in 5:41-42 under less affectionate circumstances. The laughing in all three is a scornful laugh. For Mark's "child" and Matthew's "girl" Luke has "she." Mark's question about weeping, which is omitted in Matthew, becomes a demand in Luke.

Mark 5:40-41

Then he put them all outside, and took the child's father and mother and those who were with him, and went in where the child was. He took her by the hand and said to her, "Talitha cum," which means Little girl, get up!

Matthew 9:25

When the crowd had been put outside, he went in and took her by the hand.

Luke 8:54

[Luke says nothing here about anyone being put out or entering a place where the child was]

He took her by the hand and called out, "Child, get up!" Earlier Luke had said that Jesus "did not allow anyone to enter with him" (Luke 8:51).

As Mark likes to do, he uses Aramaic words and then gives the meaning in Greek for his non-Jewish readers. See also 3:17; 7:11, 34; 11:9-10; 14:36; and 15:22, 34. For *"girl"* Matthew uses *korasion*, which he had used in 9:24. Luke's "called out" is more forceful than "said" of Mark and was meant to be heard by others except the girl (Mark's "to her").

Mark 5:42

And immediately the girl (*korasion*) got up and began to walk about (she was twelve years of age). At this they were overcome with amazement.

Matthew 9:25

And the girl (*korasion*) got up.

Luke 8:55-56

Her spirit returned, and she got up at once. Then he directed them to give her something to eat. Her parents were astounded.

Notice the characteristic "immediately" (*euthys*) in Mark. Luke, instead, has "at once" (*parachrema*), which he uses ten times in the gospel and six in Acts. Mark never uses it, Matthew does twice, and it is nowhere else in the NT. It was customary for miracle workers to give some proof that a miracle had been performed, and the walking and reference to food serve the purpose. It is surprising that Matthew says nothing about that. In light of the reference to eating, the word "spirit" (*NRSV*; *pneuma*) would be more fittingly rendered as "breath" as an indication of restoration to physical life as before she died. Matthew has no words of Jesus to the girl after she got up.

Two additional differences here are much more evident in Greek. Mark uses a Hebrew construction, "They were amazed with a great amazement," which Luke changes into better Greek. The verb is the same in both texts, although translated differently in the *NRSV*. And, the indefinite third person ("they") in Mark is changed to "her parents" in Luke.

## What Did Jesus Really Say?

As the story of Jairus's daughter clearly demonstrates, even in passages reported to be direct quotations of Jesus, it is hard to determine what Jesus actually did say. The following passages illustrate how an author's own literary style and thought influenced how he reported sayings of Jesus. The Beatitudes provide an excellent example of this, so we include several in our discussion. The Beatitudes are sayings in the beginning of Jesus' Sermon on the Mount, which is in both Matthew and Luke (mostly from Q). Jesus is speaking to his disciples.

Matthew 5:3

Blessed are the poor in spirit, for theirs is the kingdom of heaven.

Luke 6:20

Blessed are you who are poor, for yours is the kingdom of God.

What does "poor in spirit" mean? Matthew was probably influenced by the OT, where poor and spirit are sometimes combined. "It is better to be a meek-spirited person with lowliness than one who divides the spoil with the proud" (LXX, Proverbs 16:18-19; see also Isaiah 66:2). "Kingdom of heaven," Matthew's favorite, occurs nowhere else in the NT, whereas Luke's "kingdom of God" occurs a few times in Matthew and in Mark and Luke, Acts, and Paul's letters. Luke's "poor" are people in poverty and reflect his favoritism toward the poor and his prejudice against the rich. This is emphasized by his matching woes, absent in Matthew: "But woe to you who are rich, for you have received your consolation" (6:24). Luke's "your" and "yours" are more personal than Matthew's "theirs" and are directed to those among "a great crowd of his disciples" (Luke 6:17) who are poor and rich respectively.

Matthew 5:6

"Blessed are those who hunger and thirst for righteousness, for they will be filled."

Luke 6:21

"Blessed are you who are hungry now, for you will be filled."

Again, Luke's language is more direct, and his prejudice is emphasized by his contrasting woe: "Woe to you who are full now, for you will be hungry" (6:25). Matthew's addition "and thirst for righteousness" show influence from the OT, where the two are sometimes combined. In Isaiah 49:10 the people saved by Yahweh so that they could return to Jerusalem "shall not hunger or thirst" (see also Deuteronomy 28:49). Moreover, righteousness is a special concern of Matthew (7, 0, 1), whereas Mark never mentions it and Luke does only once.

Luke omits a crucial Beatitude: "Blessed are the peacemakers, for they will be called children of God" (Matthew 5:9). In light of Luke's special interest in "peace" (4, 1, 14), his omission is surprising and confusing. In his birth narratives Luke mentions peace three times (1:79; 2:14, 29). In Jesus' entry into Jerusalem, instead of Mark's "Blessed is the coming kingdom...of David!" (11:10) and Matthew's "Hosanna in the highest heaven!" (21:9), Luke has "peace in heaven, and glory in the highest heaven!" (19:38). The risen Jesus greets the disciples with "Peace be with you," which is the Jewish greeting *"shalom leka"* (Luke 24:36). Here "peace" seems to be an inner tranquility, as with "Peace to this house!" in Luke 10:5 (see Matthew 9:13). "Peace" is the absence of war in Luke 11:21; 14:32; 19:42.

Given Luke's interest in "peace" elsewhere, it seems odd that he would omit Matthew's peacemakers if it occurred in Luke's Q source. Then again, "peacemakers" occurs in the NT only in Matthew 5:9, so we have to question its use there with respect to what Jesus really said. In 5:45 Matthew has Jesus call the disciples "children of your Father in heaven," which is lacking in Luke 6:27-28. For these reasons it is likely that the peacemakers and sons (Greek) of God are Matthew's additions to his Q source.

There are numerous examples of the same kinds of challenges in trying to get back to what Jesus really said. Study the following and notice the differences: reasons for divorce (Mark 10:11-12; Matthew 5:21-32; Luke 16:16-18), the Lord's Prayer (Matthew 6:9-15; Luke 11:2-4; see also Mark 11:25, with note in the *NRSV*), the building of a house (Matthew 7:24-27; Luke 6:47-49), the sending out of the disciples (Mark 6:6-13, 34; Matthew 9:35–10:16; Luke 9:1-6; see also Luke 10:1-16), and the reason for Jesus speaking in parables (Mark 4:10-12; Matthew 13:10-15; Luke 8:9-10 and Mark 4:21-25; Matthew 13:12; Luke 8:16-18).

# The Gospel of John

## John and the Synoptic Gospels

From beginning to end there is a noticeable difference between John and the other gospels. Jesus is not only presented in a very different way, but the location of his activity is also different. In the Synoptics Jesus teaches mostly in and around Galilee, whereas in John his activity centers in Judea, with frequent trips to Jerusalem. There is also a difference in the length of Jesus' activity. In the Synoptics Jesus goes to Jerusalem only once and attends only one Passover, at the time of his death. In John he attends three Passovers (2:13; 6:4; 11:55), so his career lasted at least two years, probably longer.

John seems to assume that his readers knew some gospel traditions. He uses "disciples," not "apostles," for Jesus' followers, and he mentions "the Twelve" without saying that they had been called (6:67, 70-71; 20:24). Both the Synoptic gospels and John mention activity of the Baptist first and his inferiority to Jesus, but John emphasizes it more. In the Synoptics Jesus succeeds the Baptist, whereas in John both men are active at the same time.

In the Synoptics most of Jesus' teaching is in the form of parables, whereas in John he teaches mostly in discourses, especially with his Jewish adversaries and his disciples. The synoptic word for "parable" (*parabolē*) does not occur in John. John composes passages in which Jesus speaks as *egō eimi* ("I am"), a prominent form of his teaching, some of which is allegory or symbol.

Significant incidents in the Synoptics are absent in John: temptations of Jesus; actual baptism of Jesus; teaching about the kingdom of God, what it is like, and its coming; healing of demoniacs and lepers; Jesus' association with outcasts and sinners; institution of the Lord's Supper; Jesus' transfiguration; and agony in Gethsemane.

These incidents are in both the Synoptics and John: feeding of the 5000, the only miracle in all gospels; a last meal with disciples; special entry of Jesus into Jerusalem; prediction of Peter's denial of Jesus; Jesus before the Sanhedrin and Pilate; request for release of Barabbas; crucifixion and burial of Jesus; and empty tomb and resurrection.

Four miracles are only in John: changing water into wine, healing of the man at Beth-zatha, restoring of sight to man born blind, and the raising of Lazarus. Other incidents in John not in the Synoptics are meeting with Nicodemus, the woman of Samaria, Greeks wanting to see Jesus, Jesus washing the disciples' feet, trial of Jesus before Annas, and Jesus' resurrection appearance to Thomas.

Some scholars believe that the likenesses and differences between John and the Synoptic gospels are to be explained by John's use of an independent source. Some think that John knew and supplemented the Synoptics either from other traditions or by his own imaginative creation. A minority of scholars, including myself, believe that John actually used one or more of the Synoptics. Our further study of John as an author will show his uniqueness and that there is no simple answer to what "the Bible says" with respect to sayings of Jesus.

*Literary Style of John*

John writes some of the easiest Greek, and his vocabulary is limited. He repeats the same words a lot, and they become themes of the gospel. Here are some examples (Mark, Matthew, Luke, John): light (1, 7, 7, 23); life (4, 7, 5, 36); two verbs "to love": *agapaō* (5, 8, 13, 37) and *phileō* (1, 5, 2, 13); love (*agapē*; 0, 1, 1, 7); truth (3, 1, 3, 25); true (1, 1, 0, 14); the noun "witness" (3, 0, 1, 14); verb "to witness" (0, 1, 1, 33); "to judge" (0, 6, 6, 19); "to know" (12, 20, 28, 59); and "to believe" (14, 11, 9, 98). The noun "faith" does not occur in John.

The most characteristic feature of John's literary style is the repetition and variation in language and thought, even to the point of contradiction. John is fond of using synonyms, words with multiple meanings, and the devices of misunderstanding and avoiding an answer to a question but giving a reply that expresses John's theology. For example, in 1:5 when Jesus says "the light shines in the darkness, and the darkness did not overcome it," John is using a word with multiple meanings. The word translated as "overcome" in the *NRSV* is *kataballō*, which may also mean "grasp with the mind" or "comprehend." So, did the people not overcome the light, or did they fail to understand its significance? John uses three different forms of two different words for "see," all translated as "see" in the *NRSV*, two of which might better be "Behold!" (5:14) and "observe" (5:19). They may be synonymous for John, perhaps with different nuances as suggested.

In John 2:18-22 the Jews ask for a sign, to which Jesus replies: "Destroy this temple, and in three days I will raise it up." Thinking he is talking about the temple of the Jews, they reply that the temple was being constructed for 46 years, and will he raise it in three days? Then John, who was using the device of misunderstanding, adds that he was speaking about his body as a temple that would be raised in three days. Likewise, in 4:7-15 the Samaritan woman thinks Jesus is speaking about drinking water, but he is talking about the water that gives eternal life. John's theme about Jesus giving eternal life is brought out again in the discourse with Jews about the bread of life given by Jesus, yet another example of misunderstanding. It is not the manna like Moses gave them in the wilderness, as the Jews think; it is the bread given by the Father for the life of the world. Jesus is the bread of life that comes from heaven, and those who eat it will not die (6:25-51).

Jesus' discourse with Nicodemus is an excellent example of John's fondness for using words with more than one meaning, misunderstanding, and repetition with variation. Jesus says, "No one can see the kingdom of God without being born *anōthēn*." The word for "see" *(horaō)* can also mean "perceive" or "experience," and *anōthēn* may mean "again," "anew," or "from above" (3:1-10). So, how are we to understand those words? Nicodemus misunderstands when he thinks of physical birth: "Can one enter a second time into the mother's womb and be born?" Jesus replies by repeating what he had said but in a different way: "No one can enter the kingdom of God without being born of water and Spirit… Do not be astonished that I said to you (singular), You must be born *anōthēn*."

Is "enter" to be taken as synonymous with "see" or in a different sense? Jesus says, "What is born of the flesh is flesh, and what is born of the Spirit is spirit." Notice that the first "Spirit" has a capital letter, but the second does not. Is "Spirit" the Holy Spirit or another spirit? Nicodemus is not to be astonished because Jesus said, "I said to you, You must be born from above" (3:7). Here the first "you" is singular, indicating that Nicodemus personally is addressed. However, the second "you" is plural. Nicodemus had approached Jesus by saying, "Rabbi, we [plural] know…" Apparently John wants it to be understood that through Nicodemus Jesus is speaking to a larger audience. These are linguistic twists that are not evident in translation.

Consider the wordplay on the double meaning of *pneuma* as "wind" or "spirit" in 3:8: "The wind (spirit) blows where it chooses." Jesus' words must leave readers flustered when Jesus continues: "And you (singular) hear the sound of it, but you do not know where it comes from or where it goes. So it is with everyone who is born of the Spirit." Is this a variation of, or an explanation for, what it means to be born *anōthēn*? Nicodemus still does not understand, so he asks, "How can these things be?" Jesus asks, "Are you a teacher of Israel, and yet you do not understand these things?" This is a good example of John avoiding a question by giving a different answer. See also John 11:25-27.

The passage in John 3:1-10 is usually given to support the view of some that Christians must be "born again." However, can we be sure what Jesus actually said or what he (or John) meant? We might think that "again" and "anew" mean the same thing, but that may not be true. "Again" may imply "in the same way," while "anew" may mean being born in a different way. If one is born "from above," does that mean from heaven or God or the Spirit (see John 19:11; James 1:17; 3:15, 17). If one is born in that sense, must one be born "again"? Compared with the Synoptics, it is likely that we are more removed from what Jesus actually said in the gospel of John, which becomes even more evident in studying John's portrayal of Jesus.

*Jesus as Teacher and his Teachings*
Turning from the Synoptic gospels to John, we discover a very different Jesus from start to finish. In John's first chapter there are numerous titles and characterizations of Jesus from the preexistent Word to the heavenly Son of Man. The person of Jesus and the content of his teaching are also very different. Although Mark lacks the Sermon on the Mount as it occurs in Matthew, some teachings that appear to be from it are in Mark. In contrast, in John there is no Sermon. Moreover, John's teaching method is mainly discourses, especially with the Jews and his disciples, and a basic feature of John's discourses, absent in the Sermon on the Mount, is that persons often interrupt Jesus to criticize him or ask him questions. The discourses are sometimes connected with "signs," John's distinctive word for miracles performed by Jesus.

The story of the healing of a man ill for years (5:2-16) is followed by a discourse on Jesus' work (5:17-47). The feeding of 5000 (6:1-21) is followed by a discourse with the crowd (6:22-32) and one on Jesus as the bread of life (6:35-59). The longest discourse is that with his disciples and is known as his "last" or "farewell discourse" (13:31–16:33). These discourses are on a variety of subjects, including teachings of Jesus that appear elsewhere in the gospel.

*Jesus as "I Am".* Only John uses the technical *egō eimi* ("I am") on the lips of Jesus as a person and as a method of his teaching. Although its meaning is uncertain, John was probably influenced by the Septuagint. Recall that Moses asked Yahweh what he should tell the Israelites if they asked him the name of the God who sent him. Yahweh told him to say, "I am has sent me to you" (Exodus 3:13-14).

Passages from the LXX of Isaiah may also have influenced John in portraying the divine nature of Jesus. Compare Isaiah 43:25, "I am I am, the one who" (*egō eimi egō eimi, ho*), where the second *egō eimi* is for emphasis, with John 4:25-26. The Samaritan woman said to Jesus that she knew the Messiah was coming and that Jesus responded: "I am he, the one who" (*egō eimi, ho*; John 4:25-26). For John *egō eimi*, Messiah, Son of God, Son of Man, and Savior are synonymous titles for the divine Jesus. See also 8:28:

"When you have lifted up the Son of Man, then you will realize that I am he" (*egō eimi*).

John uses *egō eimi* either with or without a description that follows it. *Egō eimi* sayings with a description are more obvious to modern readers, such as the following: "I am the good shepherd. The good shepherd lays down his life for the sheep" (10:11). In the allegory in this passage, the "sheep" are some believers, the sheepfold the believing community of John, and the strangers adversaries of that community, either other Christians or Jews. John was writing to a second generation of Christians who had not seen or known Jesus, a group of believers in the process of separating from Judaism, and the allegory was intended to enlighten his readers about the nature of Jesus. It coincides with John's theme elsewhere of Jesus bringing life and eternal life for believers (20:31, e.g.). See "I am the resurrection and the life" (11:25-26).

It is more difficult to understand John's use of the "I am" without a descriptive phrase. Jesus says to the Jews, for instance, "I told you that you would die in your sins...unless you believe that I am" (he; *egō eimi*; 8:24; see also 13:19). John may have been influenced by LXX Isaiah 43:10-11. There the author says that the servant of Yahweh is a special person to come, who is chosen by him, "in order that you may know and believe and understand that I am he (he; *egō eimi*)...I am God, and besides me there is no savior."

In conversation with the Jews, who boast that Abraham is their father, Jesus says, "Before Abraham was, I am" (8:39, 58). Jesus came into existence before Abraham did, and John's thought may be influenced by Psalm 90:1-2: "Lord, you have been our dwelling place in all generations. Before the mountains were brought forth, or ever you had formed the earth and the world, from everlasting to everlasting you are God" (see also Isaiah 43:13). Here "you are" is the equivalent of "I am." John transfers these ideas from God to Jesus, in consistency with the Word being with God in the beginning and that through him "all things came into being" (1:1-3).

The differences between what is said about Jesus and his teaching in John, compared with the Synoptics, clearly shows how difficult it is to determine what "the Bible says" with respect to Jesus. The following sayings of Jesus on specific themes illustrate how John's literary style and thought influenced what he reports Jesus said.

### Sayings of Jesus on Specific Themes

With regard to Jesus testifying about himself, the gospel of John has obvious contradictions in what Jesus says. "If I testify about myself, my testimony is not true" (5:31). Contrast that with Jesus saying, "Even if I testify on my own behalf, my testimony is valid" (true; 8:14).

The same kind of contradiction occurs also about Jesus judging: "God did not send the Son into the world to condemn the world, but in order that the world might be saved through him. Those who believe in him are not condemned; but those who do not believe are condemned already, because they have not believed in the name of the only Son of God" (3:17-18). In this passage the word translated as "condemn" in the *NRSV* may also be translated as "judge." In contrast to Jesus not judging the world, Jesus says: "I came into this world for [the purpose of] judgment" (9:39) and "I have much to say about you and much to judge" (8:26). In 8:50 the Father is the judge, and in 16:7-11 judgment is associated with the *Paraklete*. The word *paraklētos* is literally "calling to one's aid" and may mean "entreaty," "evaluation," "encouragement," "consolation," "comfort," "advocate," or "helper." It is translated as "Advocate" or "Helper" in the *NRSV*; "Counselor," *RSV*; "advocate," *REB*; "Comforter," *ASV*; and left untranslated as "Paraclete," *NJB*.

The above passages seem to make judgment a part of the present existence with Jesus and the Father judging. Compare them with those that follow, which make judgment a part of the future. "The Father judges no one but has given all judgment to the Son" (5:22). However, in 5:24 Jesus says that anyone who believes him (God) who sent him "has eternal life, and does not come under judgment," which contradicts what was said in 3:17-18. In 5:30 Jesus says that he can do nothing on his own, and then immediately says, "As I hear, I judge; and my judgment is just." With this and 5:22 compare 8:15: "I judge no one. Yet even if I do judge, my judgment is valid (true); for it is not I alone who judge, but I and the Father."

In John 8:21-23 Jesus says to the Jews: "Where I am going, you cannot come." The Jews ask: "Is he going to kill himself?" They do not understand that he is from above and not of this world, and they will die in their sins unless they believe that Jesus is *egō eimi*. In the last discourse with the disciples the words are repeated with variations: "As I said to the Jews so now I say to you, 'Where I am going, you cannot come.'" Peter asks why he cannot follow Jesus now, because he will give his life for him. Jesus predicts Peter's subsequent denial (13:33-38).

Jesus says that he is going to prepare a place for his disciples, he will take them to himself, and they know the way to where he is going. This time Thomas responds by saying that they do not know where he is going, so how can they know the way. Jesus answers: "I am the way, and the truth, and the life. No one comes to the Father except through me" (14:3-7), a repeated theme in John. He uses the disciples and their questions as ploys for conveying his own beliefs about Jesus. Other persons in the gospel serve the same purpose.

The theme of life and eternal life are just as varied and inconsistent as other themes. Eternal life comes through believing (3:15-16, 36; 6:40). After Martha confesses that Lazarus will rise in the resurrection at the last day, Jesus says: "I am the resurrection and the life. Those who believe in me, even though they die, will live, and everyone who lives and believes in me will never die." Then Jesus asks if she believes this, but she evades the question and replies: "Yes, Lord, I believe that you are the Messiah, the Son of God, the one coming into the world" (11:21-27). Thus, Martha is a ploy for the three-fold confession of John's faith (see 20:31).

John has numerous other variants on the theme of life. As the Father gives life, so does the Son (5:21). These things also bring life: believing in the one whom God sent (5:24; 17:3); the coming of Jesus (5:40; 10:10); the Spirit (6:63); the words that Jesus speaks (6:63, 68); having done good (5:29); working for the food that endures (6:27); the bread of God (6:33); Jesus, the bread of life (6:35); following Jesus (8:12; 10:27-28); hating one's life (12:25); the Father's commandment (12:50); and honoring the only true God and Jesus Christ (17:3).

## Chapter Summary

In our study of Acts and the synoptic gospels we learned how difficult it is to separate fact from faith in trying to decide what "the Bible says." Our study of the gospel of John has made that task even more difficult. Sayings of Jesus in that gospel, both outside and within the many discourses, have been influenced by John's special literary style of variation and repetition. In doing so he uses words with more than one meaning, synonyms, misunderstanding, and questions put to Jesus by various characters. Misunderstanding and replies that often avoid answers, but instead state a belief of John, serve as ploys for the expression of his beliefs. John was probably interested in stylistic variation so much that he overlooked the inconsistencies within his gospel.

Given everything we have learned about the writers of the four gospels and how their own religious views, interests, and literary styles influenced what they wrote, it becomes clear that it is very difficult to be certain what Jesus really said. Fortunately, there are ways to help us decide what is most likely the best representation of Jesus' thought and teachings. With the help of those scholarly techniques, we can conclude that there seems to be more evidence that content about Jesus is more reliable in the first three gospels than in the fourth. But even those gospels leave many unanswered questions and provide differences and discrepancies that make determining the "truth" difficult and sometimes impossible. Keep this in mind as we turn to the stories of Jesus' birth, which appear only in Matthew and Luke.

Chapter 15

THE STORIES OF JESUS' BIRTH

## Introduction

Celebrated each year with the many traditions and festivities of the Christmas season, the birth of Jesus is probably the best known and, perhaps, most beloved biblical story to Christians. From childhood on, we learn about Mary and Joseph finding no room in the inn as they were approaching Bethlehem on their way to register for the census. Wrapped in swaddling clothes and laid in a manger, the baby Jesus began his life in very humble circumstances. The three wise men and the gifts they brought, the star of David announcing the birth of the Messiah, and the stir that was caused by his birth, are all part of what most Christians remember about Jesus' birth.

Interestingly, though, a critical examination of the birth narratives in the gospels would probably reveal that many Christians are least well informed about these stories. A careful look into what "the Bible says" about the birth of Jesus might, indeed, surprise many devout and faithful Christians. So, as we examine the biblical birth narratives in this chapter, you will probably come to understand those stories in new and more insightful ways. Take your Bible and relax as you prepare to be surprised about what you learn.

## *Mary's Conception of Jesus (Matthew 1:18-25; Luke 1:26-38)*

Matthew says that Mary and Joseph were engaged, "but before they lived together [a euphemism in *NRSV* for sexual intercourse], she was found to be with child from the Holy Spirit" (1:18). However, Matthew then calls Joseph Mary's husband when he says that the righteous Joseph, upon learning that Mary was pregnant, wanted to "dismiss" her quietly and prevent public disgrace (1:19). This latter statement could certainly lead the reader to question Mary's character. In Jewish society, a woman who became pregnant before being married was disgraced, which is why Joseph would have wanted to "dismiss" Mary quietly. The word translated as "dismiss" (*apoluō*) in the *NRSV* means "set free," "release" or "divorce" (*RSV*, *NJB*; see Mark 10:4, 11; Matthew 5:31-32; Luke 16:18).

Later, though, Matthew goes on to say that "an angel of the Lord appeared to him [Joseph] in a dream and said, 'Joseph, son of David, do not be afraid to take Mary as [not in Greek text] your wife, for the child conceived in her is from the Holy Spirit'" (1:20). And, as the Lord commanded, "he [Joseph] took his wife" (1:24; Greek: *RSV*). The literal translation of the RSV is changed in the *NRSV* to "he took her as his wife," an excellent example of how translators often depart from the biblical text in order to preserve theological belief. Observe that, according to Matthew 1:25, Joseph "had no marital relations with her [Mary] until she had borne a son." This is said in spite of the fact that Joseph had taken Mary "as his wife."

So, if you follow Matthew's account carefully, you will see that Mary was engaged, became pregnant, was to be divorced, was married, bore a son, and then had marital relations, in that order. "The Bible Says So!"

Luke's account of the conception of Mary differs from that of Matthew because he had a separate source. Like Matthew, Luke attributes Mary's conception to the Holy Spirit, but the angel brought the news to Mary rather than to Joseph. From the beginning Mary, the virgin, doubts what the angel tells her about conceiving a son: "How shall this be since I do not know a man?" (Luke 1:34, Greek). In answer to Mary's question, "How shall this be...?" the angel responded, "The Holy Spirit will come upon you, and the power of the Most High will overshadow you" (Luke 1:35).

In the Canaanite religion gods had intercourse with humans for producing offspring. Since Most High is a metonym for God and the two are in parallel, it has been suggested that God shared a physical union with Mary. Plutarch, the biographer and philosopher in Luke's time, says that the Egyptians think a spirit of God can approach a woman without sexual intercourse and start conception. See Rebekah's conception in Genesis 25:21: Isaac prayed to the Lord, who granted his wish, "and his wife Rebekah conceived." Plutarch also says that it is not terrible if God by some touching or other contact, but not as a man does, changes the mortal nature and impregnates it with a more divine child (Plutarch, *Lives*, "Numa" 4; *Morals*, "Symposiacs" 8.3).

Luke's words about the Holy Spirit/Most High coming upon (*eperchomai*) Mary may have been influenced by such thought. Luke is the only gospel writer to use the word, and he uses it also in Acts 1:8 of the Holy Spirit coming upon the disciples. As in the gospel, in Acts Luke associates "power" with the Spirit. The author of the *Psalms of Solomon*, writing about the Messiah to come, says: "For God will make him powerful by means of the Holy Spirit." According to Isaiah 1:1-2, the spirit of the Lord will rest upon the descendant of Jesse. See Luke 4:14: "Jesus, filled with the power of the Spirit." The Jewish philosopher and allegorist Philo also provides helpful understanding of Luke. According to Exodus 2:21–3:1, Jethro, father-in-law of Moses, gave Moses his daughter Zipporah in marriage. Then the LXX reads: "The woman conceived and gave birth to a son." Philo says that when Moses took Zipporah, without even praying, he "found her pregnant through absolutely no mortal being" (Philo, *Cherubim* 13).

Notice that Mary never uses the word "virgin," and her statement, "I do not know a man," is ambiguous (Luke 1:35). In Matthew 1.19 the word translated as "husband" is *anēr*, the same word for "man" in Luke 1:34. Meaning either "man" or "husband," *anēr* is the counterpart of *gynē*, meaning either "woman" or "wife." So, Mary's words could also be taken as "I do not know a husband" or "I do not have sexual relations with a man" or with "a husband." It was said of Jephthah's daughter: "She did not know a man" (LXX, Judges 11:39), which the *NRSV* renders as "She had never slept with a man," a euphemism for sexual intercourse, as it would be understood by the Israelites.

The verb "know" (*ginōskō*) can mean "know" in the sense of "know something" or "know someone." For example, Nathanael asked Jesus, "Where did you get to know me?" (John 1:48). In the LXX "know" is also used for sexual relations, the translation of a Hebrew word with the same meaning. In Genesis 4:1 the *NRSV* translates literally: "The man knew his wife Eve, and she conceived and bore Cain." So, some translators change "not knowing a man" to "virgin" and thus avoid the difficulties with the word "know." The *KJV*, *ASV*, and *NKJV* translate the text literally; the *RSV*, "I have no husband"; the *NIV*, *REB*, and *NRSV* use "virgin"; the *NEB*, "I have no knowledge of man," which makes no sense.

So, Matthew's Mary being engaged to Joseph has a counterpart in Luke's a virgin being engaged to Joseph. However, Luke adds that she was expecting a child (2:3) and says nothing about the two not having intercourse until after Jesus was born. In fact, if we had only Luke's account, we would assume that Mary's conception occurred through sexual relations, which could arouse suspicion about the illegitimate birth of Jesus, as would Joseph's wanting to "dismiss" her quietly in Matthew. But, if Mary's statement that she does not know a man is taken as "I do not know a husband," it is in contradiction to Matthew's "her husband Joseph" and Luke's words that Mary was pregnant by Joseph before being married.

These observations have prompted some scholars to suggest that some Jews rejected Jesus because of an illegitimate birth. If that should be the case, then Mary's pregnancy with the Holy Spirit would be a defense against the Jewish accusation. According to this view, Joseph represents the Jews in perceiving that there was something wrong with Mary's conduct, a matter completely lacking in Luke's account. Since sexual relations were a very private matter, Jews did not talk about that subject in public. It seems, then, that the couple's sexual relations would not have been known. Again, this raises questions. How did the person who first reported the story of Mary's conception learn about the couple's private lives? Did Joseph or Mary tell someone? What the Bible says here defies a single, simple conclusion. Perhaps the most likely answer is that each author composed his account from unknown sources in his own literary style and from his own faith perspective.

Paul mentions nothing about a virgin birth, but he does say that Jesus was descended from David in "accord with human nature" (Romans 1:3-4). As with Paul, Mark does not mention a virgin birth. For John a virgin birth would have been entirely inconsistent with his view of the pre-existent Word who assumed human form. John does mention the mother of Jesus, but he never uses her name. The disciple Philip tells Nathanael that they have found "Jesus son of Joseph of Nazareth" (John 1:45). After Jesus speaks to the Jews about God as his Father, they say, "We are not illegitimate children" (John 8:41). The implication here that Jesus was illegitimate supports the view that some Jews rejected Jesus for that reason.

### Mary and the Women in Matthew's Genealogy

The conception by the Holy Spirit (Matthew) or the Most High (Luke) and Matthew's claim that it fulfilled OT prophecy were attempts of the authors, especially Matthew, to refute the Jewish accusation that Christians were proclaiming a Messiah whose birth was illegitimate. In spite of Luke's interest in women in both the gospel and Acts, he does not include Mary in his genealogy (3:23-38). Matthew does include Mary at the end of his genealogy when he says, "Joseph the husband of Mary, of whom Jesus was born; who is called the Messiah" (1:16). In other words, Matthew stresses the special role of Mary as mother of Jesus the Messiah. Interestingly, Matthew names four women from the OT in his genealogy, all of whom were disreputable: Tamar, Rahab, Ruth, and the wife of Uriah (Bathsheba; Matthew 1:5-6). However, what is important is that, in the course of Jewish history, these women came to be looked upon favorably. They each served a purpose which made them worthy of the acclaim they eventually received. Similarly, although Mary was thought to give birth to Jesus illegitimately, she achieved favor by becoming the mother of the Messiah.

*The Women in Early Christian Literature*
In some early Christian literature the four women were all declared innocent of wrongdoing because of the role God or the Holy Spirit played in their lives. That was reason enough for Matthew to insert their names in his genealogy, in order to defend the character of Mary against Jewish accusations. By the end of the first century CE, for example, Rahab was regarded as virtuous in one way or another. The author of Hebrews includes her among the faithful. "By faith Rahab the prostitute did not perish...because she had received the spies in peace" (Hebrews 11:31; Numbers 21:32; Joshua 2:1-8; 6:17, 26). The author of James 2:25 writes that Rahab the prostitute was also "justified by works when she welcomed the messengers and sent them out by another road." The author of *1 Clement* also praises Rahab: "Rahab the prostitute was saved because of her faith and hospitality." The crimson cord in her window was a clear sign that "for all who believe and hope in God there will be redemption through the blood of the Lord" (*1 Clement* 12:7-8).

*Understanding Matthew's Account of Mary's Conception*
It appears that Matthew was defending Mary against the Jewish charge of the illegitimacy of Jesus' birth in three main ways. First, after emphasizing that Mary's conception was "from the Holy Spirit," he supports his belief by a quotation from LXX Isaiah 7:14, where the word "virgin" appears instead of "young woman" as in the Hebrew text. Second, instead of having Joseph divorce Mary, Matthew has him take Mary his wife and give Jesus his name as an angel of the Lord had commanded. Third, Joseph accepts Mary, not a bearer of an illegitimate child, as Jews were charging, but as a virtuous woman who was to give birth to the Messiah as prophesied (Matthew 1:1, 16 17).

With the use of Form Criticism, some scholars have proposed that the legends and myths surrounding Jesus' birth were actually among the latest oral traditions about him. The tradition of Joseph as Jesus' father had been well established before the stories of a virgin birth circulated. As the gospel writers became aware of the stories of Mary's conception by the Holy Spirit, they added this to their accounts. Many scholars agree that Matthew and Luke added their stories of Jesus' birth after they had completed the bodies of their gospels. Christians could not have Jesus' birth both ways. He could not be born of a virgin and have Joseph as his father. A virgin birth, in fact, conflicted with the genealogies of Matthew and Luke that trace Jesus' ancestry from David to Joseph through male lineage. But, they never addressed that contradiction, and so, today, many Christians accept without question the virgin birth. "The Bible Says So!" Or, does it?

## Ideas behind the Birth Stories

As with many other accounts in the Bible, insightful understanding of the birth stories in Matthew and Luke necessitates a critical examination of prevalent thinking and beliefs that could help to explain the origin and content of the biblical stories. Recall that in Genesis 1:3 a wind or spirit from God was associated with the creation of the earth. A psalmist writes that living things are created by God's spirit: "You shall send forth your spirit and they shall be created" (LXX Psalm 103:30). Hebrews believed that sexual intercourse was defiling, so virgins were respected as pure and undefiled: "Blessed is the barren woman who is undefiled, who did not know conception in transgression" (Wisdom 3:13).

Moreover, Philo writes allegorically about Rebekah as steadfast "in virtue" and says that through the power of God she became pregnant (*Cherubim* 13). Some Jews familiar with these ideas may have been more receptive to Jesus the Messiah being born through the power of God than through sexual relations between Mary and Joseph. No wonder that, in Luke's account, he declares, "The Holy Spirit will come upon you, and the power of the Most High will overshadow you; therefore the child to be born will be holy; he will be called Son of God" (Luke 1:35). Belief in the virgin birth then gave rise to the belief that, because of it, Jesus was without original sin, unlike all others born naturally.

Remember, also, that pagan societies believed that prominent men were thought to be sons of god, lords, even gods, and that Paul proclaimed Jesus as the Son of God and Lord. According to Greco-Roman myths, Plato, Julius Caesar, and Augustus were said to be born through sexual relations between a god and a human. When considering these prevalent beliefs, it is possible to see how biblical authors could have been influenced to report a virgin birth.

A legend about Apollonius of Tyanna, sage and miracle worker born about the time of Jesus, offers another interesting insight. One of his pupils wrote some memoirs used by Philostratus (born c. 170 CE) in writing his *Life of Apollonius of Tyanna*. Philostratus writes that, before Apollonius was born, Proteus, god of the sea, appeared to the prospective mother and informed her about the child she was about to bear. Told in a dream that she was to walk in the meadow, she fell asleep. Swans awakened her, and when she heard the sound, she leaped up and bore her child. People of the countryside said that at the time of his birth a thunder bolt sounded, a portent that indicated the great distinction Apollonius was to attain. The star in the East (Matthew 2:1-12) and the appearance of angels praising God (Luke 2:13-15) are portents at the time of Jesus' birth.

## Date of Jesus' Birth

A date for Jesus' birth is not mentioned anywhere in the NT, and Christians did not think about it until centuries after the event. Therefore, in order to determine a date, we must consider persons or events associated with the birth whose dates are relatively certain. Matthew says, "In the time of King Herod...Jesus was born in Bethlehem" (2:1, 3). Luke writes that Zechariah was a priest "in the days of King Herod of Judea" (1:5). This was Herod the Great who ruled Judea from 37-4 BCE, when he died. Matthew also says Herod killed all children "who were two years old or under" (2:16). If we take into account those two years, Jesus would have been born sometime between 6-4 BCE, if born before Herod died.

Matthew also says that Archelaus, son of Herod, "was ruling over Judea in place of his father Herod" (2:22) when Joseph wanted to take the boy Jesus back to Israel. Archelaus ruled from 4 BCE–6 CE. According to this information, Jesus was born shortly before Herod died. However, further information complicates the problem of determining a date for Jesus' birth.

Luke mentions a decree from Caesar Augustus, who ruled over the Roman Empire, including Palestine (27 BCE–14 CE), at the time of Jesus' birth (2:1-2). Luke also mentions that the registration (census for tax purposes) took place when Quirinius was governor of Syria. Since Herod ruled Judea from 37–4 BCE and Augustus ruled over the Roman Empire from 27 BCE–14 CE, we might conclude that Jesus was born sometime between 37 BCE and 14 CE. However, Quirinius ruled Syria from 6-9 CE. This cannot be reconciled with Luke's dating of Jesus' birth during the reign of Herod the Great (37–4 BCE).

This provides an excellent illustration of the complexities involved not only in trying to learn what "the Bible says" when confronted with inconsistent information in it, but also in determining actual historical truth. In Acts 5:36-37 Luke makes another chronological mistake when he places the rebellion against Rome by Theudas, a false messiah, in the time of the procurator Fadus (44-46 CE) before Judas the Galilean in 6 CE. Despite Luke's reputation for being a historian, there are obvious flaws in his "history." Yet another example is his reference to Bethlehem as "the city of David" (2:3, 11), which in the OT is always used of Jerusalem, not Bethlehem. Although Matthew also says that Jesus was born in Bethlehem (2:1), he never refers to it as the city of David. Taking into account the historical inaccuracy of Luke with respect to the registration (census), it is widely believed that the most likely date of Jesus' birth is sometime between 6-4 BCE. It is impossible to be more specific than this.

## *Place of Jesus' Birth*

Jews believed that God knew the Messiah, but no one knew the time or the place of his coming. Paul seems to imply that Jesus existed with God before his birth, because he says: "When the fullness of time had come, God sent his Son, born of a woman" (Galatians 4:4). That the place of the Messiah's coming was unknown is alluded to in John 7:25-27, where Jews from Jerusalem question if the Jewish authorities really know that Jesus is the Messiah. They do not think so, because they know where Jesus is from, which contradicts their belief that "when the Messiah comes, no one will know where he is from." This belief is also behind the questions of the wise men and Herod about where the Messiah was to be born (Matthew 2:2-4).

Matthew places the birth in Bethlehem because he believed that it had been prophesied (2:5-6). However, Luke says that Jesus was born there because Joseph and Mary had to go to Bethlehem for the registration (census). Matthew probably did not know the tradition of Luke that Joseph and Mary lived in Nazareth prior to the registration. Matthew says that the wise men entered the house and found the child and his mother (2:11). If we did not have Luke's statement that Joseph "went from the town of Nazareth" to Bethlehem (2:3-7), where Jesus was born near a manger, we would have to assume that Jesus was born in the usual manner in a house. Although present in every other scene in Matthew's account, Joseph is absent in the scene with the wise men. Could that absence be an unwitting indication of the Jewish accusation of Jesus' illegitimate birth? See "the son of Mary" in Mark 6:3.

The tradition of Nazareth as the home of Joseph before the birth of Jesus was well established. Moreover, according to Mark, "Jesus came from Nazareth of Galilee" (1:9, 24). In early material in Acts Luke mentions "Jesus the Nazorean" and "Jesus Christ the Nazorean" (2:22; 3:6; 4:10). No Jewish sources speak of Bethlehem as the place of the Messiah's birth until the fourth century CE. Bethlehem was a Christian tradition, which Matthew put on the lips of priests and scribes (2:3-5) and John in the mouth of the crowd (7:42). Apparently Luke was aware of the Bethlehem tradition, which he may have gotten from Matthew, and he used the registration as a literary device for getting Jesus to Bethlehem. Such discrepancies caused no difficulty for early Christians, but they do for us who want to learn what "the Bible says" about the time and place of Jesus' birth. And if the birth in Bethlehem was a fact, why would there be two such conflicting stories to prove it?

*The Manger Scene*
Luke not only places Jesus' birth in Bethlehem, but he also includes the inn and a manger. These are the center of the Christmas festival, so let's consider them. The "bands of cloth" in the *NRSV* is a form of the Greek verb *sparganoō*, meaning "swathe" or "swaddle," that is, wrap in strips of cloth to restrict movement of the baby. This tradition appears in Wisdom 7:4, where Solomon says of himself, "In swaddling clothes I was nourished with care." Where would Mary have gotten those bands after a long ride on a donkey and being turned away from an inn? Perhaps even more perplexing is the thought of a woman at the end of a pregnancy making a long journey on a donkey or even being seen in public, for that matter.

Recall that Luke had a special interest in the poor and women, so did he want to show the humble beginnings of Jesus, who was born near a manger, and Mary's motherly care of her baby? The Greek for "manger" is *phatnē*, meaning "feeding trough," a place holding food for animals. Troughs were usually under a lean-to at best, but generally out in the open, not in a barn or stable. Luke's words about "shepherds living in the fields" in the region support this understanding.

*The Inn*
Luke wants the manger to be contrasted to the inn, for which the Greek *katalyma* is more fittingly translated as "lodgings" or "lodging place." This was a crude structure with a roof to protect weary travelers from the weather, especially the hot desert sun, and perhaps to provide a place to sleep. Instead of *katalyma* used here, Luke uses a more classy word of inn (*pandocheion*) in his parable of the Good Samaritan (10:29-37). In addition to lodging, in a *pandocheion* there was an innkeeper and a place to buy food and other necessities. Luke's *katalyma* may have been influenced by several passages is the LXX, where it and related words are used for "lodgings." In LXX Jeremiah 14:8 the prophet laments Yahweh's unconcern during a severe

drought, and he acts like "a sojourner turning aside for a lodging place" (*katalyma*; see also 1 Samuel 1:18). Yahweh says to Ezekiel: "Turn aside, do not lodge in this place where you were born; in your land I will judge you" (LXX Ezekiel 21:30).

## *The Family of Jesus*

The genealogies of Jesus were written to show that he was a descendant of David, from whom the Messiah was to come. But lineage through a male line and a virgin birth cannot be reconciled. Matthew had no difficulty doing that, however, because after he gets to "Jacob the father of Joseph the husband of Mary," he adds: "of whom Jesus was born" (1:16). Is this, perhaps, an attempt on Matthew's part to stress a legitimate birth? It was not typical in patriarchal societies to identify men as husbands or to include women in genealogies. This was done only in rare instances in order to show the historical significance of the woman. This might have been another reason for Matthew's wording.

If we consider the birth stories as a whole, including the circumcision of Jesus (Luke 2:41-52) and Jesus at 12 years of age, we learn real clues about Jesus' parents. We have learned that Matthew calls Joseph Mary's husband and Mary his wife. Luke reports that Joseph and Mary were devoted Jews who went to Jerusalem to be purified after childbirth according to Jewish law. Jews considered childbirth defiling, but why would the couple have to be purified if Mary had been a virgin? Luke also refers to the couple as "the child's father and mother" (Luke 2:33) and twice calls them "his [Jesus'] parents" (2:41, 48). Luke shows the loving concern of parents when he reports Mary as saying: "Look, your father and I have been searching for you in great anxiety" (2:48). If anyone knew who Jesus' father was, it should be Mary, should it not?

Luke begins his genealogy with Jesus, "the son (as was thought) of Joseph son of Heli" (Luke 3:23). "As was thought" was added by a scribe to resolve the contradiction with the virgin birth. If Joseph were not the father of Jesus, the genealogies would be pointless. Notice that Luke lists Heli as Joseph's father, whereas Matthew has Jacob. Did Jesus have two paternal grandfathers? This is just one of many differences between the two genealogies, thereby, once again, defying simple answers about what "the Bible says."

We learn more about Joseph as the father of Jesus in the story of the rejection of Jesus in his "hometown" (Mark 6:1; Matthew 13:54), for which Luke has "Nazareth" (4:16). In Mark the people ask: "Is not this the carpenter, the son of Mary?" Since a man was referred to in Jewish society as the son of his father, not the mother, regardless of whether the father was still alive, Mark's "son of Mary" may be a subtle inference of illegitimacy. Perhaps that is why Matthew changes Mark's reading to: "Is not this the carpenter's son? Is not his mother called Mary?" Here the carpenter is surely not the Holy Spirit or God, but Joseph. In keeping with Luke's view of the paternity of Jesus elsewhere, Luke has simply: "Is not this Joseph's son?" In John 1:45 Jesus is called "Jesus son of Joseph from Nazareth," and in John 6:42 the paternity of Jesus is expressed more strongly: "Is not this Jesus, the son of Joseph, whose father and mother we know?"

In the hometown story Mark refers to Jesus as "brother of James and Joses and Judas and Simon" and to Jesus' "sisters here with us." Matthew turns the statements into questions, and Luke omits the reference. The fact that Jesus' brothers were named may show how well known they were. Is it not likely that if the gospel writers believed that Mary and Joseph were Jesus' parents, they also believed that his brothers and sisters were genuine siblings?

### Perpetual Virginity of Mary

The Roman Catholic and Eastern Orthodox Churches subscribe to a doctrine called the Perpetual Virginity of Mary. In essence, this means that, because of a miracle of God, Mary remained a virgin, even physically, during and after the birth of Jesus. Naturally, according to that doctrine, Jesus could not have had natural siblings. Consequently, other explanations arose by mid-fourth century CE. Some church officials known as Church Fathers maintained that Jesus' "brothers" were sons of Joseph by a former wife and, therefore, half-brothers. Others maintained that they were cousins of Jesus, that is, sons of Mary, wife of Cleopas and sister of Jesus' mother (see John 19:25). On the other hand, a lay theologian held that Mary had a normal life after her marriage to Joseph and that she had other children.

Another view of the siblings of Jesus is that they were brothers and sisters as his followers or people of "the faith." Defenders of that view quote Mark 3:31-35: Jesus' "mother and his brothers" came by and the crowd said, "Your mother and your brothers and sisters are outside, asking for you." Seeing those around him, Jesus replied metaphorically: "Here are my mother and my brothers! Whoever does the will of God is my brother and sister and mother." The passage is reproduced in Matthew 12:46-50 and Luke 8:19-21 in essentially the same way.

## Chapter Summary

Biologically, the virgin birth of Jesus raises serious questions for many persons today. Without a human father, could Jesus be truly human, with flesh, bones, and blood like other men? Some geneticists even say that if parthenogenesis (virgin birth) were biologically possible, Jesus would have been a girl, not a boy. Furthermore, if we accept Paul's view that Jesus was "declared to be Son of God... by resurrection from the dead," this conflicts with the view that Jesus was the Son of God already at his birth (Matthew 1:23; 2:15; Luke 1:32, 35).

The belief that Jesus was the Messiah and a descendant of David developed early (see Romans 1:3). After that it was natural to think that Jesus was born in Bethlehem, the hometown of David. But how are we to reconcile that tradition with the fact that some scholars believe Jesus was born in Nazareth? Does Matthew carry more weight because he used OT quotations to support both traditions? Or is that a good reason for questioning what he writes? Is the Nazareth tradition more likely to be historical because there are no definitely authentic OT texts that support it?

That some of Jesus' followers came to believe he was more than a good man and superhuman, even divine, is beyond doubt. There is also no doubt that legends and myths developed about Jesus which were influenced by the culture of the times. Because of them we are left with many unanswered questions about the sources of the stories, the unresolved differences in the accounts, and how much of the birth stories reflects particular beliefs of the individual biblical authors.

It seems certain that the tradition of Joseph as Jesus' father had been established before the birth narratives were composed. In composing them the authors were not concerned with historical accuracy or consistency but with persuading Jews that Jesus was the Messiah and Son of David and with persuading Gentiles that he was the Son of God and Lord. The idea of a virgin birth caused difficulty for some Jews who thought it a sign of the illegitimacy of Jesus. Matthew as a Jew writing especially for Jews presented the prophecy of the OT and the four Hebrew women who came to be regarded as paragons of virtue, whom Mary also exemplified, in response to the Jewish charge.

Again, it is impossible for persons who want to know what "the Bible says" to come to an absolute conclusion. Perhaps we should understand the narratives of Jesus' birth somewhat as follows. Jesus was born as a human being and may have been a descendant of David. A pious elderly conservative, but open-minded, professor of mine once said, "Some persons believe that the Christmas stories are myths. If that is true, they certainly are inspirational myths." No matter what the background and origin of the birth narratives are, Matthew and Luke have presented the beliefs of some early Christians in the forms of legends and myths in beautiful prose and poetry, which centuries later inspired the Christmas festival and which still inspire many people today.

Chapter 16

THE RESURRECTED JESUS

*Introduction*

Ash Wednesday, Lent, Palm Sunday, Good Friday, Easter. Think of all the sacred Christian traditions surrounding the crucifixion and resurrection of Jesus. We remember the Last Supper that Jesus shared with his disciples, and we feel the quiet despair of Jesus in Gethsemane when we "come to the garden alone." Christians mourn the suffering and death of Jesus on "the old rugged cross," and they celebrate early Easter morning the joy when "Up from the grave He arose, With a mighty triumph o'er His foes... Hallelujah! Christ arose!" After all, central to the faith of Christians is their belief that, through the sacrifice God made in the death of his Son, we are given the opportunity for eternal life. If we accept Jesus as our Savior, we are forgiven for our sins through his death and suffering and given eternal life through his resurrection. What could be more sacred than the Easter season?

In this chapter we will examine what "the Bible says" about the resurrection in an attempt to gain insightful understanding into this very central part of the Christian religion. In contrast to the birth of Jesus, his resurrection is a prominent part of Paul and is mentioned or assumed by every other NT writer. As with the birth stories, those of the resurrection are probably among the best known to Christians but also rarely studied critically by them. That is what we are about to do, as you open your mind and Bible for new insights and understanding.

*Stories of Jesus' Resurrection*

Belief in the resurrection of Jesus did not come immediately after his death. It took some time for these traditions to develop. Visionary appearances of the resurrected Jesus, beginning with Cephas (another name for Peter), are among the oral traditions known to Paul (1 Corinthians 15:3-9). After listing other appearances of Jesus, Paul says, "Last of all, as to one untimely born, he appeared also to me." What Paul mentions vaguely was filled in as the tradition about Jesus' resurrection developed further. First we consider the appearance to Cephas (1 Corinthians 15:5).

The Greek for "he appeared to Cephas" is "it was seen to Cephas." The word for "see" or "appear" is *horaō*, which Paul uses in 1 Corinthians 9:1, where he says, "Have I not seen Jesus our Lord?" There the word may also mean "perceive" or "experience," but how is it to be understood in 1 Corinthians 15:8, where the Greek is "it was seen to me also"? Perhaps the following passages will help in understanding its meaning.

The two men on the way to Emmaus reported to the 11 disciples: "It was seen to Simon [Peter]" (Luke 24:34). The phrase "it was seen to" was the standard formula used to introduce various kinds of manifestations or appearances. For example, see LXX Genesis 18:1-2: "God was seen to him [Abraham]... He looked up and saw three men standing beside him." Here what was first a perception of God turns physical with the three men. Is this what happened in the tradition of the "appearance" to Cephas in 1 Corinthians 15:5 and then in Luke 24:34 to Simon?

## The Empty Tomb and the Women (Mark 16:1-8; Matthew 28:1-10; Luke 24:1-12; John 20:1-18)

These passages, the first in the gospels about the resurrection, immediately pose a challenge in deciding what "the Bible says." Mary Magdalene appears in the four gospels, but in John she is the only one who goes to the tomb. Matthew is probably closer to Mark than are Luke and John. Luke does not mention names of women until the end of the tomb story (Luke 24:10-12). However, he has already mentioned them as the nameless women who had come with Jesus from Galilee and are introduced in the tomb story as "they" (Luke 23:55–24:9). In addition to Mary Magdelene, Mark and Luke also mention Mary mother of James, but instead of Salome, only mentioned in Mark, Luke lists Joanna. Instead of the mother of James, Matthew has the other Mary, but who she was nobody knows.

In Mark the women questioned who would roll away the "very large" stone that sealed the tomb, but they found it already removed. The size implies that it would take more than human power to move it. Matthew leaves no uncertainty by mentioning a "great earthquake" and an angel that rolled back the stone and sat on it. This harks back to the miraculous tearing of the temple curtain at the death of Jesus in Mark 15:38 and Luke

23:45 and Matthew's addition of the shaking of the earth, the opening of the tombs, and the rising of the dead saints (Matthew 27:51-53).

John's account of the empty tomb is very different. When Mary Magdalene saw the stone was away, she ran to tell Peter and "the other disciple, the one whom Jesus loved": "They have taken the Lord out of the tomb, and we do not know where they have laid him" (20:2). Mary Magdalene says "we" although she had been alone, and who the "we" refers to remains unknown. Later, in typical fashion, John has Mary repeat what she said earlier to the two angels: "They have taken away my Lord, and I do no know where they have laid him" (20:13). According to John 20:4-5, "Peter and the other disciple set out and went toward the tomb. The two were running together, but the other disciple outran Peter and reached the tomb first. He bent down to look in and saw the linen wrappings lying there, but he did not go in." Then Peter went into the tomb and saw the wrappings, and the other disciple also entered the tomb "and he saw and believed." But what did he "believe," since they did not yet "understand the scripture, that he [Jesus] must rise from the dead" (John 20:9)?

The accounts of the women at the tomb and what they saw differ widely, as evident in the following passages.

Mark 16:5

As they entered the tomb, they saw a young man, dressed in a white robe, sitting on the right side; and they were alarmed.

Matthew 28:3

[With respect to the angel that rolled the stone]
His appearance was like lightning, and his clothing white as snow. For fear of him the guards [at the tomb; only in Matthew] shook and became like dead men.

Luke 24:3-5

When they went in, they did not find the body. While they were perplexed about this, suddenly [only in Luke] two men in dazzling clothes stood beside them. The women were terrified [what follows is only in Luke] and bowed their faces to the ground.

John 20:11-12

Mary stood weeping outside the tomb. As she wept, she bent over to look into the tomb; and she saw two angels in white, sitting where the body of Jesus had been lying, one at the head and the other at the feet.

In the verses that come next (Mark 16:6-7; Matthew 28:5-7), Matthew follows Mark very closely in what the "young man" or "angel" tells the women. They are not to fear, they are looking for Jesus who was crucified but is raised, they see where he had been laid, and they are to tell the disciples and Peter (omitted in Matthew) that Jesus has been raised from the dead and that he is going to Galilee where they will see him. Luke has a much abbreviated version (24:5): "Why do you look for the living among the dead? He is not here, but has risen." Mark ends with "just as he told you" and Matthew with "This is my message for you," which become a theological statement in Luke 24:6-7: "The Son of Man must be handed over to sinners, and be crucified, and on the third day rise again." These words from the gospels follow:

Mark 16:8

So they went out and fled from the tomb, for terror and amazement had seized them; and they said nothing to anyone, for they were afraid.

Matthew 28:8

So they left the tomb quickly with fear and great joy, and ran to tell his disciples.

Luke 24:8-9

[The women remembered Jesus' words]
and returning from the tomb, they told all this to the eleven and to all the rest.

These passages show how the news spread from Mark, who says that the women did not tell anyone, to Matthew, where they told the disciples, to the women who told "all this to the eleven and to all the rest" in Luke. Mark's gospel ends with the empty tomb but with no one being told about it. There are no resurrection appearances in Mark. The shorter and longer endings given in some translations, including the *NRSV*, were added later and do not belong to the original Mark. It seems that the stories of the resurrection might have been embellished over time, even in some later manuscripts of Mark.

Apparently Matthew changed Mark's "amazement" to "great joy" perhaps in anticipation of the words that follow. Jesus greets the women, "And they came to him, took hold of his feet, and worshiped him." Jesus tells them not to be afraid but to go tell his "brothers to go to Galilee" where they will see him (Matthew 28:9-10). These verses cause some difficulty. Did the tradition behind them take the "young man" of Mark to be Jesus? The taking hold of Jesus' feet (Matthew 28:9) is intended to show that he has risen as a human, the only proof in the synoptic tomb story that he is alive again. The words "Do not be afraid" repeat the words of the angel in Matthew

28:5. The exhortation to tell Jesus' brothers repeats the one to tell his disciples in 28:7. These things tend to indicate that Matthew 28:9-10 is a later addition.

Luke 24:9-12 is comparable to John's account. For the first time Luke names the women who came from Galilee with Jesus – "Mary Magdalene, Joanna [Joanna is peculiar to Luke], Mary the mother of James, and the other women with them." Luke had mentioned the women, without naming them, in 23:55-56, where "they saw the tomb and how his body was laid." They went home and prepared to anoint the body but rested on the Sabbath, according to the Law. This accords with Luke's statement later that they did not find the body when they returned to the tomb, and it is his confirmation of an empty tomb (24:2-3). The women told the disciples and others about the empty tomb, which is inconsistent with Mark's statement that they did not tell anyone. According to Luke, the news "seemed to them [apostles] an idle tale," and the apostles did not believe them. This is in contrast to the other disciple in John who went into the tomb and "saw and believed" (20:8). According to Luke, Peter ran to the tomb, looked in, and saw the cloths. "Then he went home, amazed at what had happened" (24:12). This coincides with John's statement that after Peter and the other disciple saw the empty tomb they went back home. In accordance with Mark and in contrast to Matthew, Luke gives no proof that Jesus is alive.

*Understanding the Empty Tomb Stories*

Perhaps the empty tomb story began somewhat as follows. Paul writes that in a tradition passed on to him Jesus was first seen to Peter. But there is no evidence that the risen Jesus appeared to Peter. After listing some other appearances, Paul says that Jesus was seen to him as to one untimely born, but he gives no concrete evidence for what he says. Moreover, some of his converts at Corinth were saying, "There is no resurrection of the dead." Paul believed that Christ's resurrection was the guarantee that there would later be a general resurrection of believers. But then doubters asked that if there is a resurrection, "With what kind of body do they come?" (1 Corinthians 15:12-13, 35). After a long soliloquy on the perishable/physical and the imperishable/spiritual, Paul concludes that the raised body will be a spiritual one: "This perishable body must put on imperishability, and this mortal body must put on immortality" (1 Corinthians 15:42-54).

Remember that Paul believed that God had revealed his Son in him before he was born (Galatians 1:15). Nowhere, though, does Paul give tangible proof for his experiences. Any hint of Jesus' resurrection was based on reports of burial cloths in an empty tomb, but some thought that was an "idle tale" and did not believe the women (Luke 24:11). The church needed concrete evidence of the resurrection – a living body. The women taking hold of Jesus' feet, reported in the controversial passage in Matthew 28:9, was a step in that direction. John also has Jesus call Mary Magdalene by name. That makes the empty tomb story more personal and reflects a living body, especially with her reply in Jesus' own language: "Rabbouni," that is, "Teacher" (John 20:16). Then Jesus tells her, "Do not hold on to me," which is in contrast to the women taking hold of Jesus' feet in Matthew 28:9. This sets the stage in John for what follows with the disciples and doubting Thomas.

So what are we to conclude about the empty tomb stories? Are they historical or the first major step in the efforts of the church to convince early followers of Jesus that he was raised from the dead? It seems that if Paul had known about the empty tomb, he would have mentioned it. Therefore, the tomb stories must have been written after Paul wrote 1 Corinthians. His experience of the risen Jesus, both in 1 Corinthians and elsewhere in his letters, was personal and within. Although he knew from oral traditions about the appearances of the risen Jesus to numbers of people, there were none that indicated concretely a physical body. Probably for that reason he had enough trouble trying to convince the Corinthian doubters of a physical resurrection.

Paul knew Peter, James the brother of Jesus, and other authorities in the church in Jerusalem (Galatians 1:18-24). If Peter was aware of the empty tomb, would he not have given that evidence to Paul? It is quite likely that the church first came to believe in the resurrection of Jesus and then invented the empty tomb story as one of the proofs for it. The stories of the resurrection appearances of Jesus were the ultimate proof.

### Resurrection Appearance in Matthew (28:16-20)

There are no two resurrection appearances of the same kind reported in the gospels. In Matthew the resurrection occurred on a mountain in Galilee. There the emphasis is not so much on the appearance of Jesus, but on overcoming doubt that still persisted. Some onlookers worshiped Jesus, "but some doubted" (28:17). Written after the church came to believe in the deity of Jesus, Matthew 28:16-20 served as mission preaching in order to make converts among Jews and Gentiles – "disciples of all nations."

However, the church still needed proof that the resurrected Jesus was real. That proof was later provided in Luke and John.

## Resurrection Appearances in Luke

### On the Road to Emmaus (24:13-35)

After the empty tomb, Luke continues the story with the two men on the way to Emmaus. They correspond to the two men whose dazzling clothes terrified the women and inspired them to reverence (Luke 24:4-5). The element of surprise is added in that the two men on the road to Emmaus did not recognize Jesus as truly alive until he later acted as a human. When the "stranger" asked the men what things had happened, their answer is a blending of Luke's theology and a report of the crucifixion of Jesus and the women at the empty tomb (24:19-27). The suspense of wanting the ultimate proof of Jesus' resurrection continues in Luke's literary creation with its variations and repetitions. It begins with Jesus meeting the two men, then with the conversation on the way and their meal together. The men recognize him at the meal, but Jesus "vanished from their sight" without the readers being told that he actually ate food. The men reflect on Jesus as he revealed the scriptures to them, and they returned to Jerusalem to the Eleven and their companions and stated emphatically: "The Lord has risen indeed, and he has appeared to Simon [Peter]!" (recall "was seen to Simon").

### To the Eleven Disciples (24:36-49)

In the last of the appearances Luke blends in features of the former scene, the unexpected appearance of Jesus, who startled and terrified his audience. This time the disciples thought they had seen a ghost or spirit. Probably from the same tradition as Matthew 28:9-10, Luke has Jesus assure any doubters by saying that a spirit does not have flesh and bones as he does, and he shows them his hands and feet. However, it is not said that anyone touches him. Some were still disbelieving and wondering, so he ate some fish for them to see. The surprise ends, but nothing is said that doubts were overcome. Readers are left to assume that.

The rest of Luke's story is anticlimactic, with repetitions of what Jesus had already told the disciples. The words about the disciples as witnesses and being clothed with power from God and Jesus' ascension prepare readers for what is to follow in Acts. In Acts during the course of 40 days, Jesus appeared and showed "many convincing proofs" that he was alive. He also spoke "about the kingdom of God," which, by the way, had not come as he had previously predicted. The two men on the road to Emmaus "had hoped that he was the one to redeem Israel" (Luke 24:21). Because that had not happened was surely a strong reason for disbelieving a resurrection.

### At the Ascension (24:50-53)
In the story of Jesus' temptation Luke says that when the devil asked Jesus to worship him, Jesus replied: "Worship the Lord your God, and serve only him" (Luke 4:8). In Luke 24:51-52 Luke says that the disciples worshiped Jesus after he "was carried up into heaven" (see also Matthew 28:9). The word for "worship" is *proskyneō*, which literally means "bend the knee" or "do obeisance to." In typical Jewish fashion the disciples bow in adoration to the Messiah (see Luke 24:46). Then they returned to Jerusalem and blessed God in the temple. Thus, the gospel of Luke ends as it began – with worship of God in the temple (Zechariah in 1:5-10).

### Resurrection Appearances in John (20:19-29)

The apparition of Mary Magdalene at the tomb and her report to the disciples that she had seen the Lord sets the stage for what follows. Notice that Jesus is now "Lord," a designation repeated several times. In the Synoptics only Luke mentions "Lord" in the resurrection scenes (Luke 24:34). Mary's word was not enough; concrete evidence was needed. So, John has the disciples experience an apparition. Despite locked doors, Jesus stood among them and conferred the Holy Spirit upon them. However, Thomas was absent and did not believe when they told him that they had seen the Lord. Thomas wanted to see marks of the crucifixion. Later, again with the doors shut, Jesus stood among the disciples and greeted them as before. He asked Thomas to look and touch the marks, which coincides with Luke 24:39-40. But without doing that, Thomas confesses, "My Lord and my God!"

The confession that Jesus is Lord and God is the confession of Christians in John's church. Jesus responds, "Blessed are those who have not seen and yet have come to believe" (20:29). Most members of John's church were of the second generation of Jesus' followers who had never seen Jesus as a man. They wanted assurance that what they had been taught was true. Thomas represented those Christians, and by changing from doubt to belief he gave them that assurance. They did not have to "see" Jesus to believe.

## What Kind of Body Did the Resurrected Jesus Have?

We learned how difficult it was for Paul to persuade his converts at Corinth about Jesus' resurrected body. He solved the problem metaphysically, not concretely. Have you thought about how hard it is to determine the nature of Jesus' resurrected body? It had both human and superhuman characteristics. There are supernatural beings of various kinds in connection with the empty tomb and the resurrection: a young man in a white robe (Mark 16:5-6), an angel whose appearance was like lightning, clothes as white as snow (Matthew 28:2-6), two men in dazzling clothes (Luke 24:4-5). Suddenly, out of nowhere, Jesus appears as a nonhuman figure to the women on the way to tell the disciples about the empty tomb, but he speaks to them and they take hold of his feet, both human qualities (Matthew 28:9).

On the Emmaus road Jesus comes to the two men and walks with them, a human trait; but they do not recognize him because of his nonhuman quality (Luke 24:15-16). Although he interpreted the scriptures to them, they did not recognize him until he blessed some bread and gave it to them. Those are human traits reminiscent of the Lord's Supper with the disciples (Mark 14:22-25; Matthew 26:26-29; Luke 22:10-20). Then he vanished from their sight but later reappears, and they believe he is a spirit or ghost (same word in Greek), with superhuman traits (Luke 24:36-37). Jesus assures them by saying: "Look at my hands and feet; see that it is I myself. Touch me and see; for a ghost does not have flesh and bones as you see that I have" (Luke 24:39). However, Luke does not say that the disciples actually touched him. Although Jesus had not eaten in the previous scene, he now eats fish in plain sight. Then he speaks to them but loses his human traits when he is "carried up into heaven" (Luke 24:51).

In John there are the same kinds of human and superhuman qualities of the resurrected Jesus. He appears from nowhere with doors locked, apparently unrecognized until he showed the disciples his hands and side. However, Thomas never touches Jesus' hands and sides.

## Chapter Summary

So, what kind of body did the resurrected Jesus have? There are no simple answers about what "the Bible says." As with the birth narratives, the traditions about Jesus' resurrection developed over time, and there is no agreement among the gospels about what took place. Mark, the earliest gospel, does not even have a resurrection appearance. According to

Matthew, the resurrection took place in Galilee, whereas in Luke it occurred in Judea.

Paul's apparition, followed by the empty tomb stories, began the tradition of a resurrected body. That the body was missing naturally inspired stories to explain what had happened. And, since biblical writers lived in a world that was filled with beliefs about demons, spirits, and other supernatural phenomena, it is understandable that their explanations would have included such phenomena. As the resurrection stories evolved, the resurrected body was reported as having both human and nonhuman traits. The human characteristics, such as talking and eating, provided necessary proof of a body, yet the body remained supernatural as it suddenly appeared out of nowhere and through closed doors.

So, as you ponder questions about what "the Bible says" about Jesus' resurrection, questions that leave uncertainty because of conflicting accounts, we move on in the next chapter to consider two questions asked of the human Jesus that were also left unanswered.

# Chapter 17

## The Man Jesus

### Introduction

In John 12:21 some Greeks said to the disciple Philip, "We want to see Jesus." However, they never got to see him because their request was a literary device on the part of the author to set the stage for Jesus' monologue on his glorification (John 12:23-26). As with the Greeks, we can never get to see Jesus or completely understand him. Our sources are not only secondhand and sometimes inconsistent, but they also provide little information about him as a person. Yet, ever since the gospels were written, people have been trying to understand Jesus and writing about him.

For more than 20 centuries scholars, clerics, students, and lay persons have been discussing the person of Jesus and his teaching. There is much said about him not only in formal literary compositions, but also in the media, especially television and movies. And what is said ranges from plausible ideas with a factual basis to other ideas that attract a lot of attention but, in reality, have absolutely no factual support. Some even are disrespectful and disgusting. Three of the most preposterous ideas are that Jesus arranged with Judas to betray him because as the Messiah he had to be betrayed; Jesus and John the Baptist were twin messiahs; and Jesus married Mary Magdalene and had a child with her, and the fetus in her womb was the real Holy Grail.

Stories of Jesus' childhood were mentioned in gospels of the second and third centuries that were known as apocryphal, that is, spurious. Greatly divergent views were regarded as heresy, and heretics were burned at the stake. Occasionally others were excommunicated from some church because of widely divergent views. Isn't it ironic that today persons with all sorts of absurd views are given multi-million-dollar book or movie contracts? Without that kind of moneymaking sensationalism, in this chapter we discuss Jesus, the "Man," given what "the Bible says." We consider two questions that remain unanswered in the Bible but that can provide important insights.

### "What Is This? A New Teaching - with Authority!" (Mark 1:21-28)

Even those around Jesus did not understand, so the gospels have questions about him that are either ignored or answered with another question. Now study carefully Mark 1:21-28, and notice that verses 23-26 are a miracle story, which was probably in Mark's source. Recall that in Mark's time people believed in miracle workers and miracles and in magicians and magic. In order to present Jesus as a teacher and to appeal to potential converts, Mark had to present Jesus also as a miracle worker. Do some Christians today still believe in Jesus, the kind of person he was and his teaching, because of his miracles?

What was new in Jesus' healings is that he was not concerned with miracles as such, but for the welfare of the poor, sick, lepers and other outcasts. Many persons despised such persons as ungodly and unworthy of association. Nevertheless, some of Jesus' hearers were confused about his miracles, and they reacted differently. His family thought "he has gone out of his mind" (Mark 3:21), and his adversaries said that he cast out demons "by the ruler of the demons" (Mark 3:21-22). By enclosing the miracle story with reference to Jesus' teaching, Mark emphasizes Jesus as teacher, not as miracle worker. Regarding Jesus teaching in the synagogue in Capernaum, Mark (1:22-27) says: "They were astounded at his teaching, for he taught them as one having authority, and not as a scribe... They were all amazed and they kept on asking one another, 'What is this? A new teaching – with authority!'"

### What Was New in Jesus' Teaching?
It has often been said that there is little, if anything, new in the teaching of Jesus, because he was not a Christian but a Jew. He did not teach a new faith or a new religion. How could he avoid repeating things that had been said before? His originality arises precisely on some subjects shared with the Judaism of his time. Newness or originality in an ethical teacher is not the same as that of an inventor who makes something new. Sometimes what seems like new teaching is new only because we have not thought about it or heard it before. That was surely true for some of Jesus' followers, yet there must have been something new or different about his teaching or it would not have caught on so soon after his death and endured so long. Nor would

his adversaries have opposed him if he had taught only old ideas. He taught "not as the scribes" (Mark 1:22).

Many Greeks were always seeking to hear something new, a view reflected in 2 Timothy 4:3. There the author says that those opposed to "sound doctrine" have "itching ears," that is, they desire to hear something new. Luke writes in Acts 17:21 that Athenians "would spend their time in nothing but telling and hearing something new." Jesus' teaching surprised his hearers, who questioned his authority, but they never accused him of novelty, as had been the case with Socrates.

*The Surprising and Unexpected.* Imagine how surprised Jesus' hearers were when they heard: "Blessed are you who are poor" (Luke 6:20). Who would have expected the poor to be in a state of happiness, the underlying meaning of the word *makarios* ("blessed")? It was used in congratulations: "You who are poor are to be congratulated." The feeling is like that of an athlete who wins the race or makes the winning basket. When the disciples were arguing about who was the greatest among them, Jesus responded, "Whoever wants to be first must be last of all and servant of all" (Luke 9:35; see also 22:26; Mark 10:43-44; Matthew 20:26-27). Imagine the surprise of the disciples when Jesus said that.

Another surprise was when Jesus said that the tax collector, who was generally regarded as a sinner, was the one justified before God, not the self-righteous, praying Pharisee (Luke 18:9-14). The Jews and a people known as Samaritans, who differed from the Jews on the extent of the law, the coming of a messiah, and other matters, did not associate with each other. But Jesus did mingle with Samaritans. Recall the Samaritan woman whom Jesus asked for a drink of water. She was surprised that Jesus, a Jew, was asking for a drink from her, a Samaritan woman (John 4:1-10).

When a lawyer asked Jesus what he had to do to inherit eternal life, Jesus told him to love the Lord and his neighbor as himself. Not satisfied, he asked Jesus, "And who is my neighbor?" (Luke 10:25-28). Jesus tells the parable of the Good Samaritan. Most Jews thought of a neighbor as a fellow Jew. Jewish travelers would have been expected to help the Jew who was beaten and abandoned along the roadside. But the help of the Samaritan, who went out of his way to help the Jewish man, was surely unexpected. The neighbor is no longer just a fellow Jew, and all people are to show mercy to anyone in need, no matter the race or religion (Luke 10:36-37).

The Pharisees were very fussy about ceremonially washing their hands. They were not only surprised but took offense when Jesus said that it is not what goes into the mouth but what comes out of it that defiles a person.

From the human heart come evil intentions that lead to wicked deeds (Mark 7:1-23; Matthew 15:1-20). The rich young man, like the righteous Pharisee, had kept all the commandments, but he went away shocked and sorrowful when Jesus told him: "You lack one thing; go, sell what you own, and give the money to the poor" (Mark 10:20-22; Matthew 19:20-22; Luke 18:21-23).

*Concern for the Most Essential.* Hillel, a distinguished Jewish teacher in Jesus' time, and some of his contemporaries made summaries of the Law. Paul did the same thing: "The whole law is summed up in a single commandment, You shall love your neighbor as yourself" (Galatians 5:14; Romans 13:8-10; see Leviticus 19:18). When a scribe asked Jesus which commandment was first of all, Jesus replied by quoting the Jewish statement of monotheism: "Hear, O Israel: The Lord is our God, the Lord alone" (Deuteronomy 6:4). And then Jesus added that the second commandment is the love of neighbor as oneself (Mark 12:28-31; Matthew 22:34-40; Luke 10:25-28). Hillel and other Jewish teachers never intended that summaries of the law meant that all else could be ignored. That is precisely what Jesus meant, as some of the following examples show.

Jesus challenged the Jewish law of sabbath observance. He could ignore that law if it meant healing a man or saving a person's life. When his critics watched to see if Jesus would heal a man on the Sabbath, he asked them if it is lawful to do good or harm on the Sabbath, "to save life or to kill?" His critics were silenced, but Jesus was angry and healed the man (Mark 3:1-6; Matthew 12:9-14; Luke 6:6-11). This is a good example of what Jesus thought was essential in religion – and certainly something new.

According to ancient laws murderers should be punished. But for Jesus anger toward one's fellowmen and lack of forgiveness are also punishable. Reconciliation among brothers made acts of worship effective. "First be reconciled to your brother or sister, and then come and offer your gift" (Matthew 5:21-26). This is another new teaching of what is essential in religion.

*Practice Goodness to the Extreme.* In Judaism there was strong emphasis on moral conduct and doing good deeds rather than on faith. Jesus shared that view, especially with goodness to the extreme. Jesus' hearers knew the Jewish commandment to love one's neighbor and hate one's enemies. According to Jesus that was half right: "Love your enemies and pray for those who persecute you" (Matthew 5:43-44). Luke extends the saying further: "Do good to those who hate you, bless those who curse you, pray for those who abuse you" (Luke 6:27-28).

Jesus' teaching about goodness in the extreme sometimes included the motive or intention behind the deed, and that was as important as the act itself. The law of the Jews on adultery was well known, but what Jesus said was not only new and surprising, but extreme. "Anyone who looks at a woman with lust has already committed adultery with her in his heart" (Matthew 5:28; see Matthew 7:21). That is a tough one for men and seems extreme, does it not? That attests its originality with Jesus.

The saying of Jesus, "Be perfect, therefore, as your heavenly Father is perfect" (Matthew 5:48), is the acme of extremeness in Jesus' teaching. The word for "perfect" is *teleios*, which means "having reached its end," "mature," "complete," "perfect," the Greek equivalent of the Hebrew *tamim*. It is related to the idea of holiness in the OT: "You shall be holy, for I the Lord your God am holy" (Leviticus 19:2). Paul prays that the Thessalonian converts may be "blameless in holiness" (1 Thessalonians 3:13; Greek; see also 2 Corinthians 7:1; Philippians 1:9-10).

The saying on perfection is a good example for showing how a Jewish idea is used in a novel way by Jesus. Noah was characterized as "a righteous man, perfect in his generation" (Genesis 6:9). Yahweh commanded Abram, "Be perfect" (Genesis 17:1). In contrast to the wicked Canaanites, the Israelites were to "be perfect before the Lord" their God (Deuteronomy 18:13). In the context of Matthew 5:48 "Be perfect" is to be taken as a summary of the teaching about love that precedes it; but it is, nevertheless, a virtue taken to the extreme. The change in Luke, whether by Luke or his source, weakens the meaning considerably: "Be merciful, just as your Father is merciful" (Luke 6:36).

The sayings we have been discussing illustrate aspects of Jesus' teachings that were new. Undoubtedly, they were surprising and unexpected to his hearers, as they may well be to some readers today. Most of the sayings considered are in Matthew, the most Jewish gospel. If the sayings do not originate with Jesus, Matthew the Jew saw fit to attribute them to Jesus. On the other hand, if they do not go back to Jesus, it is unlikely that Matthew would have preserved them because they differ from Jewish teaching.

### *"What Sort of Man Is This?" (Matthew 8:27; see Mark 4:41; Luke 8:25)*

Jesus' disciples were scared by a storm at sea and Jesus calmed both their nerves and the storm. Then they wondered: "What sort of man is this, that even the winds and the sea obey him?" (Matthew 8:27; Mark 4:41; Luke 8:25). Christians continue to want to learn about Jesus as a man and generally begin with presuppositions of his divine nature based on the stories of his birth, miracles, and resurrection. Jesus' hearers, in contrast, took his humanity for granted. They knew him as the carpenter or the son of Joseph; they knew his brothers and sisters. That is why his Jewish hearers were surprised by some of his teachings that were unexpected. They were so different that some of his hearers questioned his teachings and authority. When we consider what kind of human being Jesus really was, you may be surprised at what we do not know. For that reason we must leave much unanswered as did the gospel writers.

Luke thought that already at 12 years of age Jesus was a precocious youth. The story in Luke 2:41-52 is comparable to similar stories by Jewish authors of his time. Remember that Paul writes of his advance in Judaism beyond many of the same age (Galatians 1:14). Josephus boasts that when he was a boy about 14 years of age Jewish authorities came to him for answers about their customs (*Life*, 2). Josephus writes that Moses' "understanding was not in accordance with his stature." The words for "understanding" (*synesis*) and "stature" (*helikia*) are both used by Luke of Jesus. People were amazed at Jesus' understanding (Luke 2:47), and Jesus "increased in wisdom and stature" (2:52). According to Josephus, by the end of "his twelfth year" Samuel was already a prophet (*Antiquities* 5.10.4). According to pagan authors, both Alexander the Great and Augustus were precocious youths.

Only Luke writes about Jesus as a youth and that he "was about thirty years old when he began his work" (3:23). What did he do in the meantime? Did he ever play as a boy? We do not know, but writers of the apocryphal works of the next century came up with fantastic tales about the boy Jesus. For example, at five years of age he was playing with some other boys on the Sabbath and made two sparrows out of clay. When Joseph was told that Jesus had done that on the Sabbath, he scolded his son. But Jesus clapped his hands and yelled at the birds, and they flew away chirping. The Jews were amazed and reported his deed to their elders. When Jesus was six years old, he was bringing a pitcher of water home for his mother. On the way he fell and broke the pitcher, but he spread out his garment, filled it with water and took it to his mother. When she saw the miracle, she kissed him but kept what she had seen to herself. Compare Mary's statements about Jesus in Luke 2:19, 51.

What about Jesus' family relationships? He had brothers and sisters, but does that mean he was part of a large family? According to Mark, Jesus was a carpenter (6:3); according to Matthew he was the son of a carpenter

(13:55). The word for "carpenter" is *tektōn*, which means a craftsman in stone, metal, or wood, but it was usually used of a wood worker. We do not know what kind of craftsman the gospel writers meant, but later tradition supplied an answer. Justin Martyr, a church father in mid-second century CE, writes that among Jesus' crafts were "ploughs and yokes" (*Dialogue*, 88). Did you ever see pictures of the young Jesus working in the shop with his father? I have.

We get some insight into the emotions of Jesus as a man. We have learned that Matthew and Luke tended to eliminate human character traits occurring in Mark. Jesus looked at the Jews "with anger" (Mark 3:5), but those words are omitted in Matthew 12:9-14 and Luke 6:6-11. John was especially interested in the deity of Jesus, but he writes much more about Jesus' humanity than any synoptic writer. The reason for this is that by the time of John some heretical persons were saying that Jesus never really had the features and emotions of a human being. John wrote to counteract that view by stressing Jesus' human traits. Jesus and his disciples are invited to and attend a wedding, where he rebukes his mother for her concern that the wine was gone (2:1-17). He drives people and animals out of the temple with a whip (2:13-15). He is tired from his journey and asks a Samaritan woman for a drink of water (4:6-7). Jesus tells his brothers that he is going to Jerusalem, then says he is not going, but later he goes (7:1-10). Only John writes about Jesus loving Martha, Mary and Lazarus (11:3, 5, 36), a special disciple (13:23), and other disciples (15:9). Jesus cries when Lazarus has died (11:35). Only John reports that Jesus thirsts when on the cross (19:28).

*Questions about Jesus the Man*
Given limited information and few simple answers about Jesus the Man, it is difficult to try to assess Jesus' character by modern standards. Below are some questions for you to consider, questions that remain largely unanswered. As you ponder them, stop to realize how little we actually know about Jesus the Man.

What about Jesus' manner and his personality? What were his likes and dislikes? Did he have a sense of humor or ever speak ironically? What is your general impression of his health? What about his intellectual ability and his emotional stability? Did he hide his emotions or reveal them openly? Was he an introvert or extrovert, an optimist or pessimist? Was he at ease or uneasy when meeting people? Did he tend to be a leader? Could he easily persuade others to work with him? Did he have a keen sense of responsibility, or did he shirk his duty? In general, was he a likeable person, the kind you could get along with easily, or was he too unusual?

What were Jesus' own interests? What concerned him most? Did he have a definite plan or goal in his life? Was he interested in the social problems of the day? What was his religious affiliation, if any? What about his politics: was he a Pharisee, Sadducee, or Essene? Did he want religion and politics to mix? Was he liberal or conservative? Did he easily adapt himself to unforeseen and changing situations?

If you close your eyes and imagine you see Jesus, what picture comes into your mind? How would you describe his general appearance? Did he have a beard? Was his hair long or short? What about his stature and deportment? Did he look kind and loving, or did he appear stern or intimidating? Have you ever thought about how artists portray Jesus? What hints can they get from the gospels about his physical stature or his complexion, and what is said about the color of his hair and his eyes? Interestingly, and perhaps surprisingly, there is absolutely no clue in the Bible as to Jesus' physical appearance, yet, most Christians share an image of what he looked like, don't they?

It doesn't appear that the gospel writers were really interested in Jesus' appearance or in his personality. In fact, NT writers emphasized his divine nature as the Son of God and Savior much more than his humanity. People did not follow Jesus because of the way he looked but because of what he said and did. And, Jesus was primarily concerned with human beings and their relationships with God and fellow human beings. Jesus concerned himself least with himself. And, he certainly had very little to say about the superficialities in religion, such as ritual and creeds. In fact, it took a long time for the creeds of Christianity used today to be formulated.

## Chapter Summary

Christians have tended to stress two poles in Jesus' life – his birth and resurrection – and to ignore what came in between these two events. Do Christians always remember and abide by the ethical standards for which Jesus both lived and died? Do they sometimes emphasize faith at the expense of what they should do? Suppose that, like the good Samaritan, Christians always loved their neighbors as themselves. Would the world not be a better place? According to Acts, authorities at Thessalonica said of the apostles: "These people who have been turning the world upside down have come here also" (17:6). Are Christians today still turning the world upside down?

Christianity arose because Christians did not blend in with the evil ways of the world at that time. The first Christians were known primarily for their moral behavior, as the remarks in 1 Peter remind us. The ethical teachings of Jesus and Paul were greatly influenced by those of the OT prophets. In the next chapter, we will focus on the ethical teachings of Paul in relation to the topics of love, family, marriage, and sex.

Part IV

BIBLICAL VALUES

Chapter 18

LOVE, FAMILY, MARRIAGE, AND SEX

*Introduction*

Although the Bible was written for people who were living during the times when its authors were living, it certainly has important teachings, including values, which can be applied to our lives today. A value can be defined as a very important kind of belief, that is, a belief specifically about what is "good" or "desirable." A value, then, can also mean "degree of excellence," or something equivalent to the Greek idea of "virtue." Values, of course, vary significantly from one culture to another and can be judged as right or wrong only in relation to a particular belief system. So, if we consider values that are appropriate for Christians living in today's world, we certainly can use the Bible, as the basis of the Judeo-Christian belief system, as a kind of standard against which to determine "how right" or "how wrong" a particular value or corresponding behavior is.

Take a few moments to consider important values in your life. What beliefs are of central importance to you? Do you believe, for example, that love of family is an important value? Or, is the desire for material possessions and wealth more of a guiding value than love of family? How do you feel about sexual relations outside of marriage? What value do you have regarding faithfulness of marriage partners in contrast to extramarital affairs? What do you believe about homosexuality? Do you believe that it is important to love all people, or do you believe that love should be reserved only for those who are "righteous" according to your beliefs or, perhaps, only for those of your own race or social class or cultural or religious background? Perhaps even more importantly, does your behavior coincide with your values? Do your values truly motivate you to do certain things and to refrain from others? What values do you cherish enough to teach to your children or to stand up for in society?

All of these questions might seem, at first glance, to have simple answers. Yet, with considerable honest reflection, it is probably fair to say that they pose some difficult dilemmas if we examine how closely we actually carry out behavior that truly reflects our values. The same difficulty arises when considering what "the Bible says." While it is very easy to declare that "The Bible Says So!" when we quote a particular passage to support a value that is important to us, it is much more difficult to ferret out simple answers when looking more deeply into biblical values. True insightful understanding is really quite elusive, and in this chapter we look at the topics of love, family, marriage, and sex with that in mind.

## *Love as the Primary Value*

There is no doubt that love is a primary value in the Bible. But, exactly how do we define love? When we speak of "making love" and this involves sexual relationships with multiple partners, is this truly "love?" Is that the same kind of love as that between a man and a woman deeply devoted to one another, whether married or unmarried? How about love between monogamous, committed gay or lesbian partners? What about a man who says he loves his wife so much that he cannot bear to see her suffer during some terminal illness and who, therefore, takes her life? How is the love between a parent and child different from love between the child's parents or between siblings or friends? What about the "love" some persons say they have for their pets or for dark chocolate, for that matter?

Unlike the Greek language, English has only one word for love, and it is used in various ways. In Greek there are four words for love, each with a special meaning: *eros, philia, storgē,* and *agapē. Eros* is the oldest word, the name for the god of love in Greek mythology. It refers to sexual love. In the LXX *eros* occurs only in Proverbs 7:18 and 24:51, and it never occurs in the NT. In Proverbs 7:18, "Come, let us enjoy love until morning; come, let us embrace in love," the first word for love is *philia*, and the second is *eros*.

The basic meaning of *philia* is "affectionate regards," as that between friends, or "friendship." It occurs one time in the NT and considerably more often in the LXX, for example, "The person who reviles a friend breaks up a friendship" (*philia;* Sirach 22:20). According to Sirach 25:1, three things are pleasing to the Lord and men: "harmony of brothers, friendship (*philia*) of neighbors and a wife and husband who live happily together." These values should be good for people everywhere, should they not? The verb *phileō*, meaning "love with emotion and friendship" occurs about as often in the LXX as in the NT.

*Storgē* means "love" or "affection," especially of parents and children. In the LXX it occurs only in *3 Maccabees* 5:32 and *4 Maccabees* 14:13-17, and it does not occur in the NT. *Agapē*, our last word, was rarely used before the time of the LXX, but it occurs very often in the Septuagint and the NT and assumes all the meanings of the other words, but rarely of *eros*. In the NT *agapē* is used of human love toward one another (John 13:35) and toward God (1 John 2:5) and of God's love toward humans (Romans 5:8) and to Christ (John 17:26). It is also used of Christ's love toward humans (Romans 8:35).

### Love for Aliens

Israel was to love God with its whole heart, soul, and might and its neighbors as itself (Deuteronomy 6:5; Leviticus 19:18). The Israelites were often reminded that they were aliens in the foreign land of Egypt (e.g., Genesis 12:10; 49:4; Exodus 22:21; Deuteronomy 26:4-5), and that was the basis for their view toward foreigners or aliens. Key passages are Leviticus 19:33-34 and Deuteronomy 10:17-19. According to the former, Israelites are not to oppress aliens who reside with them, for they are as fellow citizens. According to Deuteronomy 10:17-19, God loves strangers and provides them sustenance, so the Israelites are to love aliens as Yahweh loves them.

Today there are millions of strangers or aliens or refugees living in lands all around the world. Do you think that the passages about love just mentioned express values that should be considered in the treatment of those individuals today? Consider the current debates about immigrants in many countries.

### Paul's Ode to Love

The acme of love in the Bible is in Paul's ode to love, which he calls a "more excellent way" (1 Corinthians 12:31–13:13). According to Paul (1 Corinthians 13:4-8):

> Love is patient; love is kind; love is not envious or boastful or arrogant or rude. It does not insist on its own way; it is not irritable or resentful; it does not rejoice in wrongdoing, but rejoices in the truth. It bears all things, believes all things, hopes all things, endures all things. Love never ends.

This presents a challenge for all of us that remains relevant today, does it not? And, what about the commandment not to covet, that is, to desire enviously or culpably what belongs to someone else? "The life of the body is a tranquil heart, but envy is a cancer in the bones" (Proverbs 14:30, *NJB*). In the NT envy is listed among vices to be avoided (Mark 7:22; Galatians 5:21; 1 Peter 2:1). Is the absence of envy a value relevant for current society? Remember, according to Paul, love is not envious.

## Family Life

The basic assumption behind Hebrew family life is the rearing of children for preservation of the family lineage. The family was the most important unit in Hebrew society. Related families made up a clan, related clans made up a tribe, and related tribes constituted the nation Israel. Hebrew society was patriarchal, and within that context the father was the supreme head of the patriarchal family. As with all aspects of Hebrew society, God was associated with marriage, which fulfilled his command to the first man and woman to be "fruitful and multiply" (Genesis 1:27-28). For that reason a man "leaves his father and mother and clings to his wife" (Genesis 2:24).

Extended families included grandparents, other relatives, male and female slaves, concubines, and aliens, in addition to brothers and sisters, until the girls were married. We have learned that members of early churches first met in homes of members for worship and instruction, a fact that reflects the Jewish heritage of the family as a religious community responsible for preserving and handing on practices of worship and moral instruction. Full responsibility was in the home. Beyond the family and the synagogue, there were no social institutions as we know them today in industrialized nations.

### Wives and Mothers

The wife was primarily responsible for the rearing of children, especially sons for carrying on family traditions. Many passages show high praise for women as wives and mothers. Recall that in our discussion of gods mentioned in the OT, Yahweh was said to comfort Jerusalem as a mother comforts her children (Isaiah 66:13). Although wives were to be submissive to their husbands and to satisfy the sexual desires and other needs of their husbands, they were shown love and respect. This is reflected in Colossians 3:18-19: "Wives, be subject to your husbands, as is fitting to the Lord. Husbands, love your wives and never treat them harshly." Consider, also, Ephesians 5:22, 25: "Wives, be subject to your husbands as you are to the Lord... Husbands, love your wives, just as Christ loved the church and gave himself up for her."

According to Proverbs 31:10-13, a capable wife is more precious than jewels, has her husband's trust, brings him gain, does him good not harm, provides food for her family, buys a field and plants crops, takes care of her body, gives to the poor and needy, is not idle but makes clothes for her family, her children call her blessed, her husband praises her, and she surpasses all women in excellence. "Strength and dignity are her clothing, and she laughs at the time to come, she opens her mouth with wisdom, and the teaching of kindness is on her tongue" (Proverbs 31:25-26). Of course, religion plays a part: "Charm is deceitful, and beauty is vain, but a woman who fears the Lord is to be praised" (see also Sirach 7:26; 26:1-18).

*Husbands and Fathers*

Fathers were the personification of greatness both for their own families and for the families of the nation Israel. They were the ancestors through whom family traditions, including devotion to God, were preserved for their descendants. Negatively, fathers had the authority to kill immediate family members and their "most intimate" friends who tried to persuade them to "worship other gods" (Deuteronomy 13:6-11). Positively, fathers were primarily responsible for the "instruction" of their sons. Both the Hebrew word *musar* and the Greek *paideia* for "instruction" literally meant "the rearing of a child" and included elements of discipline, chastisement, correction, as well as learning. Fathers were to advise their children about the commandments that the Lord has given (Deuteronomy 6:20-25). "The Lord reproves the one he loves, as a father the son in whom he delights" (Proverbs 3:12; see also Psalm 103:13). Paul dealt with the Thessalonian converts "like a father with his children" in urging them to live God-worthy lives. And, in Colossians 3:21 the author says: "Fathers, do not provoke your children, or they may lose heart."

Interestingly, there are very few biblical passages regarding husbands, in contrast to many about wives. Sirach 25:20-22 indicates that husbands are to provide for their wives, and the idea of women being dependent on men is prevalent and certainly reflective of the times. The importance of taking care of women and children is clear in Sirach 4:10: "Be a father to orphans, and be like a husband to their mother; you will then be like a son of the Most High, and he will love you more than does your mother." The depth of a mother's love is reflected here, as well.

Among the many passages that reveal how important good, faithful, sensible wives were considered to be for their husbands is Sirach 26:1-3:

> Happy is the husband of a good wife; the number of his days will be doubled. A loyal wife brings joy to her husband, and he will complete his years in peace. A good wife is a great blessing; she will be granted among the blessings of the man who fears the Lord.

Similarly, according to Proverbs 19:14, "House and wealth are inherited from parents, but a prudent wife is from the Lord." And, an insightful glimpse into husband and wife relationships in Hebrew society is provided in Sirach 36:29: "He who acquires a wife gets his best possession, a helper fit for him and a pillar of support."

Other passages discuss difficulties in having a wife who does not meet the positive criteria emphasized in the passages quoted so far. According to Proverbs 12:4, for example: "A good wife is the crown for the husband, but she who brings shame is like rottenness in his bones." And, in Proverbs 21:9, the author declares: "It is better to live in a corner of the housetop than in a house shared with a contentious wife." In Proverbs 21:19, this same idea is repeated except that it substitutes living in a desert land as being more desirable than living with a "contentious and fretful wife."

*Children*
Children were expected to obey and respect their parents as the law demanded. In Leviticus 19:1-3, reverence for mother and father is in the context of holiness as Yahweh is holy. According to Proverbs 1:8, children should obey the instruction of their fathers and not reject the teaching of their mothers. As is clear from the author's preface in 1:2-6, this is an exhortation in a textbook on wisdom and moral discipline, including righteousness, justice, and equity. The motto for such instruction, repeated many times, is "The fear of the Lord is the beginning of knowledge; fools despise wisdom and instruction" (Proverbs 1:7). A child who does not observe the instruction of a father will turn to evil desires (LXX, Proverbs 19:27). Parents should discipline children and make them obey from their youth and be concerned about their daughters' virginity and not be too lenient with them.

While the law calling for the death of disobedient children (Exodus 21:15, 17) is abhorrent to most modern minds, a value that remains important for most people today is to "Honor your father and your mother, so that your days may be long in the land the Lord your God is giving you" (Exodus 20:12; repeated in Deuteronomy 5:16). Children should honor their fathers and not forget the birth pangs of the mothers who bore them. How can children repay their parents who bore them? According to Sirach 7:23-31, this happens when they follow the Lord.

*Divorce*
It is impossible to determine accurately the current divorce rate among Jews and Christians, but some statistics suggest that up to one half of all marriages end in divorce. This is especially true in marriages that take place between very young adults. In general, there is a somewhat higher rate among Jews and conservative Christians, with Protestants having a

higher divorce rate than Catholics, and atheists and agnostics having the lowest divorce rates.

Although it was assumed among people of the Bible that marriages were to be permanent, divorce was permitted, but mostly on the husband's initiative. However, a man was not to divorce a wife whom he later slandered with false charges (Deuteronomy 22:13-19). If a man found something detestable about his wife, he could simply write a "certificate of divorce," hand it to her, and put her out of the house (Deuteronomy 24:1-4; see also Isaiah 50:1 and Matthew 1:19 for Joseph about Mary). For a likely certificate of divorce see Hosea 2:2: "She is not my wife, and I am not her husband."

According to Malachi 2:15-16, a man was not to be unfaithful to his wife, for the Lord hates divorce. In early Judaism men who married foreign women could divorce them for religious reasons (Ezra 10:2–3, 44; but see 1 Corinthians 7:12-15 below). According to Mark 10:2-9, Jesus rebuked the Pharisees by saying that Moses allowed a certificate of divorce because of hardness of heart. Jesus says that God made male and female to be joined together and not to be separated. This reflects the Eden story in Genesis 2:24. Matthew repeats the incident but adds that unchastity is an exception (Matthew 19:9). Mark reports that Jesus says that the man or woman who divorces a spouse and marries another commits adultery (Mark 10:10-12). Matthew limits the divorce to the man and again adds unchastity as an exception (Matthew 19:9). According to Matthew 5:10, in the Sermon on the Mount, Jesus says that a man who marries a divorced woman commits adultery (so also Luke 16:18).

### Paul's Views on Family Life

Paul speaks about family relationships in response to the things about which the Corinthian converts had written to him (1 Corinthians 7:1-40). Women made their presence felt in the Corinthian church. Perhaps some of them, unknowingly to their husbands, had become believers and were not content with being silent partners (1 Corinthians 7:13). By vocally participating in worship, they were exceeding what was thought proper for a woman in the male-oriented society of Paul's time. Paul was obviously trying to bring harmony into the situation. After all, God had called converts for peace (7:15). For some persons today Paul's answers still leave questions about his own position with respect to women, men, and marriage. But one thing is certain: the morality of both sexes was his main concern.

## Paul on Marriage and Sex

Paul begins his discussion of relationships between men and women (1 Corinthians 7:1-40) with words that would arouse the consternation, if not the ire, of any healthy male, even a "holy one": "It is well for a man not to touch a woman" (1 Corinthians 7:1). Paul does not give a command but uses the rhetorical formula "It is good (*kalon estin*)...but" (7:26, 38; Galatians 4:18; Romans 14:21). "Touch" (*haptō*) has sexual implications, and in the Septuagint it is used of sexual intercourse outside of marriage (Genesis 20:4, 6; Proverbs 6:29). There are many OT references against adultery and Paul's teachings add to these. He offers as one solution to prevent sexual immorality: "Each man should have his own wife and each woman her own husband" (7:2). Perhaps the fact that one of the converts had committed a detestable immoral act (1 Corinthians 5:1-5) is one of the reasons why Paul writes as he does. Or, perhaps, as some commentators have suggested, specific questions had been raised: "Is marriage permitted?" "Is sexual intercourse allowed (at all)?"

Since in Judaism men were expected to marry and have children, and since Paul's advice differs from teachings of Jesus, Paul's message is not determined by his Jewish background. His teaching, then, is due to his own physical makeup and his experience of new life in Christ. As an unmarried man, by nature emotional, Paul knew the male struggle to restrain his sexual impulses. Perhaps, as some scholars have suggested, his thorn in the flesh (2 Corinthians 12:7) was an unusually strong sex drive. This would be one way of explaining Paul's intense and incessant warnings against illicit sexual relationships. He knew what it meant to be in Christ and to live by the Spirit, not according to the flesh (Galatians 5:16-26). He could control the desires of the flesh, but he was aware that converts, especially Gentile neophytes, might not be able to do so.

Although Paul does not forbid marriage, his motive for hesitating about marriage seems to be more for avoiding sexual misconduct (*porneia*) than from feelings of love. The rule for holiness and abstention from immorality stated as the will of God in 1 Thessalonians 4:1-8 is presupposed in 1 Corinthians 7:1-2. Perhaps this was due in part to the fact that there were women believers active in the church at Corinth.

Perhaps because of the risk of being sexually immoral, each married partner should remain faithful to the other. Within the bonds of marriage sexual relationships are a mutual obligation (1 Corinthians 7:2-5). Paul may assume a "love relationship" in his response to the Corinthian converts, but according to the text, he is more concerned with morality than with love. Being an unmarried male aware of sexual temptations and yet guided by the Spirit, would he be more sensitive toward immorality than love in a marital relationship?

Paul has often been accused of supporting, if not promoting, the inequality of women. Certainly this is not true with respect to what he says about marital relationships in 1 Corinthians 7:3-4, where he is expressing equality toward the sexes:

> The husband should give to his wife her conjugal rights, and likewise the wife to her husband. For the wife does not have authority over her own body, but the husband does; likewise, the husband does not have authority over his own body, but the wife does.

Thus, the sexual relationship is reciprocal. Paul seems to be saying that the marriage relationship is so close that each partner is indebted to the other for sex. Neither should deprive the other, except when both agree for some religious reason to abstain for a limited time. But in order that Satan might not tempt them because of their abstinence, they should resume sexual intercourse again after the time agreed upon has elapsed. Paul says this, though, not as a command but as a concession, apparently allowing for circumstances (7:6). Paul knew that if married couples were to be happy and live peaceably together, nothing should interfere with the natural relations between the partners. Moreover, deprivation of sex on the part of one partner might lead to the kind of immoral behavior Paul did not want to happen.

It would be better for unmarried persons to remain single as Paul is, but if they cannot exercise self-control, they should marry. At the same time, each person has her or his own grace-gift (*charisma*) from God, which leaves open the possibility for one to abstain from marriage, as with Paul, or marry.

### Why Not to Marry

Paul gives his reasons for advising against marriage in 1 Corinthians 7:8-9, 25-31. It is well to remain single as Paul is, but it is better to marry than to burn with passion. The end of the world is coming soon, so for that reason a married man should not separate from his wife and a man free of a wife should not seek marriage. But if such persons marry, they do not sin; and if the virgin marries, she does not sin. Paul wants converts to be free from anxieties. Married people have added worries; unmarried persons have more time to be anxious about the affairs of the Lord, how to please him. Married persons might be more apt to want to please each other. Paul writes as he does for the converts' own advantage, not to put a noose around them. He wants to promote good order among families in the church and everyone to be devoted to the Lord, without distraction (7:32-35).

According to Paul, "If anyone thinks that he is behaving unseemly toward his virgin, if his sexual vigor is excessive and if it ought to be, let him do what he wishes, he does not sin, let them get married" (1 Corinthians 7:36). This is a literal translation of Paul's Greek, which, I believe, can be interpreted to mean it is permissible for a man to have sexual relations with his virgin if they subsequently marry. According to Paul, the man who has his feelings thoroughly under control and wants, deep down in his heart, to keep his companion as a virgin does well. "He who marries his virgin does well; and he who refrains from marriage will do better" (7:37-38). "Virgin" here, as in earlier verses, is to be taken as a woman who has not had sexual intercourse and is loved by a man.

*Paul on Divorce*
Paul says that married persons should not become divorced (1 Corinthians 7:10-16). However, he adds a qualification with respect to the wife alone: if she does separate from her husband, she should remain unmarried or be reconciled with her husband. Paul does not deal with remarriage as adultery but seems to want to encourage women to reunite with their husbands. He gives his charge on the authority of Jesus – "not I but the Lord" – but if Paul knew about Jesus' reported words on marriage and divorce, he uses them creatively.

Paul's advice about married persons not becoming divorced pertains to believers, because he turns to mixed marriages. On this subject he writes on his own authority (1 Corinthians 7:12-13). If any man has an unbelieving wife and she consents to live with him, he is not to divorce her. If any woman has an unbelieving husband and he consents to live with her, she should not divorce him.

In a unique way, Paul does seem to have some hope for the conversion of the unbeliever (7:14): "The unbelieving husband is made holy through his wife, and the unbelieving wife is made holy through her husband. Otherwise, your children would be unclean, but as it is, they are holy."

Paul believes that through marital sexual relationships the unbelieving partner becomes holy through the believing partner, a view analogous to that of a person who has sexual relations with a prostitute becoming immoral (1 Corinthians 6:15-18). There is always the possibility that in mixed marriages the believing partner might win the unbelieving one to faithfulness.

Throughout his discussion of marriage and divorce Paul is concerned with saving the marital relationship. He thinks of it as a holy union, and each partner should strive to preserve it. With respect to mixed marriages between a believer and an unbeliever, the basic guideline is domestic peace. "It is to peace that God has called you" (7:15).

Paul concludes his discussion of marriage, sex, and divorce by saying: "And I think that I too have the Spirit of God" (1 Corinthians 7:40). It seems he is saying that the experience of the Spirit is not limited to those who are married and have sexual relationships. As a single person (7:7-8), Paul wants to make sure that he is not thought to be devoid of the Spirit because he is unmarried.

### Homosexuality

In current society, there is considerable debate about homosexuality, what constitutes marriage, and how the structure of families should be defined. Some persons think that same-sex relationships are natural and to be desired; others think they are contrary to human nature and are to be abhorred as sinful. Compared with some other aspects of human behavior, references in the Bible to homosexuality or same-sex relationships are relatively few. And sometimes some of them are misunderstood. As with other questions dealing with values, each text must be understood in light of its context.

#### Homosexuality in the Old Testament
*Genesis 19:1-11.* This passage deals with the two angels (men) visiting Lot and the men of Sodom, discussed earlier. There the question is sexual rape between males, which never actually occurred. Of numerous references to the "sin" of Sodom, the most specific is Ezekiel 16:49-50, part of Ezekiel's allegorical history of the evils of Jerusalem. Its people are guilty of pride, excess food, luxurious prosperity, not helping the poor, and being haughty in doing evils like Sodom. Here sodomy, that is, sexual relationships among males, is not mentioned. When considering your own personal behavior, do you ever fall short of the values suggested in this passage?

In the sending out of the 12 disciples, Mark 6:11 reports that Jesus says "any place" that refuses to welcome them should be rebuked. According to Matthew 10:14-15, it will be more tolerable for Sodom on the day of judgment than for those inhospitable people (see also Luke 10:11-12). So, even if the reference to Sodom were to include homosexuality, this passage puts that behavior as a "sin" into perspective. It is unlikely that the reference to "sexual immorality and...unnatural lust" in Jude 1:7 is to homosexuality among males, as is sometimes suggested. The passage refers to the fallen angels that left their place in heaven (Jude 1:6) and married daughters of men (Genesis 6:1-40).

*Leviticus 18:22.* In this passage a male having sexual intercourse with a male is called "an abomination," a detestable act. It is one of several other abominations listed in Leviticus 18:19-23: sex with a woman during her menstrual period because her blood would defile the man (Leviticus 15:24); sex with someone else's wife which would defile the man; sacrifice of a child to the god Molech because it would profane God; sex with animals on the part of either a man or a woman because it is a perversity. A woman is mentioned only in the last abomination.

*Leviticus 20:10-16.* Here the penalties for the offenses mentioned above are given: death for both persons in an adulterous relationship, for homosexual males, and for both sexes who have sex with animals. Both partners who have sex during the woman's menstrual period are to be "cut off from their people" (Leviticus 20:18). The reason for such laws was to prevent the people of Israel from the "abominable" practices of the nations from whom Yahweh was delivering them (Leviticus 18:24-30; 20:22-26). The latter passage ends with the admonition to holiness: "You shall be holy to me; for I the Lord am holy, and I have separated you from the other peoples to be mine."

*Observations and Questions*
There is no conclusive evidence that homosexuality between females (lesbianism) is condemned in the Bible (but see Romans 1:26-27). Does that make it acceptable today because it is not condemned in the Bible? Is male homosexuality unacceptable because the Bible reproves it? Are sex during a woman's menstrual period, divorce and remarriage (Deuteronomy 24:1-4), and cross-dressing of either men or women (Deuteronomy 22:5) to be condemned because the Bible says they are abhorrent to the Lord?

Bible writers were not familiar with modern scientific advances in medicine, genetics, and psychology and other social sciences. As knowledge increases, values change. In the Western World, for example, there is widespread agreement that menstrual blood is not defiling and that intercourse during a woman's period is no longer prohibited. The scientific community is still somewhat divided on the role genetics plays in homosexuality. Some scientists are sure that because of a particular genetic makeup, homosexuality is as normal for some persons as heterosexuality is for others. Another point of view maintains that homosexual behavior is acquired, not innate.

Old Testament laws about sex in general are very severe. Sexual relations were considered defiling, and after sexual intercourse both the man and the woman were considered unclean. During her menstrual period a woman was considered unclean, her bed polluted, everything she sat on was unclean, and anyone who touched her was also unclean. For seven days after her period she was still unclean. If a woman bore a male child, she was considered unclean for seven days and if a female child, unclean for two weeks (Leviticus 12:2-5). Persons who had sexual relations during a woman's period were to be excluded from the community. But how would "the community" learn of such an act? Would the couple report their deed? Other laws regarding family relationships were equally harsh. For example, "Whoever curses father or mother shall be put to death" (Exodus 21:17; Leviticus 20:9). For other laws of the same kind see much of Leviticus 15–20 and elsewhere. So, while Leviticus condemns homosexuality, it also has numerous other dictates that simply do not apply in our present societies.

### Homosexuality in the New Testament

In dealing with biblical texts it is easy to read into or out of them what one wants to find there. Therefore, there are often different and conflicting interpretations of the same passages. There are only three passages in the NT that we can be sure specifically mention homosexuality, but another in Paul (1 Corinthians 5:9-11) also helps to provide insightful understanding. The two most significant passages are in Paul's letters, so we can omit the third one (1 Timothy 1:9-10) because it adds nothing.

Romans 1:26-27

> For this reason God gave them [Gentiles] up to degrading passions. Their women exchanged natural intercourse for unnatural, and in the same way also the men, giving up natural intercourse with women, were consumed with passion for one another. Men committed shameless acts with men and received in their own persons the due penalty for their error.

This is a very problematic passage. In the immediate context Paul is saying that the idolatry of pagans has led to their moral degeneration. Therefore, God has abandoned them because of their impurity and degraded bodies and their passions, including homosexual activity. Why does Paul imply such activity here and not mention it among the vices in similar lists in Romans 1:29-31; 13:13; 1 Corinthians 5:9-11; 2 Corinthians 12:20-21; Galatians 5:19-21? Homosexuality activity is not included in lists of vices in Ephesians 4:31; 5:3-5; Colossians 3:5-8; 2 Timothy 3:2-7 (see also Wisdom 14:22-31; *4 Maccabees* 1:24-27).

The absence of homosexuality in such lists indicates that it was not a vice foremost on the minds of the writers. A plausible reason for Paul writing as he does in Romans 1:26-27 is that homosexuality was widely practiced in the Greco-Roman culture of his time. However, gay people were a minority then, and homosexuality was not considered illicit, harmful, or odd. In our passage Paul regarded it as symbolic of the evils that originated with idolatry. Pagans served themselves as humans rather than God as the Creator (Romans 1:24-25).

There is a wide difference of opinion among scholars about what Paul means in Romans 1:26-27. It is probably true that Paul's words "natural intercourse for unnatural" mean homosexual relationships between women, as most scholars think, although a few think the relationship is that between women and men. At any rate, Paul does not specifically mention homosexuality in the list of vices that follows in Romans 1:28-32. However, he also does not mention adultery there, either. The repetition of "men" shows that Paul's emphasis is on the relationships of men with each other.

What is meant by the words "natural" and "unnatural" among women? Do they apply to "heterosexual" or "homosexual" relationships? Homosexual relationships may be implied from Paul's words, "in the same way also the men." However, such relationships are not clearly stated, as in the case of men. Is the meaning of "unnatural" to be taken differently if genetics prove, as many scientists believe, that same-sex relationships are also "natural?" Paul's emphasis is that both women and men had been immoral, but the emphasis is on the men.

1 Corinthians 6:9

> Do you not know that wrongdoers will not inherit the kingdom of God? Do not be deceived! Fornicators, idolaters, adulterers, male prostitutes, sodomites, thieves, the greedy, drunkards, revilers, robbers – none of these will inherit the kingdom of God.

There is no question that the Greek word translated here as "sodomites" refers specifically to sexual relations between males. The single Greek word (*arsenokoitēs*) is actually a combination of two words: *arsēn*, meaning male, and *koitē*, meaning marriage bed. Here Paul says nothing about homosexual relationships between women. We should observe further that "sodomites" is one kind of sinners among others. Does Paul mean that sodomites are worse sinners than the others mentioned? Notice that Paul says, "None of these will inherit the kingdom of God."

1 Corinthians 5:9-11

> I wrote to you...not to associate with sexually immoral persons...or the greedy and robbers, or idolaters... But now I am writing to you not to associate with anyone who bears the name of brother or sister who is sexually immoral or greedy, or is an idolater, reviler, drunkard, or robber. Do not even eat with such a one... Drive out the wicked person from among you.

Although this passage has no reference to homosexuality, it helps to enlighten our understanding of Romans 1:26-27 and 1 Corinthians 6:9. Notice that most of the same vices occur in both of the Corinthian passages. Are those vices more or less serious than homosexuality because Paul does not include it in 1 Corinthians 5:9-11? The Greek word translated as "sexually immoral persons" is the same as that translated as "fornicators" in 1 Corinthians 6:9 and refers specifically to males, especially male prostitutes and their immoral behavior. Paul uses it and related words a number of times to mean illicit sexual behavior of any kind. Obviously, Paul thinks poorly of persons having the vices mentioned. He advises the Corinthian converts not even to eat with such persons and to expel them from their community.

## Food for Thought

What, then, should we make of all this? It is often too easy to center attention on one "vice" to the neglect of others Paul thought were of equal, perhaps even greater, importance. The word translated as "sodomites," for example, occurs infrequently in Greek literature, nowhere in the Septuagint, and only in 1 Corinthians 6:9 and 1 Timothy 1:10 in the NT. On the other hand, drinking and drunkenness, adultery, and divorce are condemned much more widely in the Bible than homosexuality. Although frequent also in the OT, here is some evidence just in the NT (from Greek):

*Adultery* (*moicheia*): Matthew 15:19; Mark 7:22.
*Commit adultery* (*moichaomai*): Matthew 5:32; 19:9; Mark 10:11-12;
    (*moicheuo*): Matthew 5:27-32; 19:18; Mark 10:19; Luke 16:18;
    Romans 2:22; 13:9; James 2:11; Revelation 2:22.

*Adulterer (moichos)*: Luke 18:11; 1 Corinthians 6:9; Hebrews 13:4.
*Adulteress, adulterous (moichalis)*: Matthew 12:39; 16:4; Mark 8:38; Romans 7:3; James 4:4; 2 Peter 2:14.
*Become drunk (methuskomai)*: Luke 12:45; Ephesians 5:18; 1 Timothy 5:7; 1 Thessalonians 5:7.
*Be drunk (methuō)*: Matthew 24:49; John 2:10; Acts 2:15; 1 Corinthians 11:21; 1 Thessalonians 5:7; Revelation 17:2, 6.
*Drunkard (methusos)*: 1 Corinthians 5:11; 6:10.

If you read these passages, you can observe that in the places where vices are mentioned, homosexuality is not among them, nor does it occur in any of the other passages. Yet, the behaviors that are mentioned are often not given the same negative response today that homosexuality receives. In my experience within the church, alcoholism even among the clergy has been a concern. But, alcoholics are not expelled from the church; rather, they are encouraged to get counseling and treatment. In fact, it is generally accepted among social scientists that alcoholism is a disease, and modern scientific research about the brain has led to increased understanding of this very prevalent problem. It is no longer considered a moral deficiency or character flaw but a disease that can be managed with long-term support. Is is possible that scientific evidence can lead us to consider homosexuality in a new way, as well?

Gospel writers report that Jesus linked divorce and adultery together. Consider Mark 10:11-12: "He [Jesus] said to them, Whoever divorces his wife and marries another commits adultery against her; and if she divorces her husband and marries another, she commits adultery" (see also Matthew 19:9). See also Luke 16:18: "Anyone who divorces his wife and marries another commits adultery, and whoever marries a woman divorced from her husband commits adultery" (see also Matthew 5:32).

Offhand I can think of ten clergy who are divorced or have married divorced persons, and I know the president of a seminary and the chaplain of a college who are divorced. Given that, is it not fair to suggest that there may be hundreds of divorced male and female pastors currently serving parishes in the United States or in Europe? Do the people in those parishes think of their pastors or other divorced persons as adulterers? Should we not eat with them, and should we drive them from among us? In Paul's view, not ours, was homosexuality a greater vice than the other vices he mentions?

## Chapter Summary

When turning to the Bible to support or to oppose some current moral question, we must try not to say too hastily, "The Bible Says So!" Yes, Leviticus condemns homosexuality, but it says a lot about sexual relations that are not condemned today. In trying to justify a particular point of view, it is easy to choose one vice over some others, although all are equally condemned by biblical writers. Most readers would probably think it unreasonable, if not immoral, to put to death homosexual partners as mandated in Leviticus 20:13. In Leviticus 20:10 if a man commits adultery with another man's wife, both of them should be put to death. How many people in churches today think such laws should be followed, and how many churches take such drastic actions because "The Bible Says So"?

Although there are laws about adultery in some places, prosecutions for violations are very uncommon. Who does not know of persons living in adulterous situations and persons who have been divorced and remarried? Should we dismiss them from our churches? How many judges and executioners would be needed to enforce many of the laws in the Pentateuch? Who should decide which laws are justifiable and which are not? Are we to decide that some things the Bible condemns are to be observed and others equally important are not? Many members would be absent from churches if violations of the laws mentioned were carried out. In modern society it would not only be impractical, but also impossible, to observe the laws we mentioned.

Our world is far different from that of the Bible, and most biblical writers did not make the same kind of moral judgments we do or even that some later biblical writers made. It is certainly important that we use knowledge available to us today as we consider what values to uphold. That does not preclude, however, using the Bible in an insightful way to help us develop the important values that can guide our lives and that can help to define us as Christians worthy of that name. If we focus on love, rather than on judgments against those we believe violate God's law, is it not possible that we are following what might well be the most important commandment and the basis for all else that is good: "Love your neighbor as yourself."

Without insisting that wives be submissive, which was an unquestioned part of patriarchal societies as they existed in biblical times, we can still embrace the Bible's teachings about the importance of mutual respect, loyalty, and devotion of husband and wife for one another, and we can still appreciate the importance of teaching our children important values. We can certainly also strive for "harmony of brothers, friendship of neighbors and a wife and husband who live happily together" (Sirach 25:1). Remember, too, that Jesus taught the importance of goodness to the extreme, which seems applicable to all times and in all places. And, there seems to be infinite wisdom in remembering that love "endures all things." There is no doubt, in fact, that "The Bible Says So!"

Chapter 19

THE BIBLE AND SELECTED SOCIAL ISSUES TODAY

## Introduction

A multitude of social ills that face societies today pose a major threat to the well-being of humankind and, at times, even to our existence. Terrorism, ethnic cleansing, political and racial strife, oppression, human rights violations, the threat of nuclear attacks, and many additional, serious social issues create ongoing challenges to people around the world. Beyond these global concerns are others that impact many individuals and families, regardless of culture, such as crime, domestic violence, sexual abuse, AIDS and other life-threatening diseases, pornography and a growing sex trade victimizing children, drug abuse and other addictions, untreated mental illness, and poverty and homelessness.

What can we learn from the Bible about important social issues today? In this chapter, we approach this question in a general way and then focus on more specific issues that are at the center of much current religious and political controversy. While it is difficult, if not impossible, to address many important issues directly, because today's world is so radically different from the world of the Bible, we can certainly gain some important insights about what "the Bible says" in terms of underlying values that are relevant in a general way. And, interestingly, when we pause to contemplate issues that impacted individuals and societies in the centuries during which the Bible was written, it becomes surprisingly clear that there are more similarities between then and now than what we might expect.

## The Bible in Today's World

Perhaps the best way to start a discussion of what "the Bible says" that is relevant to social issues today is to explore what it says about life itself. In the OT God is thought of as the Creator of life, as reflected in Job 33:4: "The spirit of God has made me, and the breath of the Almighty gives me life."

(See also Psalms 21:4; 104:29-30; 1 Samuel 2:6.) For centuries, it was thought that the conception of a child was a sign of God's mysterious ways. And, as Creator of life, only God can take life away. According to Genesis 1:27, humans were made from dust, God breathed into them the breath of life, and to dust they would return (Genesis 3:19; see also Psalm 139:7-18). Remember, too, that Jesus healed a man on the Sabbath, even though rebuked by his critics, saying: "Is it lawful to do good or to do harm on the Sabbath, to save life or to kill?" (Mark 3:4; Matthew 12:12; Luke 6:9). He gave life priority over laws about working on the Sabbath.

A long life was an indication of the good life, as seen in Proverbs 10:27: "The fear of the Lord prolongs life, but the years of the wicked will be short" (see also Acts 17:25 and 1 Timothy 6:13). This is true because the Hebrews/Jews did not believe in life after death until the second century BCE, but even then the Sadducees did not accept the doctrine of an afterlife (see Acts 23:6-8; Mark 12:18; Matthew 22:23; Luke 20:27). Paul's belief in Christ influences what he says about life and death, but, again, only because of the value of life would eternal life be important: "The wages of sin is death, but the gift of God is eternal life" (Romans 6:23).

A case could probably also be made that the Bible supports the importance of quality of life, as, for example, in John 10:10: "I came that they [Jesus' followers] may have life and have it abundantly." The word translated as "abundantly" is *perissos,* which means "more than sufficient," "over and above," or as in the *REB*, "in all its fullness." According to Paul, baptism brings "newness of life" (Romans 6:4; 1 Thessalonians 4:9-12; see also Ephesians 4:1, 22-24; Colossians 1:9-10), that is, a life with enhanced quality.

When we think of life, should we think of it as mere existence or as quality of life? That would certainly have some bearing on decisions about any number of issues of life and death, in at least some situations. In fact, let's consider God's command to Adam and Eve that they "be fruitful and multiply." The context of that passage is the beginning of the world and God's creation of human beings. Does that still apply to today's world, given issues of overpopulation and millions of people who die each year from starvation and abject poverty? Is creating new life more important than sustaining life that already exists or in providing quality of life beyond mere survival? Is it more of a sin to abort a fetus than it is to live in relative abundance while tens of thousands of children around the world starve to death each day or die from preventable or curable disease? For some reason, abortion seems to get more attention than "death by default," so let's see if the Bible can offer any insight about such complex issues of life and death.

## Abortion, Capital Punishment, and Other Issues of Life and Death

Abortion is certainly a social issue that has raised considerable controversy and that has deeply divided people who are referred to as "pro-choice" from those who are referred to as "pro-life." At the core of the debate about abortion is whether or not women should have the right to control choices about their bodies to the point of terminating a pregnancy and at what point life begins. Members of both groups are probably equally convinced that they are "right" and that what "the Bible says" supports their views. Without attention to the complicated ethical issues of a biomedical nature, we can explore several passages in the Bible that are often quoted in debates about abortion.

### Abortion and the Bible

There is no passage in the NT dealing with abortion and just a few references to it in the OT. There is also no word in the Bible for abortion in the sense of its use today, but there are passages referring to a fetus showing signs of life. Recall that Jacob and Esau as "children struggled together within" Rebekah (Genesis 25:22), which indicates that they were thought of as children before they were born. A comparable passage is Luke 1:41, 44, where "the child leaped" in the womb of Elizabeth. Then Elizabeth calls Mary the mother of her Lord and tells her that "the child" in her womb "leaped for joy." The word translated as "child" is *brephos*, and it refers to the unborn John the Baptist, the same word used of the born Jesus in Luke 2:13, 16.

These passages are used to support a "pro-life" view that the Bible treats the fetus as a person, so, for that reason, abortion is taking life or killing, and, therefore, wrong. The type of prenatal activity mentioned in these passages, however, is clearly indicative of a fetus at a stage of development considerably later than the first trimester, when the vast majority of abortions occur. It is highly unlikely, in fact, that women of biblical times would even have been aware that they were "with child" at the time in a pregnancy when most women seek abortions. So, these passages actually do not address the issue of abortion nor do they provide valid arguments in favor of or against it.

Related ideas in the Bible that are used for the same purpose include Jeremiah's belief that before he was formed in the womb God knew him and consecrated him to be a prophet (Jeremiah 1:5). Similarly, Paul says that before he was born God revealed his Son in him to proclaim him to the Gentiles (Galatians 1:15-16; see also Job 3:3; 10:8-12; Psalm 139:13-16; Isaiah

44:1-2). As with the passages cited earlier, the Bible is not actually addressing abortion in these passages, either. So, what *does* the Bible say?

Exodus 21:22, quoted below, is particularly pertinent to a discussion of abortion and the Bible:

> When people who are fighting injure a pregnant woman so that there is a miscarriage, and yet no further harm follows, the one responsible shall be fined what the woman's husband demands... If any harm follows, then you shall give life for life, tooth for tooth.

While this passage is often used to support a "pro-life" view, a closer examination makes it less clear that "The Bible Says So!" It appears that a miscarriage – or the loss of the unborn "child" – is given less significance than harm to the mother. After all, the only penalty for the miscarriage is a fine to be determined by the woman's husband. This might well reflect that, in societies that depended upon the contributions of children to help sustain their families, a miscarriage represented more of a monetary loss than a loss related to life itself. Yet, with regard to harm that "follows," which must mean harm to the woman, it is to be settled, instead, by the *lex talionis*, that is, "eye for eye..." The fine for the fetus is certainly less serious than the *lex talionis* for the woman, suggesting that the fetus was not regarded as having equal value with the woman. In fact, it is not absolutely clear from this passage that there was compensation for the loss of the fetus or whether it was just for the woman and her injury from the miscarriage.

The LXX Exodus 21:22-23 differs from the Hebrew in important points:

> If two men are fighting and strike a woman with child, and the child be born imperfectly formed, he shall be forced to pay a penalty as the woman's husband assesses. He shall pay with a monetary value. But if it be perfectly formed, he shall give life for life.

This passage raises more interesting questions. Here the law of injury is applied to the fetus rather than to the woman, as in the Hebrew text. There is also a distinction between a fetus imperfectly formed and one perfectly formed, although it is not clear what was actually meant by "perfectly formed." Did that refer only to a fetus that would have been viable outside the womb? In biblical times, that would have been a child nearly full-term. Or, did it refer to a fetus that did not show any signs of birth defects or deformities, regardless of the stage of its development? There are no definitive answers to these questions.

The word for child is *paidion*, meaning "young child," "little one," or "baby." While there was no word to differentiate a child after birth from a fetus, as is true today, the death of a "perfectly formed" unborn child was apparently regarded as murder, because the penalty was "life for life." Yet, since the penalty for harm to an "imperfectly formed" fetus was, in contrast, a monetary one, does this suggest that abortion of a child known to have birth defects or before it is developed enough to sustain life outside the womb is acceptable? Given advances of modern medicine, when we discover that a diseased or deformed fetus, if left to develop into birth, would mean a miserable existence for the child and untold agony for the parents, would the Bible support abortion? Would the importance of life itself and of quality of life – or even the value of "love" – suggest that, for all involved, abortion would bring the most "abundant" life?

To add to these uncertainties, those arguing a "pro-choice" position sometimes take the complicated passage in Numbers 5:11-31, especially verses 29-31, to mean that God induces a miscarriage if a woman has had intercourse with a man other than her husband. They appeal to the translation of the *REB*, which uses "miscarriage and untimely birth" several times for Hebrew words translated otherwise in other translations. The *NRSV* has "make your womb discharge," which might be taken as miscarriage. The *NJB* has "make your belly swell and your sex organs shrivel." How's that for trying to decide what the Bible says? Is this passage truly suggesting that God himself causes abortions to occur? If one agrees that the passage in Numbers 5:11-31 shows that God induces abortion as a punishment for sin, then should pregnant sinners be allowed to have abortions and then be punished? If only we could claim easy answers, because "The Bible Says So!"

Whether the debate is about abortion or premarital sex or adultery or other decisions of a moral nature, the ultimate choice of any individual is a matter of that person's values, which are often impacted by faith and religious beliefs. What makes abortion particularly significant, of course, is that it raises questions about life – and when life actually begins – and about killing or murder, which then raise legal concerns, as well. Yet, killing, as in capital punishment, is sometimes a legal solution to murder. Can we gain any insightful understanding about this controversial issue of life and death by turning to the Bible?

### Capital Punishment and the Bible

In the OT, Hebrew laws and moral teachings were closely related. Beyond the sixth Commandment, "You shall not murder" (or "kill"; Exodus 20:13; Deuteronomy 5:17; "Thou shalt not kill," *KJV*), there are numerous other passages that address murder. And, reflecting the *lex talionis,* the penalty for murder, according to Hebrew law, was death. Does this mean that the Bible supports capital punishment? Well, yes, we could say that, but it would be far too simplistic an answer. Death, indeed, was the punishment for murder, but it was, as well, for striking or cursing a parent (Exodus 21:15, 17), for kidnapping (Exodus 21:16), for sex with an animal (Exodus 22:19; Leviticus 20:15-16), for a person who owns an ox that kills a man (Exodus 21:28), for profanity or working on the Sabbath (Exodus 31:15; 35:2), for sacrificing a child to a pagan god (Leviticus 20:2-4), for adultery, incest, and homosexuality (Leviticus 20:10-14), for being a medium (Leviticus 20:27), and for blasphemy (Leviticus 24:16). That should give all of us some food for thought.

What is also thought-provoking is that God himself, who was seen in the OT as responsible for life and death, did not punish Cain by death for killing his brother (Genesis 4:14-17). Remember, too, that Adam and Eve were supposed to die if they ate from the tree of the knowledge of good and evil, but that did not happen, either. And Matthew, the Jew, reports that Jesus said to his disciples: "You have heard that it was said, 'An eye for an eye... But I say to you, Do not resist an evildoer. But if anyone strikes you on the right cheek, turn the other also... Give to everyone who begs from you...'" (Matthew 5:38-42; see also Luke 6:29-30) So, does the Bible support capital punishment? We can hardly say "The Bible Says So!"

*Insightfully Understanding the Bible*
If we are to truly hold life as a gift from God, we can certainly say that abortion is wrong, if we believe that a fetus, even in its earliest stages, is "life." Knowing that a heartbeat can be detected at two weeks, we could use that as a sign of "life," yet whether or not a *sign* of life is the same as *life* itself is unclear. And, in the Bible it appears that a fetus was not given the same value as the woman who was pregnant.

Although it would be wonderful to be able to turn to the Bible to resolve complex issues like abortion, it is more a matter of interpretation than insightful understanding that is possible, because the Bible just simply does not present clearcut answers. And, when we add to that reality the fact that our world today has knowledge not even imagined in biblical times and an awareness of bioethical, moral, social, and philosophical questions that we raise because of that knowledge, it is best to turn to the Bible for direction when we can be reasonably positive about what it says that applies to today's world.

## Poverty

There is a recurring theme of concern for the poor and needy in the Bible, which is an area where we can say, with absolute certainty, what "the Bible says." Literally hundreds of passages address this social issue. And, there is no doubt that poverty is a global issue of global importance, even in our modern world! Worldwide, statistics are shocking. For millions of people, including far too many infants and children, poverty is a death sentence. It is estimated that, at the present time, hunger affects a billion people around the world and that every five seconds a child dies from starvation or other effects of hunger. That means that almost 16,000 children die each day from hunger-related causes. In the United States alone, 30,000,000 people go to bed hungry each night, and every night there are about 300,000 more people who are homeless than there are beds for them. While a relatively small proportion of the world's population lives affluently, many more people struggle just to survive. More than a billion people, in fact, live on just one dollar a day, and one third of the world's population dies prematurely or develops disabilities due to lack of adequate nutrition.

### In the Old Testament

*The Prophets.* The prophets, those great moral and social reformers of Israel and Judah who generally appeared in times of relative peace and prosperity, predicting adversity, spoke against all persons, no matter who they were, who took advantage of the poor. Amos, for example, appeared during the long and prosperous reign of King Jeroboam II of Israel (c. 786-746 BCE). There was crime and corruption in the cities, persons in rural areas were committing evils of all kinds, and the rich and noble were taking advantage of the poor. People whose stomachs were full were not troubled by the hunger pangs of the poor. According to Amos 5:11-13, for people living in luxurious houses and beautiful surroundings, it was easy to ignore the poor in the slums.

Many of the rich could afford to live down south in winter and up north in summer. Amos believed that God had spoken against such wealth: "I will tear down the winter house as well as the summer house" (Amos 3:13). Even wealthy women, whom Amos compared to the "cows of Bashan" and "Samaria," had become alcoholics and were begging their husbands to take them to the club for a drink. Those women, too, were oppressing the poor and subduing the needy (4:1-4). Some people did not know how to do right and hated those who tried to do so and to speak the truth. At the same time, the poor were oppressed and cheated out of what belonged to them (5:10-11; 8:4-6). But no one could fool Yahweh: "I know how many are your transgressions, and how great are your sins – you who afflict the righteous, who take a bribe, and push aside the needy" (5:12).

Many persons thought they were religious by participating in ceremonial practices, but they were mistaking rituals for true religion. According to Amos, if such persons were unwilling to serve God by ministering to the poor and needy, such practices did not count as true religion (4:4-5; 5:21-23). While the needy were suffering, wealthy persons reveled in rich feasts, drinking, and improvising idle songs and music.

During the time of King Uzziah (c. 783–743 BCE) the kingdom of Judah was at the peak of its power. After Uzziah died, Isaiah tried to keep the kingdom on a strong and steady course. Read the beautiful poetry in Isaiah 1:2-23 that describes the deplorable situation of his time. Amidst all the luxury and evil, the rich and powerful "do not defend the orphan, and the widow's cause does not come before them" (1:23). The hungry survivors were moved to curse the king who had deceived them and the God in whom they had trusted. No matter where they looked, they could find no relief. In Isaiah 29.1-8 the prophet uses the simile of a hungry and thirsty man among the woes Yahweh will inflict upon the wicked Jerusalem: "It will be like the dream of a hungry man: he eats, then wakes up with a hungry belly; or like the dream of a thirsty man: he drinks, then wakes up exhausted with a parched throat" (*NJB*).

In the glorious age to come, which will be a time of social justice and moral and spiritual revival, the wise man and the fool will be known for what they really are. "A fool will no longer be called noble, nor a villain said to be honorable." Fools "leave the craving of the hungry unsatisfied" and "deprive the thirsty of drink" (Isaiah 32:5-6; see also 49:8-12).

The author of Isaiah 58:7-11 thought that only the wealthy could afford to fast because only they could deprive themselves of food. The hungry are on a perpetual fast. Effective fasting means that the rich share with the poor so that all are equal in the sight of God. Isaiah reminds his readers that they are to share their bread with the hungry, bring the homeless poor into their houses, and cover the naked when they see them. If the people who can offer their food to the hungry and satisfy the needs of the afflicted, Yahweh will satisfy their needs. For Ezekiel giving bread to the hungry is a sign of a righteous man: "If a man is righteous…gives his bread to the hungry and covers the naked with a garment…he shall surely live, says the Lord God" (18:5-9).

*The Pentateuch.* As the result of teachings of the prophets, a genuine concern for all people, including the poor and hungry, became a part of Hebrew law, especially in Deuteronomy. Special consideration was not given to persons because of their wealth or other seeming advantage, but because of their needs. This was in sharp contrast to other nations. A primary purpose of the Law was to assure the welfare of the poor and the weak. If there is anyone in any town that is in need, persons should "not be hard-hearted or tight-fisted" toward needy neighbors. People should give willingly to meet any need because the poor will always be present. The command is: "Open your hand to the poor and needy neighbor in your land" (Deuteronomy 15:7-11).

A sense of humanitarianism helped shape Hebrew social law. For six years people were to sow and reap from the land, but not the seventh year. Every seventh year some land was to lie fallow, "so that the poor of your people may eat; and what they leave the wild animals may eat." People should do the same for vineyard and olive orchards (Exodus 23:10-11). Again and again in the Law attempts are made to instill moral values that should pervade all decisions. Humans, like God, should show no partiality in making decisions (Deuteronomy 10:17-19). "You shall not render an unjust judgment; you shall not be partial to the poor or defer to the great" (Leviticus 19:15; see also Exodus 23:2-3; 25:35).

*Psalms and Proverbs.* Psalms and Proverbs say much concerning the poor and needy. Some Psalms relate personal experiences or situations of others of various kinds and generally associate God with the situations. For example, the first part of Psalm 107 is a thanksgiving to God for help in the past. Some persons, "hungry and thirsty," wandered in desert places; they called to God, who delivered them. God "satisfies the thirsty, and the hungry he fills with good things" (107:4-9). The second part of the psalm deals with God's punishment of the unfaithful and his compassionate treatment of the poor and righteous. This was a prominent Deuteronomic theme and appears also in Psalms 10, 37, 146. Psalm 41:1-3 expresses the belief that help to the poor brings happiness and that the Lord protects them from their enemies.

In Proverbs there are short sayings about the poor and hungry, who are sometimes contrasted with the rich. "The wealth of the rich is their fortress; the poverty of the poor is their ruin" (Proverbs 10:15). "Those who oppress the poor insult their Maker, but those who are kind to the needy honor him" (14:31; see also 21:13). Here, as usual, the sayings about rich and poor are written from the perspective of faith in God.

The author of Proverbs 28:15 was aware that a malevolent ruler will always have poor people as victims of his power and greed. "Like a roaring lion or a charging bear is a wicked ruler over a poor people." Isn't this true even today in some countries where powerful but unsympathetic and greedy rulers are responsible for the poverty and oppression of their subjects?

*New Testament*
*Synoptic Gospels.* Although it is very difficult to determine which sayings of Jesus are authentic, there is general agreement that, in spite of the special interests of each gospel writer, Jesus' concern for the poor was a genuine part of his life and teachings. We have also learned that Luke had a special concern for the poor. This is clear already in his Magnificat, where he says that Jesus would be born to fulfill the OT words about filling the hungry with good things and sending the rich away empty (Luke 1:53; see Psalm 107:9).

Recall Jesus' reading from the prophet Isaiah in the synagogue about his mission to the poor and oppressed (Luke 4:18-21; Isaiah 61:1-2). Recall, also, the two versions of Jesus' words about the beatitude and the woe on the poor (Matthew 5, 6; Luke 6:20-21, 24-25). And, in the story of the rich man who told Jesus that he had kept the law since his youth, Jesus told him that he lacked one thing, that is, he was to sell all he owned and give the money to the poor (Mark 10:20-21; Matthew 19:20-21; Luke 18:21-22). By changing Mark's "give" to "distribute," Luke emphasizes the distribution of the money to the poor.

*Acts and Paul's Letters.* In the times of Paul and Acts Jews provided two kinds of aid to the poor. Travelers and temporary residents received daily distributions of food and wine from officers appointed for that purpose. Other officers collected food and clothing from local residents and then distributed them to the poor people of the community on every Friday. As churches became more and more independent of their Jewish heritage, they had to develop their own systems for providing help to the poor. In Acts 2:44-45 believers shared things in common and sold some of their possessions and distributed the money to the poor. As the result of that practice, there was no poor person among them (Acts 4:32-35). As the number of disciples increased, some of their widows did not receive the daily distribution. Therefore, seven persons were chosen to fulfill that task (Acts 6:1-6; see also 11:27-30).

Paul was aware that early followers of Jesus had regular and systematic methods for the care of the poor. He writes to the Galatians that, when it was determined that he and Barnabas should preach among Gentiles, the only requirement was that they remember the poor. Paul said that he was actually eager to do that (Galatians 2:9-10). In Romans 15:26 Paul writes that people from Macedonia and Achaia were glad to share their resources with the poor holy ones in Jerusalem.

Paul writes at length in 2 Corinthians 9 about the special collection for the poor in Jerusalem. He sent some brothers ahead of him to make sure that the bountiful gift they had promised would be ready when he arrived. Some people from Macedonia had already made a generous contribution to the fund, and he did not want to be embarrassed by any small amount the Corinthians might give. Paul exhorts them to give liberally and supports what he says by alluding to Deuteronomy 15:10 about giving liberally and ungrudgingly and being blessed by the Lord in return (see also Proverbs 11:24-26).

In Romans 12:20-21 Paul quotes LXX Proverbs 25:21-22 in the context of overcoming evil with good as a means of avenging one's enemies: "If your enemy hunger, feed him; if he thirst, give him drink; for by doing so you will heap coals of fire upon his head, and the Lord will reward you with good things" (see also Matthew 5:44; 25:35).

*Letter of James.* James wants his readers to know that their faith is not compatible with preferences shown to people because of their prestige, social class, influence, power, eminence, or wealth. If believers pay special attention to persons entering the assembly who wear fine jewelry and clothing and invite them to sit in one place, and if believers ask poor persons to stand over there or sit at their feet, they make distinctions among themselves and judge with evil thoughts (James 2:1-4).

Then the writer echoes the OT attitudes that the poor are the special object of God's care and that the oppressiveness of the rich is to be condemned. The author's words not only reveal his own attitude toward the poor; they also reflect the situations of his times. His personal faith is that God has "chosen the poor in the world to be rich in faith" and to be beneficiaries of God's love. But James's readers have "dishonored the poor" (2:5-6).

*Revelation.* The writer of Revelation believes that members of one church may be physically poor yet spiritually rich. That is the case with the church at Smyrna to whose members he writes: "I know your affliction and your poverty, even though you are rich" (Revelation 2:9; see also 2 Corinthians 6:8-10; James 2:5). On the other hand, members of the church at Laodicea, a city made wealthy because of its commerce, industry, and banking, could boast of its riches, but spiritually they were poor. "For you say, I am rich, I have prospered, and I need nothing. You do not realize that you are wretched, pitiable, poor, blind, and naked" (Revelation 3:17; see also Luke 12:13-21; 1 Timothy 6:17-19).

For the writer of Revelation hunger was one of the afflictions in his present evil age, but he believed it would be absent in the glorious heavenly age to come. Of those who have washed their robes white in the blood of the Lamb (Christ), he says, "They will hunger no more, and thirst no more" (7:14-16; see also Isaiah 49:10; Psalms 107:35-36; 146:6-7).

## *Conclusion*

Perhaps concern for the poor and oppressed is the least controversial among the issues we have considered. Individuals and nations often respond immediately to persons suffering as the result of natural disasters and regularly to oppressed people in some parts of the world. Yet, there is so much suffering and need in today's world, despite scientific advances, knowledge, and wealth unimaginable in biblical times. The devastation of wars, the negative consequences of greed, exploitation, and immorality, the human suffering caused by disease that could be prevented or cured, social and economic injustice, religious persecution, and a seemingly endless list of social issues remain a blight on our global landscape.

In striving for insightful understanding about what "the Bible says," it seems most important to remember what the Bible is and how it originated. As a collection of writings that were generated over many centuries, it has *become* a sacred book that provides both inspiration and moral teachings for Jews and Christians. However, when studying the contexts of biblical passages and the meanings that were undoubtedly intended by biblical authors, it becomes clear that much is unclear.

There are innumerable contradictions and discrepancies, often due to different sources and different motives behind the writings. Unfortunately, it is often impossible to say, with certainty, what the prophets of the OT might have said, or what actually happened with the Patriarchs or if they even existed, or what Jesus really said and did. Yet, with techniques used by biblical scholars, it is possible to determine, with some sense of accuracy, what was meant by some of the most important teachings recorded in the Bible. If we focus on what is truly relevant in today's world, then what "the Bible says" can be a valid and valuable source of guidance today.

First and foremost, the Bible reflects the understanding and faith of its authors. The creation stories, for example, were an explanation of the beginning of the world, explanations that were understandable in the context of biblical times. Yet, the creation stories are just that – stories. They were based on prototypes that evolved out of a pagan world, and the biblical writers adapted them to fit their monotheistic beliefs. Perhaps we need to take a lesson from those writers. Today, given the tremendous scientific advances that enlighten us about the world and the origin of life as we know it, we need to adapt those creation stories for our times. "Believing" was "knowing" for the biblical authors. Today, however, we have science to balance religion. And whatever we can learn from science, whether it is about our expansive universe or genetic causes of mental or physical illness or brain research, must help to inform our decisions, on both personal and societal levels.

The Bible has never been and never can be science, nor can science be religion. To confuse the two is to lose the value of both. As Galileo said, "I do not feel obliged to believe that the same god who has endowed us with sense, reason and intellect has intended us to forego their use." So, should we teach creationism in science classes? Perhaps the best answer to that is another question. Should we rewrite the Bible to include science or teach evolution in Sunday School or Parish School of Religion classes?

Are we not losing sight of what's really important when we focus on teaching creationism or on condemning the sexual orientation of people, for example, because "The Bible Says So," or on using the Bible to argue for or against issues like abortion or capital punishment when there is no conclusive evidence to support either view? As we have moved from the perspective of biblical authors that the world is flat, sandwiched between the heavens above and the seas below, to a much more accurate conception, the creation stories and the pagan myths on which they were based are simple answers that just do not remain valid today. And not one of us suffers because of this.

We can appreciate, with insightful understanding, the historical and literary roots of the creation stories without misrepresenting them as scientific explanations. Yet, when we ignore or fail to abide by the humanitarian values that have derived from important Judeo-Christian principles taught in the Bible, human suffering and needless death occur daily. Likewise, when we turn away from modern medical advances and discoveries in the social and physical sciences that can shed new light on longstanding issues, we are not fully using the "life" we have today to enhance *quality* of life.

So, what is important? Support or condemnation of evolutionary *science?* Support or condemnation of homosexuality? Support or condemnation of abortion? Or, should we focus on what we can do to make the world a better place? Are we not supposed to be our brother's keeper? We might look scornfully at someone who chooses abortion or is gay, but are we any less sinful, if indeed they are sinful, when we turn our backs on the millions of starving and homeless people suffering worldwide? What would the OT direct us to do? What would Jesus say?

Isaiah believed that with the Lord's help nations would come to arbitration: "They shall beat their swords into ploughshares, and their spears into pruning hooks; nation shall not lift up sword against nation, neither shall they learn war any more" (Isaiah 2:4). Perhaps we should invest our time and resources into pursuing peaceful solutions to world problems. As individuals and as faith-based communities, would we not benefit from remembering the words of Isaiah 1:10-12, 16-17:

> Listen to the Lord. Hear what he is telling you! I am sick of your sacrifices. Don't bring me any more of them... Who wants your sacrifices when you have no sorrow for your sins? The incense you bring me is a stench in my nostrils. Your holy celebrations...all are frauds! I want nothing more to do with them. Oh, wash yourselves! Be clean! Let me no longer see you doing all these wicked things; quit your evil ways. Learn to do good, to be fair and to help the poor, the fatherless, and widows.

As Jesus said, he was coming "to bring good news to the poor...release to the captives...sight to the blind...to let the oppressed go free" (Luke 4:18), and he would want us to do the same. According to Matthew and Luke, Jesus sent out his disciples to "cure the sick, raise the dead, cleanse the lepers, cast out demons" (Matthew 10:8; see also Luke 9:1-2; 10:9). Although set in an apocalyptic context of the coming of the kingdom soon and in the language of the times, its thought is appropriate for any age. Likewise, both Matthew and Luke report that Jesus said, in the Sermon on the Mount, that people cannot serve two masters: "You cannot serve God and wealth" (Matthew 6:24; Luke 16:13). Or to go back again to an even earlier time, consider the relevance in today's fast-paced world of the psalmist's words (*REB*):

> Lord, let me know my end and the number of my days; tell me how short my life is to be. I know you have made my days a mere span [width of a hand] long, and my whole life is as nothing in your sight. A human being, however firm he stands, is but a puff of wind, his life but a passing shadow; the riches he piles up are no more than vapour, and there is no knowing who will enjoy them (Psalm 39:4-6).

Remember, too, that in the Sermon on the Mount Jesus says that his disciples are "the light of the world," so they are not to hide their light "under the bushel basket." They are to let their "light shine before men, so that they may see your good works and give glory to your Father in heaven" (Matthew 5:14-15). According to Paul, the kinds of virtues that come to us when the Holy Spirit controls our lives certainly seem relevant as a basis not just for personal moral and ethical choices, but for societal decisions, as well: "love, joy, peace, patience, kindness, goodness, faithfulness, gentleness and self-control" (Galatians 5:22-23, 26). Or, consider the following teachings of Paul in Romans 12:9-21:

> Let love be genuine; hate what is evil, hold fast to what is good; love one another with mutual affection; outdo one another in showing honor. Do not lag in zeal, be ardent in spirit... Rejoice in hope, be patient in suffering... Contribute to the needs of the saints; extend hospitality to strangers.

Paul directs us to bless, not curse, persecutors, rejoice with those rejoicing and weep with those weeping, live in harmony with each other without haughtiness, and mingle with the lowly. Do not pretend to be wiser that you are, do not return evil for evil, leave vengeance to God, provide food and water to those who need it, let good prevail over evil. "The Bible Says So!"